KIDS ONLINE

Opportunities and risks for children

Edited by Sonia Livingstone and Leslie Haddon

This edition published in Great Britain in 2009 by

The Policy Press
University of Bristol
Fourth Floor
Beacon House
Queen's Road
Bristol BS8 1QU
UK

Tel +44 (0)117 331 4054
Fax +44 (0)117 331 4093
e-mail tpp-info@bristol.ac.uk
www.policypress.co.uk

North American office:
The Policy Press
c/o International Specialized Books Services
920 NE 58th Avenue, Suite 300
Portland, OR 97213-3786, USA
Tel +1 503 287 3093
Fax +1 503 280 8832
e-mail info@isbs.com

British Library Cataloguing in Publication Data
A catalogue record for this book is available from the British Library.

Library of Congress Cataloging-in-Publication Data
A catalog record for this book has been requested.

ISBN 978 1 84742 438 9 paperback
ISBN 978 1 84742 439 6 hardcover

Cover design by The Policy Press
Front cover: image kindly supplied by www.istock.com
Printed and bound in Great Britain by Hobbs the Printers, Southampton

Contents

List of figures and tables

Figures

Tables

Notes on contributors

Elena Aristodemou has a Bachelor of Science (BSc) in psychology from Monash University, Australia and a Master of Science (MSc) in psychological research methods (pending defence) from The Open University, UK. Her research interests lie in the fields of education, learning disabilities and cognitive processes. Elena is the science coordinator in the New Media in Learning Laboratory at the Cyprus Neuroscience & Technology Institute and coordinator of the Hotline SafenetCY. She is a research associate in several projects such as CyberEthics, Hajj and MAPS.

Joke Bauwens is a media sociologist in the Centre for Studies on Media and Culture (CEMESCO) at the Free University of Brussels, where she teaches courses on media sociology, media and culture and communication research methods. She is also a senior researcher, and her research interests include digital culture, young people and media culture. She coordinated a Belgian research project on 'Teens and ICT: Risks and Opportunities' (TIRO).

Petter Bae Brandtzæg joined SINTEF Information and Communication Technology, the Department of Cooperative and Trusted Systems and the HCI (Human–Computer Interaction) Group in 2000. His expertise lies in analysing user trends, user motivations and user typologies of new media, with a particular focus on social networking sites and young people. He is the author of more than 30 international publications. At present he is a PhD candidate at SINTEF in the Department of Media and Communication at the University of Oslo, Norway.

Thorbjörn Broddason is Professor of Sociology in the Department of Sociology, University of Iceland. He has been instrumental in establishing sociology, media and communication studies and journalism and mass communication at the University. His research includes the long-term project 'Children and Television in Iceland', which began in 1968 and continues to this day, with repeated questionnaire surveys among random samples of 10 to 15 year olds at intervals of six years in order to chart the constantly changing media landscape. His other research has been aimed at Icelandic media structures and a theoretical investigation of media professionalism.

Elza Dunkels is a senior lecturer in the Department of Interactive Media and Learning at Umeå University, Sweden. Her PhD thesis, 'Bridging the distance: children's strategies on the internet' was published in 2007 by Umeå University. Her research interests include young people's internet use in general, and their strategies against threats in particular.

Leen d'Haenens is an associate professor at the Centre for Media Culture and Communication Technology at the Catholic University of Leuven, Belgium, and at the Department of Communication at Radboud University, Nijmegen, the Netherlands. Her research interests include western media policy, media responsibility and accountability mechanisms, media and minority ethnic groups and patterns of news use among young people. She held a Jean Monnet Chair in European Media Policy from 2001 to 2007.

Verónica Donoso is a senior researcher at the Centre for User Experience Research (CUO) at the Catholic University of Leuven, Belgium. She completed her Master's degree in educational sciences (University of Chile) in 2000 and her PhD in communication sciences (Catholic University of Leuven) in 2007. Since 2002 Verónica has been researching use-related risks and the developmental and social impacts of adolescents' internet use. She is currently involved in Belgian and European projects about users' experience of new digital applications, with a focus on technology-enhanced learning, social relationships and the development of identity.

Andrea Dürager is a research assistant in the Department of Communication at the University of Salzburg, Austria, where she is working towards a PhD. She completed her first degree in communication studies with a focus on public relations in 2004; one of her postgraduate degrees was also in communication (2006), the second one in educational studies (2008). Her special interests are in television as well as internet studies, in higher education research, and in quantitative research, especially methods of data acquisition, statistics and evaluation.

Cédric Fluckiger teaches in the Department of Education Science and is a researcher in the CIREL (Centre Interuniversitaire de Recherche en Education de Lille) laboratory at the University of Charles-de-Gaulle Lille 3. He worked as a network and telecoms engineer (1999-2003) in France Telecom R&D (research and development), before studying for a PhD in education science on the appropriation of information and communication technology by young teenagers (ENS Cachan – Ecole normale supérieure de Cachan). His main research interests include processes of gaining independence during childhood, the role of new relational tools and the acquisition of practical and technical skills in diverse environments.

Carmelo Garitaonandia is Professor of Journalism at the University of the Basque Country (with a PhD in political sciences, a BA in law from the Complutense University of Madrid and a Master's degree in information and audiovisual communication from the University of Paris 7). His books and articles include: *Decentralisation in the global era* (edited with Miquel Moragas, University of Luton Press, 1995); *TV on your doorstep* (edited with John Libbey, Miquel Moragas and Bernat Lopez, University of Luton Press, 1999); and, with J.A. Oleaga, 'Media genres and content preferences', in S. Livingstone and M. Bovill (eds) *Children and their changing media environment* (Lawrence Erlbaum Associates, 2001).

Maialen Garmendia has a PhD in sociology (University of Deusto, Bilbao, Spain) and has been teaching at the University of the Basque Country, Spain since 1990. Her interests are in applied research, social research techniques, statistics and audience research and in the audiences of new communication technologies. Since 1997 she has also been on the editorial board of ZER *Revista de Estudios de Comunicación* (www. ehu.es/zer/).

Jos de Haan is head of the research group, Time, Media and Culture, at the Netherlands Institute for Social Research, and Professor of Information and Communication Technology (ICT), Culture and Knowledge Society at the Erasmus University Rotterdam. He was awarded a PhD in sociology from Utrecht University (thesis: 'Research groups in Dutch sociology'). His research into the spread, use and consequences of new ICT includes work with digital divides, digital skills among the youth and the rise of e-culture. During 2003-07 he was editor of the Dutch yearbook, *ICT en Samenleving* [*ICT and society*], and is a member of the Dutch UNESCO working group on Culture, Communication and Information.

Leslie Haddon is a senior researcher and part-time lecturer in the Department of Media and Communications at the London School of Economics and Political Science (LSE), and a visiting research associate at the Oxford Internet Institute and the Institute for Social and Technical Research, University of Essex. His work focuses on the social shaping and consumption of information and communication technology. In addition to numerous articles, chapters and co-edited books he is the author of *Information and communication technologies in everyday life* (Berg, 2004) and is co-series editor for a collection of textbooks on new media to be published by Berg in 2009. He has worked on various academic and European Commission-funded projects as well as those commissioned by companies and trade associations, including several international collaborations. He is part of a European network of researchers in COST Action 298.

Ingunn Hagen is Professor of Media and Communication Psychology in the Department of Psychology at the Norwegian University of Science and Technology. Her research fields include audience reception studies, political communication, consumption of popular culture, young people and new media, and recently children and consumption. Her books include *Medienes publikum. Fra mottakar til brukar? [Media audiences. From receivers to users?]* (Ad Notam Gyldendal, 2004/1998); *Consuming audiences? Production and reception in media research* (co-edited with Janet Wasko, Hampton Press, 2000); and *Mediegenerasjonen. Barn og unge i det nye medielandskapet [The media generation. Children and young people in the new media landscape]* (with Thomas Wold, Samlaget, 2009).

Uwe Hasebrink is Director of the Hans Bredow Institute for Media Research at the University of Hamburg, Germany and Professor of Empirical Communication Research. His main research interests include individual patterns of media use, the development of media use in Europe, programme quality and the public service function of media. He was a member of the sixth Framework Programme Co-ordination Action 'International Radio Research Network' (IREN) and the European Union-funded project 'European Association for Viewers Interests'. He is on the Executive Board of the European Communication Research and Education Association (ECREA).

Veronika Kalmus is Associate Professor of Media Studies at the University of Tartu, Estonia. She leads the research project 'Children and Young People in the Emerging Information and Consumer Society', financed by the Estonian Science Foundation. She has published in collections of papers and international journals including *Discourse & Society, Journal of Curriculum Studies, Journal of Baltic Studies, East*

European Politics & Societies, Childhood, Young, Journal of Computer-Mediated Communication and *Cyberpsychology: Journal of Psychosocial Research on Cyberspace*.

Lucyna Kirwil is an assistant professor at the Warsaw School of Social Psychology, Poland. She is an expert adviser for the Ombudsman for Children in Poland on the protection of children against the harmful effects of screen violence, and co-author of the present system of TV ratings used in Polish media.

Yiannis Laouris is a senior scientist at the Cyprus Neuroscience & Technology Institute, where he heads the New Media in Learning and the Neuroscience Laboratories. He publishes in the areas of neuroscience, systems sciences, learning through computers, the web and mobile phones and the potential of information technology. He participates in COST 219ter: Accessibility for All to Services and Terminals for Next Generation Networks, and COST 2102: Cross-modal Analysis of Verbal and Non-verbal Communication. He was co-founder of an international chain of computer learning centres for children, known as CYBER kids. He is also the Director of CyberEthics, the safe internet awareness node and hotline for Cyprus.

Sonia Livingstone is Professor of Social Psychology in the Department of Media and Communications at the London School of Economics and Political Science and author/editor of 14 books as well as articles on media audiences, children and the internet, the domestic contexts of media use and media literacy. Recent books include *Young people and new media* (Sage Publications, 2002); *The handbook of new media* (edited, with Leah Lievrouw, Sage Publications, 2006); *Media consumption and public engagement* (with Nick Couldry and Tim Markham, Palgrave, 2007); *Harm and offence in media content* (with Andrea Millwood Hargrave, Intellect, 2009), *The International handbook of children, media and culture* (edited, with Kirsten Drotner, Sage Publications, 2008); and *Children and the internet* (Polity, 2009). She serves on the Executive Board of the UK Council for Child Internet Safety (UKCCIS), the Ministerial Taskforce for Home Access to Technology for Children and, until recently, the Board of the Internet Watch Foundation (IWF).

Bojana Lobe completed her PhD in social sciences methodology at the University of Ljubljana, Slovenia, in 2006. She is Assistant Professor of Social Science Methodology in the Faculty of Social Sciences, University of Ljubljana and a coordinator of the Slovenian national study '*What Slovenian children do online*' (2009-11). She is on the editorial board of the *International Journal of Multiple Research Approaches* and has recently published *Integration of online research methods* (Faculty of Social Sciences Press, 2008). Her current research interests include methodological issues in mixed methods research, new technologies in social science data collection (virtual ethnography, online focus groups, online qualitative interviews), systematic comparative methods and methodological aspects of researching children's experiences.

Marika Hanne Lüders is a research scientist at SINTEF Information and Communication Technology in Oslo, Norway. She received a PhD in media and communication studies from the University of Oslo in 2007, and has for several years been working with emerging uses of personal and social media, with a particular focus on young people. Marika was co-editor of the Norwegian anthology *Personlige Medier* (*Personal media*) and her work has been published in Norwegian and international anthologies and journals.

Helen McQuillan is an Arnold F. Graves postdoctoral scholar at the Dublin Institute of Technology, Ireland. Her doctoral research was carried out on the Ennis Information Age Town (EIAT), and she has been involved in digital inclusion research and practice for almost 10 years. Helen was a senior research consultant for the Information Society Commission (ISC), Ireland, and co-authored *eInclusion: Expanding the information society in Ireland* (ISC, 2003). From 2003-06 she was research manager for England's €800 million e-government programme, and was also a strategic adviser on community engagement and e-inclusion. She is currently a member of the e-inclusion advisory group for the government's Information Society Policy Unit.

Gemma Martínez Fernández has a Bachelor's degree in journalism from the University of the Basque Country, Spain. She is a PhD candidate and research scholar with a scholarship from the Ministry of Education and Science. Professor Carmelo Garitaonandia is supervising her dissertation 'Youth, ICTs and the role of parental mediation'. She has also collaborated on a variety of papers on youth and new technologies.

Giovanna Mascheroni is a research fellow at the University of Torino, Italy, and a senior researcher at Osscom (Osservatorio sulla Comunicazione). Her research interests are focused on social networks, virtual and physical mobility, the internet and mobile media. She has published two books: *Breve Dizionario dei nuovi media* [*Short dictionary of new media*] (with F. Pasquali, Carocci, 2006) and *Le comunità viaggianti. Socialità reticolare e mobile dei viaggiatori indipendenti* [*The traveller. Sociality and the mobility lattice of independent travellers*], (Franco Angeli, 2007). Her international publications include (2007) 'Global nomads' network and mobile sociality. Exploring new media uses on the move', *Information, Communication & Society*, vol 10, no 4: 527-46.

Maria Francesca Murru is a PhD candidate in the Department of Media and Communication at the Catholic University of Milan. She graduated in 2006 with a thesis analysing the concept of media literacy through the theoretical perspectives of the diffusion of innovations theory and the social shaping of technology approach. She is currently working as a researcher at Osscom (Osservatorio sulla Comunicazione), an academic research centre for media and communication based at the same university. Her PhD dissertation examines online public spheres and she recently published with Fausto Colombo 'Weblogs between counter-information and power: an Italian case history', *Observatorio (OBS★) Journal*, vol 2 (2007), 001-013.

Kjartan Ólafsson is a lecturer in the Faculty of Humanities and Social Sciences at the University of Akureyri, Iceland. He has worked on several research projects related to youth and/or the media, including the long-term research project 'Children and Television in Iceland', the international World Health Organization project 'Health Behaviour in School-aged Children', the European School Survey Project on Alcohol and Other Drugs (ESPAD) and the Icelandic School Survey Project. He was principal researcher on one of the largest social science research projects in Iceland, monitoring the social and economic impacts of construction projects in East Iceland.

Brian O'Neill is Head of the School of Media at Dublin Institute of Technology, Ireland. His research fields include media literacy and media education practice. He is the author of several commissioned reports on media literacy and articles on media policy in relation to children, technology and new media. He was a founder member of Ireland's Teachers' Association for Media Education and the Irish contact for Euromedia, an international network for the comparative study of media education policy and practice. He is a member of the Digital Radio Cultures in Europe (DRACE) research group (COST Action A20) and Deputy Head of the International Association for Media and Communication Research (IAMCR) Audience Section.

Ingrid Paus-Hasebrink is Professor of Communication and head of the section on audiovisual communication at the Department of Communication, and Vice Dean of the Faculty of Cultural and Social Sciences of the University of Salzburg, Austria. Her research includes analyses of audio-visual content (television, radio, film, internet), genres and formats as well as audience and reception analyses. She is interested in young audiences and media content targeted at children and young people, media socialisation and education, media literacy and the protection of minors in the evolving so-called 'information society'. Her recent work concerns technical convergence and digital television, including social and economic aspects of cross-media strategies and the role of the internet in relation to television programmes.

Jochen Peter is an associate professor in the Amsterdam School of Communications Research (ASCoR) at the University of Amsterdam, the Netherlands. His research interests focus on the consequences of internet-based communication and information for adolescents' development, most notably their sexual socialisation (see www. ccam-ascor.nl). His research has received multiple awards from the International Communication Association (ICA), the Association for Education in Journalism and Mass Communication (AEJMC) and the World Association of Public Opinion Research (WAPOR).

Cristina Ponte is a senior lecturer at the New University of Lisbon, Portugal, and teaches media and journalism studies in the Department of Communication. She worked in the Portuguese *Sesame Street* co-production, carried out research on the use of computers in primary education and on the representation of children in the news. She coordinated a national project 'Children and Young People in the News' (2005-07), which included children's views on news and is currently coordinating the international project 'Digital Inclusion and Participation' (2009-2011), with UTAustin (US). Her international publications include (2007) 'Mapping children in the mainstream press', *European Societies*, vol 9, no 5: 735-54.

Pille Pruulmann-Vengerfeldt is a senior researcher in the areas of media and internet studies in the Department of Journalism and Communication at the University of Tartu, Estonia. Her main research interests are the information society and the fusion of media and communication technologies in people's everyday lives. She has participated in several Estonian research projects focusing on social and cultural practices in the information society. She has published in international journals and in collections of papers. Her doctoral dissertation was published as a collection of articles entitled *Information technology users and uses within the different layers of the information environment in Estonia* (2006, Tartu University Press, http://hdl.handle.net/10062/173).

Pille Runnel is a research director at the Estonian National Museum and a research associate at the Institute of Journalism and Communication, University of Tartu, Estonia. Her research interests include media anthropology, media sociology and museology. She is currently involved in various projects dealing with internet use, content creation online and cultural participation.

Katia Segers lectures in the Department of Communication Studies at the Free University of Brussels. Since 2002 she has been the Director of CEMESO (Centre for Studies on Media and Culture) (www.vub.ac.be/SCOM/cemeso). Her current research projects and publications focus on cultural policy matters, financing of the arts (business sponsorship), the political economy of the cultural industries and creative economy (mainly the music industry) and the commercialisation of childhood. She is President of the Flemish Regulator for the Media and of the Flemish Advisory Board for the Arts.

Andra Siibak received a PhD in media and communication (2009) from the University of Tartu, Estonia, where she is a research fellow in media studies at the Institute of Journalism and Communication. Her research interests include online content creation practices of young people, visual and textual self-presentation in social networking websites and gender identity constructions in virtual environments. She is currently involved in the research project 'Children and Young People in the Emerging Information and Consumer Society', financed by the Estonian Science Foundation.

José Alberto Simões holds a PhD in sociology from the Faculty of Social Sciences and Humanities (FCSH) at the New University of Lisbon, Portugal, where he is an assistant professor in the Department of Sociology, teaching in the areas of research methodology and sociology of culture. He is a researcher at CESNova (Centre for Sociological Studies), a research unit of FCSH at the New University of Lisbon, and is also on the editorial board of *Forum Sociológico*. He completed his PhD on internet use and youth cultural practices and representations of hip-hop in Portugal. His main research areas include the sociology of culture, youth cultures, communication and media.

Elisabeth Staksrud is a research fellow and PhD candidate in the Department of Media and Communication at the University of Oslo, Norway, researching children's use of new media in relation to risk, regulation and rights. She is an appointed member of the Norwegian government e-forum, a European Commission (EC) expert on internet and public attitudes, and project director for new media at the Norwegian Media Authority, where she has coordinated several international projects supported by the EC Safer Internet Action Plan.

Gitte Stald is an assistant professor in the Innovative Communication Research Group at the IT University of Copenhagen, Denmark. She participated in the European comparative project, 'Children and their Changing Media Environment 1995-98', in the research programme 'Global Media Cultures 1999-2001' with the project 'Global Media, Local Youth', and in a project on qualitative content for young Danes and the use of mobiles. She co-heads the IT University's participation in Mobity, a research and development project on a user-driven mobile media community, and has participated in the MacArthur Foundation series on Digital Media, Learning and Education. She has published articles on media and cultural globalisation, adolescents' digital media cultures, online computer games and on mobile media.

Václav Štětka received his PhD in sociology at the Faculty of Social Studies (2005), Masaryk University in Brno, Czech Republic, where he is a lecturer in the Department of Media Studies and Journalism. He teaches on media theory and methodologies of mass communication research. In 2006 he was a visiting fellow at the Department of Social Sciences, Loughborough University, UK. His research interests include structural and cultural aspects of media globalisation and Europeanisation, as well as social functions of the internet and new media.

Liza Tsaliki completed her PhD at the University of Sussex, UK, on the role of Greek television in the construction of national identity. In 2000-02 she was a Marie Curie postdoctoral fellow at the University of Nijmegen, the Netherlands, researching digital civil society across the European Union. She was the director of international collaborations at the Hellenic Culture Organization from 2002-06. She resumed her academic duties as a lecturer at the Faculty of Communication and Media Studies at the National and Kapodistrian University of Athens, Greece, in March 2006. Her current interests involve information and communication technology, democratic participation, the public sphere, cultural policy making, pornography, online safety, blogging, online activism and audiences.

Panayiota Tsatsou is a lecturer in media and communications at Swansea University, UK. She is currently completing her PhD at the London School of Economics and Political Science where she has examined the role of societal culture and decision making in digital divides in Greece. She has been involved in research on information and communication technologies, on media regulation and policy, as well as on the role of ordinary people as users and actors in the information society. She has participated in COST Action 298, where she contributed to research on broadband society and human actors as e-users, as well as in COST ISO801 and CAN (Cyberbullying Action Network).

Kadri Ugur works at the Institute of Journalism and Communication of Tartu University, Estonia as a teacher and researcher, and works for developing media competences of children, students and adults. Her special interests include media education as a cross-curriculum theme in primary and secondary schools and teaching problems within media education. She is the author of several didactic resources.

Patti M. Valkenburg is a professor at the Amsterdam School of Communications Research (ASCoR) and Director of CcaM, the Center of Research on Children and the Media, the Netherlands. In 2003 she received a five-year Vici award for talented senior researchers from the Dutch National Science Foundation (NWO), with which she formed a research group to investigate the social implications of the internet for children and adolescents. Her research has received several awards, including an honorary fellowship from the International Communication Association (ICA), and several top paper awards from the ICA, the Association for Education in Journalism and Mass Communication (AEJMC) and the Broadcasting Education Association (BEA).

Christine W. Wijnen studied music as well as journalism and communication. She holds a PhD in communication and is a member of the steering team of the master course 'MultiMedia Leadership' at the Danube University of Krems, Austria. In addition, she is a lecturer at the University of Salzburg (Austria) and the University of Bolzano (Italy). At Aktion Film, a non-governmental organisation which focuses on media literacy education, she is responsible for the media research section and for teacher training in media literacy education, as well as organising hands-on media projects with young people. Her research interests are (international) media education, media literacy, media socialisation and audience studies with special focus on young people.

Thomas Wold is a candidatus philologiae from the Norwegian University of Science and Technology. He has been teaching mass communication psychology and is currently working as a freelance writer. His participation in the EU Kids Online network will be part of his PhD. His fields of expertise include contemporary morality and ideology reflected in popular culture, content deemed harmful and the freedom of speech.

Bieke Zaman holds a Master's degree in communication sciences at the Faculty of Social Sciences at the Catholic University of Leuven, Belgium. She is currently working towards a PhD focused on new or adapted methodologies for undertaking user experience research with digital media and young children. Bieke is also a senior researcher at the Centre for User Experience Research (CUO), where she is involved in related projects. As a teaching assistant, she lectures on Master's courses on web development and usability design.

Acknowledgements

The work presented in this book was made possible by an award of thematic network funding by the European Commission's Safer Internet Plus Programme directed by Richard Swetenham from 2006 to 2009. We worked with two project officers during this period – Christine Kormann and Evangelia Markidou.

At the London School of Economics and Political Science, Jon Deer, Bhimla Dhermojee, Dorota Rejman and Catherine Bennett ably supported the coordination of the network, while first Panayiota Tsatsou and then Ranjana Das were splendid research assistants throughout. We warmly thank them all for their support, guidance and help, along with Karen Bowler and her colleagues at The Policy Press for working closely with us to get the book published quickly, and David Brake for carefully editing the typescript.

Most of all, as editors we are grateful to our contributors and their colleagues in the wider European Union Kids Online network (see www.eukidsonline.net and Appendix C). It has been a real pleasure to collaborate with such expert, thoughtful, generous and committed researchers over the past three years. Of course, crucially underpinning the research findings discussed in this book are the voices and experiences of many children from across Europe; we hope this book represents them fairly and that it informs policy developments that will benefit them in the future.

ONE

Introduction

Sonia Livingstone and Leslie Haddon

Few issues in the past decade have so dominated the headlines or captured the public imagination as that of children as online pioneers, in the vanguard of exploring and experimenting with new opportunities on the internet. Although many adults are also online, and although parents make considerable efforts to keep up with their children, it may seem that, one decade after gaining access *en masse* to online technologies, children and young people are living in a different world from that familiar to the adults who are bringing them up, teaching them what they need to know and designing policies to ensure their well-being. This new world has become invested with all the hopes and fears we have ever had for our children, but with a dramatic new twist because, it seems, everything is so much more available and easily accessible. One no longer has to go to the library or rely on a teacher for expert knowledge. Opportunities to meet people are no longer significantly constrained by transport, time and money. Many more have the chance to get involved in decisions that matter – local, national and even international. And most can find like-minded others who share their own particular hobby or interest. All this was beyond the scope of children growing up just a decade earlier. And the list of opportunities extends far further, both because the internet is now commonplace across the developed world and because all human life can now be found online.

But although the hopes are considerable, leading parents, schools and governments worldwide to invest in information and communication technologies (ICTs) to give children new opportunities, expanded horizons and a better chance in life, it is the associated dangers of the internet that dominate the headlines. Since all human life is now online, this includes many risks – bullies, racists, cheats and, the greatest fear of all, sexual predators. Although long encountered by children in one form or another, today these risks are more available and more accessible, readily crossing national borders to reach children anywhere, anytime, too easily escaping local and national systems of child welfare and law enforcement. The first instinct of many adults observing this expanded array of risks that even reaches children at home and in their bedrooms is to turn off the computer, to ban the mobile phone and to call a halt to the march of technology. The first instinct of many children, however, is to shrug their shoulders, laugh it off and tell the worried adults that they know what they are doing.

Moving beyond this impasse has proved a fascinating and complex task for parents, educators and policy makers in many countries. It has demanded original empirical research to discover what children and young people are really doing online – what they enjoy, what they have learned, what they are good at and in what ways they struggle. Experts in diverse disciplines, such as child development, family dynamics, online technologies, youth culture, sociology, media and communication, education and many more, have conducted such research. It has also been conducted in many countries, published in many languages and discussed at many international conferences. This has enabled a valuable period of balanced assessment, asking: are young people's online activities really beneficial, are the benefits fairly distributed, do children need educational or other forms of support? In terms of risks, research has asked whether the various forms of potentially harmful content, contact and conduct children encounter online are really worrying or not, and if they are, how such risks can be managed and, indeed, minimised.

In recent years, consensus has been reached that 'magic bullet' solutions to online risks are not to be found. Moreover, although simple solutions (trust the children, rely on parents or turn off the computer) do not work, more complex solutions can only deliver if the multiple stakeholders involved each play their part and if society does not set the expectations too high. A safe childhood is unattainable – child psychologists would also say it is undesirable – but a safer one is feasible. Similar conclusions apply for the opportunities afforded by online technologies. Here too 'magic bullet' solutions do not work. Providing computers for every child does not mean all will use them, nor will they necessarily use them in intended or 'approved' ways. Moreover, patterns of use and non-use are likely to be shaped by long-established social expectations and to reproduce familiar forms of social inequality. In short, policies focused on access but not use or skills often go awry, and policies designed to benefit all children equally often result in the 'rich getting richer'. Again, complex solutions, involving multiple participants – curriculum designers, teacher training, local communities, children's charities, public service broadcasters, industry partners and many more – are required if the benefits of the internet are to be more widely and fairly enjoyed.

This volume offers an up-to-date account of current research, current policy and, especially, the current practices of children and young people as they relate to the internet and online technologies, drawing on lessons of the recent past in order to look ahead to anticipate what is coming. The very pace of change sets particular challenges to researchers, policy makers and the public, for European children have gained access to new online, mobile and networked technologies with considerable rapidity (see Appendix B to this book). In the EU27, internet penetration had reached 61% by December 2008, ranging from 33% in Romania and Bulgaria to 83% in the Netherlands and Finland (Internet World Statistics). Children and young people lead in internet use, with 75% of 6 to 17 year olds using the internet across the EU27, ranging from less than half of children online in Italy (45%) and about half of children online in Greece and Cyprus (both 50%) to two thirds of children using the internet in many countries and rising to 91% in the UK and Sweden, 93% in the Netherlands and Denmark, and 94% in Finland (EC, 2008). Parents have also recently gained access in considerable numbers, with as many now using the internet as their children in most European countries.

These changes have generated some pressing questions for policy makers, regulators, industry and the public. The most obvious is how to encourage children and young people to gain access and to make the most of the opportunities afforded by the internet, including learning, communication, entertainment, creativity, self-expression and civic participation, whether they use it at home, school or elsewhere. A further question is whether, in encouraging children to go online, society inadvertently increases the risks children encounter in their daily lives, including exposure to violent or hate content, inappropriate sexual content and contact, harassment, bullying or abuse of personal information. One may also put this problem the other way round since policy makers must also ask whether efforts to reduce online risks inadvertently constrain children in their exploration of the benefits afforded by the internet. In response to these and further questions, a critical mass of researchers and policy makers are now investigating, debating and shaping children's internet uses in new and constructive ways. Mapping these activities is the focus of the chapters that follow, but first we set out some guiding principles in the form of a theoretical framework.

Theoretical framework

Opportunities and risks are inextricably entwined at both a societal level and as experienced by individuals in their everyday lives. Thus in today's complex, modern societies, it is apparent that, somewhat paradoxically, efforts to harness science and commerce towards the grand goal of progress have themselves generated new risks; while risks associated with the internet are typical, other examples include risks associated with new forms of energy or crops or medicine. Reflecting on what he calls 'the risk society', Beck argues that modern life contains both 'the threat *and* the promise of emancipation from the threat that it creates itself' (1986/2005: 183, emphasis in original) – hence the populist rhetoric of optimism and pessimism so widely associated with innovations of many kinds, including the internet. However, processes of social and historical change are always contingent, unfolding with different inflections at different times in different parts of the world. Thus even within Europe, children's encounters with the internet differ in important ways, which is why we adopt a comparative approach in this volume.

In their everyday lives, too, people ordinarily negotiate a range of interconnected opportunities and risks in the hope of constructing a meaningful lifestyle, a valued identity and satisfactory relations with others. As Giddens puts it, these days, 'self-actualisation is understood in terms of a balance between opportunity and risk' (1991: 78). The so-called 'new sociologists of childhood' have developed this idea, showing how the construction of a meaningful identity, always a vital preoccupation task of adolescence, is no longer merely the means to an end (namely, a means of achieving psychological and economic independence from one's parents) but has rather become its own focus and source of satisfaction – a goal in its own right (Qvortrup, 1994; James and James, 2008). At the same time that young people are absorbed with experimental explorations of identity, representation and sociality – many of them mediated by the internet – society has gained a heightened awareness of new risks to the self. Thus in late modernity, 'it is not only children who are perceived as being "at risk" but the institution of childhood itself' (Jackson and Scott, 1999: 86).

Too often, research or policy on risks is conducted independently of that on opportunities, and vice versa. But as research finds over and again in the examination of distinct dimensions of internet use, the two cannot be clearly separated, not least because what adults regard as risks (for example, meeting strangers), children often see as opportunities (for example, making new friends), although also because

–

the very construction of online opportunities is, as Beck anticipated, accompanied by new forms of risk – for example to express oneself online, one must disclose personal information, and by doing this on a social networking site, one provides the data for new forms of marketing. To understand the relation between opportunities and risks, research must consider both children's agency – their motivations, interests and knowledge – and also the structures, offline and online, which enable certain actions and inhibit others (Giddens, 1984).

Research provides some good grounds to celebrate children's agency, motivation and literacy in relation to online opportunities, although it also demands recognition of their agency in perpetrating harm, whether innocently or maliciously. However, children's activities are highly constrained, both online (through the provision, construction and design of websites, interfaces, networks and services) and offline (through the defining and constraining role of schools, families and communities) (Livingstone, 2009). In this volume we explore the relation between agency and structure by taking a child-centred approach. This means first identifying children's experiences, voices and actions, and then contextualising them within the concentric circles of structuring social influences – family, community and culture (Bronfenbrenner, 1979). That permits us, on the one hand, to recognise ways in which children determine what happens in their lives, but on the other hand, it permits us to recognise the power of institutional actors – those multiple stakeholders who, in policy terms, may or may not benefit children's internet use. These include parents and teachers but also commercial and state providers of internet-related services and resources. Without the structural approach, one may fall into the trap of exaggerating children's agency, celebrating them as 'digital natives' by contrast with their supposedly 'digital immigrant' parents and teachers (Prensky, 2001) and so fail sufficiently to support their development or to address their inevitable problems.

So far we have drawn on insights from psychology and sociology or social theory in scoping a repertoire of concepts and ideas to work with. In addition, we add some insights from social studies of the internet and new technologies (Mansell and Silverstone, 1996; MacKenzie and Wajcman, 1999; Haddon, 2004; Berker et al, 2006). The first is the rejection of the technological determinism commonplace in public and policy discourses (resulting in questions or claims that begin, 'the internet impacts/affects/results in…'). After all, society shapes the process of technological innovation and its diffusion, adoption and implementation in specific historical and cultural contexts. Thus, we must ask careful questions about the dynamic and contingent relations between users and technologies, and between practices of the social shaping and social consequences of new technologies (Lievrouw and Livingstone, 2006). The language of affordances – asking how the internet may (or may not) distinctively afford certain social practices – captures the recognition that the internet enables certain consequences precisely because it has been shaped to do so (Hutchby, 2001).

Another insight, drawn from empirical work throughout the history of new media, is that, contrary to popular rhetoric, there is little evidence that the internet is revolutionising society, transforming childhood or radically changing the family or education. To be sure, the internet is implicated in complex processes of social change, facilitating some possibilities and impeding others. But questions such as, is e-learning radically different from print-based learning, or is cyber-bullying really different from offline bullying, are best approached by recognising the simultaneous influence of the old and emergence of the novel. Many use the prefix 're-' to mark this combination of continuities and change, talking of recombining or remixing media texts and formats, or reconfiguring or remediating social practices.

A third insight, also drawn from empirical work, is that there are substantial continuities between the online or 'virtual' world and the offline or 'real' world. Thus research is now rejecting early conceptions of 'cyberspace' as a qualitatively distinct place (Woolgar, 2002). Indeed, the more familiar we – as researchers, policy makers and the public – have become with the internet, the more it is recognised that while the internet extends and reconfigures information and communication, it does not constitute a virtual world wholly disconnected from the offline (Orgad, 2007). Offline practices – whether of social networking, social hierarchies or social hostilities – are typically reproduced and reinforced online. Similarly, legal frameworks increasingly insist that what is illegal or regulated offline is illegal and should be regulated online. In short, activities and structures in on and offline spheres are mutually influential, not least because the actors are the same in both.

EU Kids Online: translating principles into practice

How can these principles guide empirical investigation? The present contributors and their colleagues have been closely collaborating between 2006 to 2009 on a 'thematic network' entitled EU Kids Online, funded by the European Commission's (EC) Safer Internet Plus Programme (part of the Directorate-General [DG] Information Society and Media), precisely in order to identify the evidence base to inform policies regarding children, young people and the internet in Europe. Comprised of some 60 researchers selected to span multiple forms of expertise across 21 European countries, the network was funded not to conduct new empirical research but to identify, evaluate and compare the many recent and ongoing research studies conducted across Europe (see Appendix C to this volume). It undertook this by employing an approach to understanding children's online experiences characterised by four Cs: child-centred, contextual, comparative and critical.

Researchers working in academic, public sector and private institutions are, as a matter of course, continually conducting new projects for a variety of purposes, using a range of methodologies, to a greater or lesser degree in each country. But identifying this research and keeping track of new developments is a demanding task, especially in a field that has burgeoned so rapidly since the turn of the century (Livingstone, 2003). Policy makers may lack the expertise required to locate, evaluate or interpret the significance of available research. Researchers working in one language may never learn what has been published in another. Those with the resources to commission research in one country may not learn what has proved useful in another. For such reasons, a bridge is required between the specialist domain of empirical research and the policy imperatives of children's internet-related initiatives. Moreover, cross-national comparisons are required if findings obtained in different countries are to be meaningfully related to one another. The EU Kids Online network was therefore designed to ensure that the available empirical evidence could inform policy deliberations by examining European research (national and multinational) on cultural, contextual and risk issues in children's safe use of the internet and online technologies.

The first task was to identify and assess the available research, noting patterns and biases in the kinds of research conducted, examining whether more or different kinds of research have been conducted in different countries or for different groups of children, also pinpointing gaps in the evidence base. The outcome was a publicly accessible, searchable online database cataloguing almost 400 empirical studies conducted across Europe that met a sufficient quality threshold (see Appendix C to this volume). Although this included many studies of children's internet access and use in general, our primary interest was children's online opportunities and risks. These were classified by theme, as shown in Table 1.1, with the second, horizontal dimension distinguishing the three modes of communication afforded by the internet: one-to-many (child as recipient of mass distributed content); adult-to-child (child as participant in an interactive situation

Table 1.1: A classification of online opportunities and risks for children

	Content: child as recipient	Contact: child as participant	Conduct: child as actor
OPPORTUNITIES			
Education, learning and literacy	Educational resources	Contact with others who share one's interests	Self-initiated or collaborative learning
Participation and civic engagement	Global information	Exchange among interest groups	Concrete forms of civic engagement
Creativity	Diversity of resources	Being invited/ inspired to create or participate	User-generated content creation
Identity and social connection	Advice (personal/ health/sexual etc)	Social networking, shared experiences with others	Expression of identity
RISKS			
Commercial	Advertising, spam, sponsorship	Tracking/ harvesting personal info	Gambling, illegal downloads, hacking
Aggressive	Violent/ gruesome/ hateful content	Being bullied, harassed or stalked	Bullying or harassing another
Sexual	Pornographic/ harmful sexual content	Meeting strangers, being groomed	Creating/ uploading pornographic material
Values	Racist, biased info/advice (e.g. drugs)	Self-harm, unwelcome persuasion	Providing advice e.g. suicide/ pro-anorexia

predominantly driven by adults); and peer-to-peer (child as actor in an interaction in which s/he may be initiator or perpetrator).

Having classified research findings, the second task was to compare these across categories of children and across countries. To achieve this, an analytic model was formulated which centred on children's online activities, as shown in Figure 1.1, and which contextualises these by dividing the wider research field into an individual (child-centred) level of analysis and a country (macro-societal) level of analysis (Hasebrink et al, 2009). The individual level of analysis (shaded in darker grey) examined whether and how opportunities and risks vary depending on children's age, gender and socioeconomic status, together with findings concerning the mediating role played by parents, teachers and peers. The starting assumption, based on prior research, was that these factors are likely to influence children's opportunities and risks in a similar manner across Europe. However, since there were good theoretical and empirical reasons to expect cross-national differences, a second, country-based level of analysis was formulated to compare countries according to such contextual factors as their media environment, ICT regulation and so forth, as shown in Figure 1.1, this allowing for the explanation of observed differences in children's opportunities and risks across Europe.

Figure 1.1: An analytic model of individual and country-level factors shaping the online activities of children

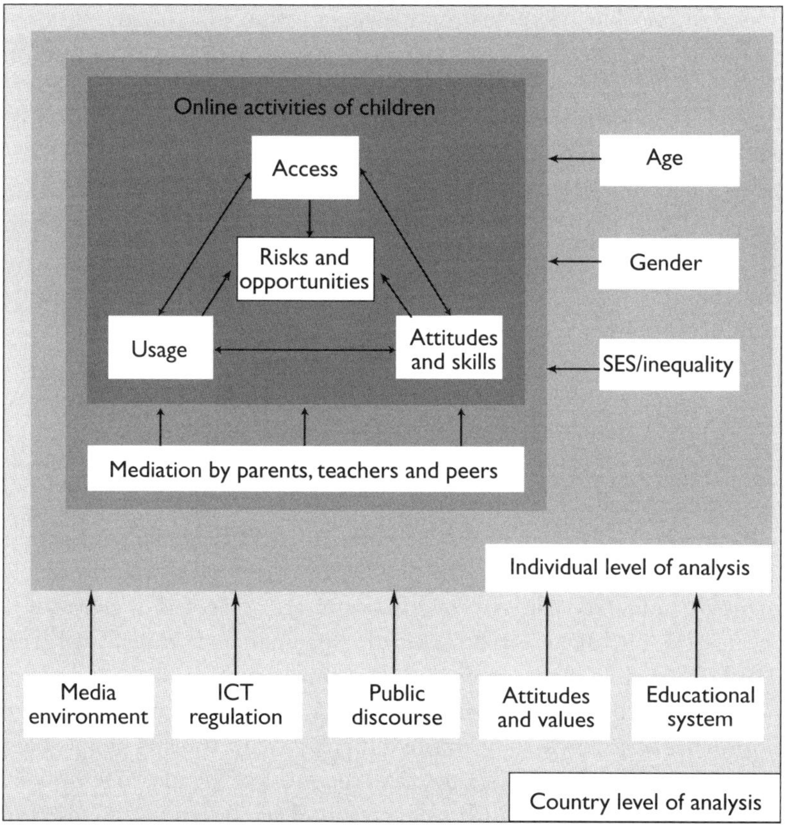

Note: SES = socio-economic status.

9

In practice, it was not feasible to directly compare the findings of almost 400 separate research studies identified in the online database, given their many differences in approach, sample, methodology and quality. Instead, the EU Kids Online network constructed a list of research questions and hypotheses to be tested against the findings – for example, are there gender differences in internet access? How do parents mediate children's internet use? Do children from middle-class families enjoy more online opportunities than those from working-class families? The body of research from each country was then interrogated by network members from that country in order to judge whether there was sufficient evidence within each country to answer each research question, and to support or contradict each hypothesis, or not. This proved an effective approach with which we draw qualified conclusions as appropriate to the evidence available.

Towards evidence-based policy

This volume has been written a decade or so after many children and young people first went online. In policy circles, many initiatives have been developed, with some success, although some mistakes have also been made and early lessons learned. Research has certainly revealed what children do online. They relish the internet, love staying in constant contact with friends, and feel free and safe in the world provided they have their mobile phone with them. They devote hours to creating art or music and sharing it with others in collaborative communities, gain confidence in knowing that information is always at their fingertips and that the most personal advice can be obtained in privacy. And, most simply, they appreciate that a source of huge entertainment is always open to them. Much of this has been enabled by public and private sector policy developments to encourage internet adoption and appropriate use in homes, work, schools, leisure, government and commerce.

However, research has also revealed some of the failures of ill-conceived policies. It shows the parents who struggle with unreadable manuals and safety guides, unused computers neglected in classrooms, 'naughty' children evading adult supervision, poor children disadvantaged anew, teachers deskilled in the face of digitally literate pupils and so on. Today, attention is switching from efforts focused on improving basic access to the more difficult task of ensuring people have the skills, or digital literacies, to make the most of the internet. Equally difficult is the question of how to respond to the growing evidence of online risk (Livingstone and Millwood Hargrave, 2009): as ECPAT

(End Child Prostitution, Child Pornography and the Trafficking of Children) International's review for the United Nations (UN) observes, although many of these risks are hardly new to society, key features of the online environment (its increasingly networked and mobile nature, convenience of distribution, permanence of images, ability to manipulate messages and conditions of anonymity and privacy) are reshaping children's risk experiences on and offline (Muir, 2005; see also ISTTF, 2008).

Just a few years ago, ministries of education promoted online opportunities while ministries of justice worried about online risks. But it is increasingly recognised that, since both research and practice reveal the many interdependencies between opportunities and risks, policies for children online must be developed in tandem with each other. In developing such policies, two points of consensus have emerged: first, that policy should be generated through multistakeholder dialogue and, moreover, be implemented by multiple stakeholders rather than just by governments; and second, that policy should be evidence-based, firmly grounded in and tested against the experiences of children and families across diverse everyday settings. Thus, recent years have seen an explosion in multistakeholder conferences, government consultations and international events all designed to bring together those players who have a stake in how the internet could and should both empower and protect children and young people (on occasion, this has included parents although too rarely has it included children directly). These are not always easy occasions, with many tensions still to be resolved, yet national and international alliances are developing and useful policies are resulting. The demand for evidence-based policy is no easier – research findings quickly become out of date, as the technologies, the institutions that promote and regulate them and children's own practices all continue to change. Further, the research agenda may not align with the policy agenda, partly because this policy agenda is not always accessible to the research community, partly because researchers seek a complex and contextualised understanding that may not generate straightforward policy implications.

In scoping the array of relevant policies, the EU Kids Online network has identified a number of facets as being central to shaping the conditions of children's engagement with the internet. One is the issue of children's rights[1], including e-inclusion[2] and equality considerations, positive content provision and promoting creative, civic and learning opportunities. Awareness raising is also important, taking into account parental mediation, as well as education and the role of the internet in schools[3]. Effective industry self-regulation, involving the development of an array of codes of conduct and institutional practices associated with content classification, age verification and social networking, is to be strongly encouraged, as are efforts towards child welfare and protection, including the operation of law enforcement agencies. Additionally, there is growing interest in programmes to promote media and digital literacy[4] and the regulation of privacy, including the protection of data and treatment of personal information.

To address these and related agendas, this volume encompasses a wide range of findings and policies concerned with the online opportunities and risks afforded by the internet. Much of the research conducted thus far has been largely descriptive of children's activities or problems associated with the internet. However, increasingly, researchers seek to go beyond description in order to guide policy more directly. In part, the agenda for this research must be informed by policy makers: they play a crucial role in shaping EC and government actions, and this in turn relies on knowledge of, for example, whether filtering software or parental supervision is more effective in making children safer online, whether girls and boys benefit equally from the internet or whether internet-related policies developed in a country with long-term experience of the internet can be applied or adapted for a country still new to it. In part, however, the research agenda must be independent of policy, drawing more widely on what researchers know of children's lives, educational systems, the risk society or cultural values in parenting and using this both to inform and at times to critique or redirect the policy agenda. Different contributors take different approaches in this volume, but we hope that, taken together, the chapters provide an insightful, valuable and multidimensional portrait of children's internet use in the first decade of the 21st century following widespread diffusion across Europe.

Notes

[1] The UN Convention on the Rights of the Child asserts children's rights to express their views freely in all matters affecting them (Article 12), freedom of expression through any medium of the child's choice (Article 13), freedom of association and peaceful assembly (Article 15), protection of privacy (Article 16) and to mass media that disseminate information and material of social and cultural benefit to the child, with particular regard to the linguistic needs of minority/indigenous groups and to protection from material injurious to the child's well-being (Article 17).

[2] 'e-Inclusion means both inclusive ICT and the use of ICT to achieve wider inclusion objectives. It focuses on the participation of all individuals

and communities in all aspects of the information society' (http://ec.europa. eu/information_society/events/ict_riga_2006/doc/declaration_riga.pdf).

[3] Developing the latter specifically, the EC's successive Safer Internet programmes have sought to increase the knowledge base to guide the promotion of a safer online environment for children and young people in Europe, initiating a series of actions to minimise online harms (via the Inhope network of hotlines) and to maximise awareness of online risk among parents, teachers and other stakeholders, including children (via the Insafe network of awareness nodes).

[4] Widely defined as 'the ability to access, analyse, evaluate and create messages across a variety of contexts' (Aufderheide, 1993: 1), this is increasingly considered vital for children and adults alike. The EC has formed an Expert Group on Media Literacy, and its enhancement is required by the Audiovisual Media Services (AVMS) Directive (November 2007) as well as supported by the Council of Europe and UNESCO.

References

Aufderheide, P. (1993) *Media literacy: A report of the national leadership conference on media literacy*, Aspen, CO: Aspen Institute.

Beck, U. (1986/2005) *Risk society: Towards a new modernity*, London: Sage Publications.

Berker, T., Hartmann, M., Punie, Y. and Ward, K.J. (eds) (2006) *The domestication of media and technology*, Maidenhead: Open University Press.

Bronfenbrenner, U. (1979) *The ecology of human development*, Cambridge, MA: Harvard University Press.

EC (European Commission) (2008) *Towards a safer use of the internet for children in the EU – A parents' perspective, Analytical report*, Flash Eurobarometer Series # 248, conducted by The Gallup Organisation, Hungary, Luxembourg: EC (http://ec.europa.eu/information_ society/activities/sip/docs/eurobarometer/analyticalreport_2008. pdf).

Giddens, A. (1984) *The constitution of society: Outline of the theory of structuration*, Cambridge: Polity.

Giddens, A. (1991) *Modernity and self-identity: Self and society in the late modern age*, Cambridge: Polity.

Haddon, L. (2004) *Information and communication technologies in everyday life: A concise introduction and research guide*, Oxford: Berg.

Hasebrink, U., Livingstone, S., Haddon, L. and Ólafsson, K. (2009) *Comparing children's online opportunities and risks across Europe: Cross-national comparisons for EU Kids Online* (2nd edn), London: London School of Economics and Political Science, EU Kids Online (Deliverable D3.2 for the EC Safer Internet Plus Programme).

Hutchby, I. (2001) 'Technologies, texts and affordances', *Sociology*, vol 35, no 2: 441-56.

ISTTF (Internet Safety Technical Task Force) (2008) *Enhancing child safety and online technologies: Final Report of the ISTTF to the Multi-state Working Group on Social Networking of State Attorney Generals of the United States*, Cambridge, MA: Berkman Center for Internet and Society, Harvard University (http://cyber.law.harvard.edu/node/4021).

Jackson, S. and Scott, S. (1999) 'Risk anxiety and the social construction of childhood', in D. Lupton (ed) *Risk*, Cambridge: Cambridge University Press: 86-107.

James, A. and James, A.L. (eds) (2008) *European childhoods: Cultures, politics and childhoods in Europe*, Basingstoke: Palgrave Macmillan.

Lievrouw, L. and Livingstone, S. (eds) (2006) *Handbook of new media: Social shaping and social consequences* (Updated student edn), London: Sage Publications.

Livingstone, S. (2003) 'Children's use of the internet: reflections on the emerging research agenda', *New Media & Society*, vol 5, no 2: 147-66.

Livingstone, S. (2009) *Children and the internet: Great expectations, challenging realities*, Cambridge: Polity.

Livingstone, S. and Millwood Hargrave, A. (2009) *Harm and offence in media content: A review of the empirical literature* (2nd edn), Bristol: Intellect.

MacKenzie, D. and Wajcman, J. (eds) (1999) *The social shaping of technology* (2nd edn), Buckingham: Open University Press.

Mansell, R. and Silverstone, R. (eds) (1996) *Communication by design: The politics of information and communication technologies*, New York, NY: Oxford University Press.

Muir, D. (2005) *Violence against children in cyberspace: A contribution to the United Nations study on violence against children*, Bangkok, Thailand: ECPAT International (www.ecpat.net/EI/Publications/ICT/Cyberspace_ENG.pdf).

Orgad, S. (2007) 'The interrelations between "online" and "offline": questions, issues and implications', in R. Mansell, C. Avgerou, D. Quah and R. Silverstone (eds) *The Oxford handbook of information and communication technologies*, Oxford: Oxford University Press, pp 514-36.

Prensky, M. (2001) 'Digital natives, digital immigrants', *On the Horizon*, vol 9, no 5: 1-2.

Qvortrup, J. (1994) *Childhood matters: Social theory, practice and politics*, Avebury: Aldershot.

Woolgar, S. (2002) 'Five rules of virtuality', in S. Woolgar (ed) *Virtual society? Technology, cyberbole, reality*, Oxford: Oxford University Press: 1-22.

Section I
Researching European children online

TWO

What we know, what we do not know

Verónica Donoso, Kjartan Ólafsson and Thorbjörn Broddason

The assumption that young people are more future-oriented, more apt and more technologically aware and interested than adults (Rushkoff, 1996) is not new. To some extent, it is believed that young people's early adoption of and adaptation to new media and technologies such as the internet are mainly the result of the inherent interest adolescents are assumed to have in new technologies as well as their massive use in formal educational settings (Lee, 2005). This group, 'the Net generation' as dubbed by Tapscott (1998), is important because, even though they may actually represent the future and, in fact, be 'the vanguard', they also constitute a vulnerable group, potentially 'at risk' from some of the new information and communication technologies (ICTs) (Livingstone, 2002: 2).

But what do we know about this age group and their online behaviour? What does current research tell us about children's experiences online? Does research provide enough evidence of the positive and negative consequences of children's uses of the internet? Based on the identification and analysis of almost 400 European studies about children and their online practices, this chapter seeks to identify the key research questions regarding children's access and uses of the internet and related online technologies[1]. Here we also attempt to map the emerging research agenda, reflecting on current pressing research gaps and on the principles that have guided research so far and those that should guide future research in the field.

An overview of existing available research

In order to get the best possible picture of research carried out in Europe, the European Union (EU) Kids Online project mapped out the available research on children's access to and use of the internet and related online technologies in the 21 countries participating in the network (see Staksrud et al, 2009).

To accomplish this, it was decided to create a repository that would contain relevant data on research carried out in the field mainly during the period 2000-08, allowing the addition of some earlier studies if they were highly relevant[2]. In total, 408 studies of children and the internet were collected and analysed (see Figure 2.1, which includes multicountry studies as well as single country ones). For each of these studies, the sampling strategy, the methodology employed, the topics researched, the countries involved, the year of data collection and publication details, as well as some other facets of the study, were registered, coded and entered into a common repository.

Even though our aim was to generate an exhaustive collection of European research in the field, it can never be absolutely comprehensive. Moreover, there will always be grey areas as regards what to include. Indeed, even if the network tried as far as possible to provide a clear sampling frame for the data collection procedure it is inevitable that the choice of studies included in the analysis depends to some extent on the individuals who collected the data, on their access to and knowledge

Figure 2.1: Number of studies identified by country (multicoded)

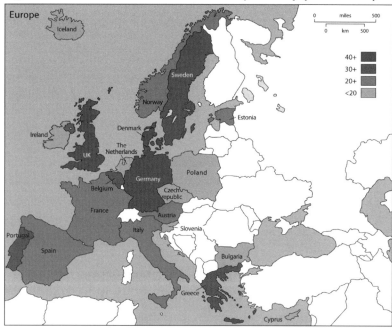

Note: Both multicountry and single country studies are included.

about research being carried out in their countries and also on their judgement regarding what to include and what to leave out from the repository. Bearing this in mind, we still believe that the data collected provide a fairly accurate picture of the research conducted on children and the internet in Europe.

What we can learn from existing research

As shown in Figure 2.2, studies on children and the internet have been growing steadily since 2000, with the exception of 2007 and 2008. Note, however, that the years reported in Figure 2.2 correspond to the date in which data collection started and not to the publication date. This may explain why the number of studies in 2007 and 2008 declined, most likely as a result of not having been published at the time the data for our repository was collected.

Figure 2.2: Number of studies by year of data collection

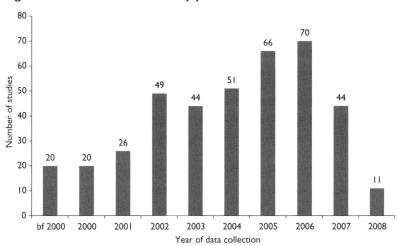

As regards research participants, teenagers are the most heavily studied age group (see Figure 2.3). Indeed, almost two out of three studies include teenagers aged 14 to 15 years old. This trend has remained rather stable since 2000. The large number of studies on teenagers may be due to the frequently expressed concern about adolescents and their exposure to and uses of the internet. Another possible explanation is the relative ease with which this age group can be recruited to take part in research compared to both younger children and older age groups.

While research also provides evidence that children aged five or under use the internet (Attwell et al, 2003; EC, 2005, Figure 2.3 shows that only a few studies consider this age group. As noted above, one possible explanation for the limited number of studies on very young children could be the complications involved in the data collection for this age group. Perhaps related to this is the fact that only 40% of the studies on children up to five years old use a quantitative approach, compared to almost 60% for the 9-12 years age group. Hence, it seems sensible to highlight the need for more studies focusing on or including younger children, especially those aged eight or younger.

Figure 2.3: Number of studies by age group (multicoded)

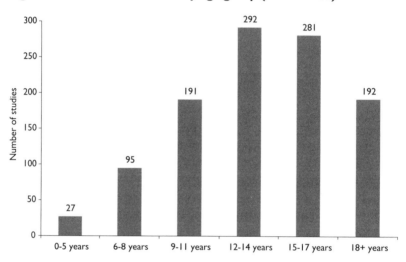

Some studies on adults' access and use of the internet include children and vice versa. Thus, adults can be present in a study both as participants in their own right or as individuals connected to the children (for example parents or teachers). Studies of the youngest children (aged 0-5 years) are most likely to include parents. Conversely, as the children participating in the study get older, parents are less likely to be involved. Unfortunately we do not have precise information about the extent to which parents are used as proxy respondents, although we are inclined to believe that this is the main reason why parents are included in research on younger children.

What has been researched?

When looking at how the focus of the studies has changed over time two general aspects are worth mentioning. First, the number of topics covered is increasing. For the studies conducted in 2000 and earlier the average number of topics covered was around seven compared to eleven for studies begun in the years 2007-08. Second, Figure 2.4 shows that while studies of parental mediation fluctuate, there is an overall increase in studies with a focus on risk. This might be an indicator of researchers' heightened awareness of risks that in turn may reflect public demand for more knowledge on this issue. It is interesting, at least, to note that non-profit organisations, regulators and the European Commission (EC) have a keen interest in studies that focus on risks (Stald and Haddon, 2008: 51).

Figure 2.4: Proportion of studies with a focus on risk/parental mediation by year of data collection

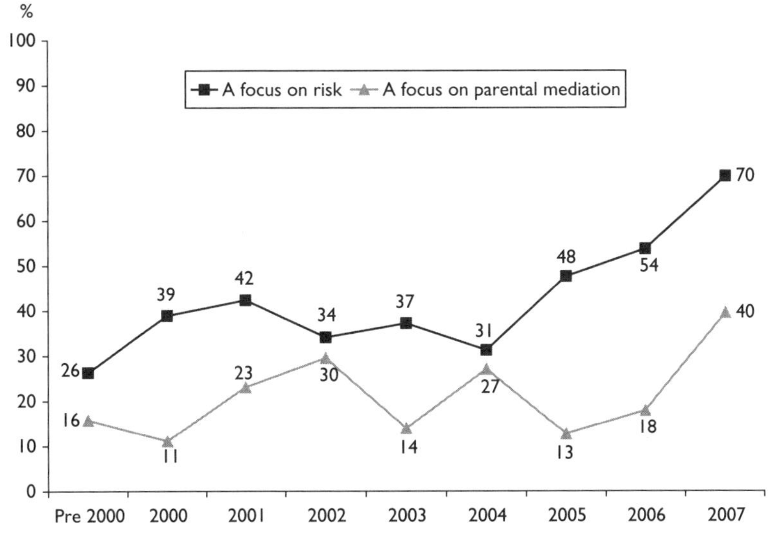

Turning to a more detailed analysis of what has been researched, of the 40 topics identified within the EU Kids Online data repository, internet access and use are the most broadly researched and well covered in all countries. Table 2.1 shows that 83% of the studies analysed include information on online usage, while 65% include information on online access. Not surprisingly, 64% of the studies include relevant information on online interests and activities. Also widely present, although not as frequently as issues relating to online access and usage, are topics dealing with online skills (42%), gender differences in terms of children's experiences of the internet (32%), children's social networking (31%) and online games (25%). Looking across the participating countries, the latter topics were fairly well covered, although less frequently than topics relating to access and general online use.

There are some important research gaps, in the sense that there is little of online civic/political participation (8%), as well as interpreting online content (12%) – relevant for the current interest in digital literacy. Also absent from the current research agenda are the factors that lead

Table 2.1: Percentage of studies by topic

Topics relating to children		Topics relating to risks	
Online usage	83	Exposure to harmful or offensive content	25
Online access	65	Contact with strangers	25
Online interests and activities	64	Encountering sexual/racist/hate material	22
Online skills	42	Giving out personal information	22
Gender differences	32	Exposure to illegal content	17
Social networking	31	Cyberbullying	15
Online games	25	Privacy	13
Effects of going online	23	Advertising – commercial exploitation	11
Learning online	23	Illegal downloading	10
Concerns and frustrations	21	Cyberstalking	9
Identity play	19	Misinformation	8
Creating online content	17	User generated content	7
Strategies for finding things	13	Hacking	6
Interpreting online content	12	Gambling	4
Seeking advice online	12	Visiting problematic sites	3
Civic/political participation	8	*One or more of the above*	46
One or more of the above	96		
Topics relating to parental regulation		Other topics relating to parents	
Style of regulation	25	Parents' competencies	17
Knowledge of children's practices	21	Concerns about online technologies	17
Parents' awareness of online risks	17	Attitudes to online technologies	15
Parents' media/information literacy	11	*One or more of the above*	22
Children's responses to regulation	10		
Effectiveness of filters etc.	8		
One or more of the above	37		

some children and teenagers to lack internet access as well as research on recent applications such as blogging or podcasting.

In total, 45% of the studies include at least one topic relating to risks while 36% include some information on regulation, in particular, regulation styles (25%) and parental knowledge of children's online practices (21%). The risk areas that had been researched more are exposure to harmful or offensive content (25%), contact with strangers (25%), encountering sexual/racist or hate material (22%) and giving out personal information (22%). The least researched topics are hacking (6%), gambling (4%) and visiting other problematic sites (such as ones on anorexia or suicide) (3%). There is clearly more scope for research here, as well as for risks associated with user-generated content (7%), given the rise in popularity of social networking sites in particular.

Lastly, although several platforms – mobile phones, games consoles and other devices – can potentially allow children to gain access to online applications, the PC remains the dominant way to access the internet. Presumably because of their lower popularity, to date there has been little research on children's use of such alternative platforms. It therefore seems relevant to explore the ways in which children are appropriating these newer platforms and to find out about the potential risks and opportunities they may offer to them.

What research methods are being employed?

Almost 60% of the studies analysed employed quantitative methodologies, whereas only 20% used a purely qualitative approach. The remaining studies used a combination of both qualitative and quantitative methodologies. Even if the number of studies has considerably increased in later years, these proportions remain fairly stable. Lee (2005) argues that the current quantitative focus of research should be shifted, while Livingstone (2002) notes that the predominance of surveys has produced reliable and representative but often not theoretically informed findings. The other problem of survey methods is that they often fail to take into account the 'life world' (Schutz, 1974), or the world of everyday life, meaning here that they lack a deeper understanding of children's own experiences and perceptions of their online practices.

That said, qualitative research on its own has its limitations: it generally relies on small samples, selected for their diversity rather than their statistical representativeness, and even though these methods seek to capture the variety of experience making for insightful accounts of the contexts and nature of internet use, they fail to support claims about distribution or scale, leaving open questions of representativeness and demographic distribution (Livingstone, 2002, 2003).

Hence there is a case for encouraging a broader range of methodological approaches, as well as approaches that combine qualitative and quantitative methods, that could ensure the quality and interpretability of the data obtained (for example Denzin, 1978; Campbell and Holland, 2005). Moreover, the systematic combination of various methods may result in increased validity and the congruence of research findings may provide more detailed, multilayered and multidimensional perspectives of the phenomenon under study (Kopinak, 1999).

Main lessons learned

It seems clear that in the last decade there has been a dramatic expansion in research on children and the internet. As the knowledge base has been built up there has also been a growing consensus regarding several key conceptual claims (Hasebrink et al, 2009). These can inform future research agendas over and above addressing some of the research gaps previously outlined.

First, researchers agree that, while internet access is an important factor because it is the prerequisite for use, access does not necessarily equal use. Hence we need more on the factors influencing children's use (or non-use) of different aspects of the online world.

Second, it is difficult to make general claims about the actual impact of new technologies as such because they exist and evolve in specific socio-cultural contexts framed within unique social institutions, norms and values, hence the need for more cross-national studies to clarify the influence of these contexts.

Third, the polarisations implied in the terms 'real' as opposed to 'virtual' and 'offline' as opposed to 'online' are problematic. The internet is real and has real consequences for real people, including real children. It also shows the necessity of researching their use of the internet in the broader context of children's everyday life and media use in general.

Fourth, and as discussed in several other chapters of this volume, if children and adolescents are to gain the necessary skills to benefit from the internet, this may involve experimenting, taking risks and pushing adult-defined boundaries. Research on risks in particular needs to be sensitive to this.

Fifth and finally, the solid tradition of research on children's television use has been extended to research on the internet. However, the internet is a much more complex type of medium which is not equivalent to television, or the radio, or the computer, but rather it remediates, reproduces and reconfigures the aspects and social practices that are connected to such technologies (Bolter and Grusin, 1999). Hence, while research on children and the internet can draw on some of the frameworks used to study television, it needs always to take this difference into account.

Conclusion

The history of television research is itself relevant when we ask whether the research on children and the internet marks new directions or continues longer traditions. In order to answer this question it is helpful to look back in order to recall some observations made with that television tradition. For instance, if we go all the way back to the very cradle of television research, we find Sir Hector Hetherington arguing (in the foreword to the pioneering work of Hilde T. Himmelweit and her collaborators) a point that could equally well apply to contemporary internet research: '[N]o research of this kind is ever final. The situation itself changes, and the methods of inquiry become more refined' (Hetherington, 1958: vi). Moreover, Hetherington went on to make a point still pertiment for our current concerns about the online risks faced by children: 'Every new medium of communication has in its time aroused anxiety.... Now it is the turn of television' (1958: xiii). Of course, to 21st-century researchers, television is no longer a 'new medium' and in the meantime other 'new media' have become objects of considerable concern. To paraphrase Sir Hector: now it is the turn of the internet.

A few years later, on the other side of the Atlantic, in the the pioneering work of Schramm and his associates, it is clear that the urgency that we now feel about research relating to children and the internet was equally present then with regard to television: 'No mass medium has ever exploded over a continent as television exploded over North America in the 1950s.... More swiftly than anywhere else, television penetrated to homes where there were young children' (Schramm et al, 1961: 11). In addtion, these researchers open on a statement that – with the replacement of a single word – could still serve as the battle cry for present-day research into children's use of new media: 'It is the children who are most active in this relationship. It is they who use television, rather than television that uses them' (Schramm et al, 1961: 1).

Moving to more recent sources, we have a very well researched and thoughtful article by two distinguished authors, Dorothy and Jerome

Singer, which was published in an issue of *The Annals of the American Academy of Political and Social Science* towards the end of the last century. Significantly, this issue was devoted to 'children and television'. Making a strong plea for improved school curricula in media literacy that would be a precursor to current calls for digital literacy, the authors point out that '[t]eaching children to understand television can yield a more critical, intelligent audience' (Singer and Singer, 1998: 175). The writing of this sensible advice coincides with a historical turn of the tide when children were beginning to be lured away from television in droves by the internet, although this was not acknowledged in this article.

Apart from the shift in research to the internet, the study of television was itself changing. In Livingstone's introduction to a special issue of the *European Journal of Communication* on 'Young people and the changing media environment in Europe', she already notes '… the shift from "television" to "the media environment"…' (1998: 437) and adds, with a lesson for current internet researchers, '[r]esearching "new media" means studying a moving target' (1998: 437). This statement, which was pertinent in 1998, fully retains its validity a decade into the 21st century.

The research discussed in this chapter clearly represents at least a partial break with the television research tradition, a break necessitated by the qualitative change in the media and communication relations of young people in the final years of the 20th century. Nonetheless, some of the questions asked in that tradition, the motivations for research, the overarching frameworks used and the understanding of the nature of the object of study continue to remain pertient for researchers of children and the internet. We may safely conclude that, although discontinuities are easily spotted, there are also clear and important continuities.

Notes

[1] Subsequently, a small number of these studies was removed from the data repository as a duplicate entry.

[2] A number of decisions had to be made regarding what to include and what to leave out from such a repository: for instance, the decision to classify the research according to the year it was carried out rather than its year of publication as a way of ensuring the comparability of the data collected. One further decision, for the purposes of charting research available, was to include Master's and PhD theses in countries where there was more limited research. Some of the later analyses, such as those on the factors influencing research in Chapter Five (of this volume), excluded these as well as the multicountry studies because of its particular focus.

References

Attwell, P., Suazo-Garcia, B. and Battle, J. (2003) 'Computers and young children: social benefit or social problem', *Social Forces*, vol 82, no 1: 277-96.

Bolter, J.D. and Grusin, G. (1999) *Remediation: Understanding new media*, Cambridge, MA: MIT Press.

Campbell, J., and Holland, J. (2005) *Methods in development research: Combining qualitative and quantitative approaches*, Rugby: ITDG Publishing.

Denzin, K. (1978) *The research act*, New York, NY: McGraw-Hill.

EC (European Commission) (2005) *Eurobarometer survey on safer internet*, Luxembourg: EC

Hasebrink, U., Livingstone, S., Haddon, L. and Ólafsson, K. (2009) *Comparing children's online opportunities and risks across Europe: Cross-national comparisons for EU Kids Online* (2nd edn), London: London School of Economics and Political Science, EU Kids Online (Deliverable D3.2 for the EC Safer Internet Plus Programme).

Hetherington, H. (1958) 'Foreword', in H.T. Himmelweit, A.N. Oppenheim and P.Vince (eds) *Television and the child*, London: Oxford University Press: i–xiii.

Kopinak, J.K. (1999) 'The use of triangulation in a study of refugee well-being', *Quality and Quantity*, vol 33, no 2: 169-83.

Lee, L. (2005) 'Young people and the internet: from theory to practice', *Young*, vol 13, no 4: 315-26.

Livingstone, S. (1998) 'Introduction', *European Journal of Communication*, vol 13, no 4: 435-51.

Livingstone, S. (2002) *Children's use of the internet: A review of the research literature*, Report to the National Children's Bureau, London).

Livingstone, S. (2003) 'Children's use of the internet: reflections on the emerging research agenda', *New Media & Society*, vol 5, no 2: 147-66.

Rushkoff, D. (1996) *Media virus! Hidden agendas in popular culture*, New York, NY: Ballantine Books.

Schramm, W., Lyle, J. and Parker, E. (1961) *Television in the lives of our children*, Stanford, CA: Stanford University Press.

Schutz, A. (1974) *The structures of the life world*, Oxford: Heinemann.

Singer, D.G. and Singer, J.L. (1998) 'Developing critical viewing skills and media literacy in children', *The Annals of the American Academy of Political and Social Science*, vol 557: 164-79.

Staksrud, E., Livingstone, S., Haddon, L. and Ólafsson, K. (2009) *What do we know about children's use of online technologies? A report on data availability and research gaps in Europe*, London: London School of Economics and Political Science, EU Kids Online (Deliverable D1.1 for the EC Safer Internet Plus Programme).

Stald, G. and Haddon, L. (2008) *Cross-cultural contexts of research: Factors influencing the study of children and the internet in Europe*, London: London School of Economics and Political Science, EU Kids Online (Deliverable D3.2 for the EC Safer Internet Plus Programme).

Tapscott, D. (1998) *Growing up digital: The rise of the net generation*, New York, NY: McGraw-Hill.

THREE

Research with children

Bojana Lobe, José Alberto Simões and Bieke Zaman

Introduction

This chapter untangles the ways in which young audiences, especially digital media and internet users, have been researched and how they can be approached. The first part is a brief discussion of the policy concept 'children and young people', since it has clear implications for how the research agenda is defined. The second part examines different theoretical approaches to the problem of whether children should be directly involved in research projects or not. In other words, should we be doing research *with* or *on* children? This distinction is important not only from a practical point of view but also from a theoretical (epistemological) point of view. The last part of this chapter addresses the issue of *how* one should research children's internet and digital media uses and experiences. More specifically, we consider whether methods conceived for working with children have to be entirely new or simply adapted from existing ones, and we discuss which methods are most appropriate for researching children's media/internet uses and experiences.

Constructing childhood and youth for digital media research

We begin this section with what might be seen as an obvious statement, but which is nonetheless of the utmost importance for our discussion: childhood and youth are social constructions; they are neither mere natural categories, nor universal ones. This assumption may be easily confirmed by the fact that both childhood and youth have changed over time and tend to assume a variety of configurations in different cultural and social contexts (Buckingham, 2000, 2007). From laws and public policies to relationships within families, from media representations to interpersonal communications, children and young people have been acknowledged and addressed in various ways (sometimes contradictorily) by different people and entities who contribute to define what they are or should be.

The media play an essential role in this process. One could say that childhood and youth are being defined to an ever-greater extent by the media. This is not just because media content reflects several aspects of children's and young people's lives, but also because children and young people are increasingly devoting their time to a vast array of media-related commodities that have been targeted at them by media industries for several decades now (Buckingham, 2007)[1]. Media-related commodities are ever more important in children's and young people's lives, not only as simple products but more essentially as resources with which particular cultures are built and identities defined.

The question of whether youth cultures are a product of the media or whether it is the media that simply tends to reproduce youth cultures has been discussed at least since the mid-1950s, when a particular consumer culture targeted at young people begun to emerge. Nowadays, this youth culture has become clearly globalised. Several youth commodities and practices are shared by most young people all over the world, even if they can be appropriated locally in different ways (Bennett, 2000). However, even if we can find the same products in remote and unforeseen parts of the globe, this does not mean that the world has become culturally homogenised (Featherstone, 1995). In this context, online technologies have offered new opportunities for self-expression and communication, since their advent has ineluctably challenged the traditional power relations between diffusion and reception, producers and consumers.

There is no consensus of opinion regarding these changes. There is a parallel between discourses about technology in general and what might be its effect on children and young people in particular. This has to do with a tendency for media history to repeat itself: the emergence of a particular medium is usually followed by polarised views, either welcoming its adoption for its unquestionable – and even revolutionary – benefits, as in most rhetoric regarding the 'information society' (Webster, 1995; May, 2002); or demonising it for the threats it embodies. These views not only represent a simplified perspective about media influence in society, emphasising certain features and overlooking others, but they also show an inclination to see technology by way of a certain determinism (Robins and Webster, 1999), ignoring the fact that the relation between technology and society is far more complex and interactive.

We may find versions of these hyperbolic discourses about technology that explicitly address children's and young people's digital media use. On the one hand, young generations are seen as empowered by technology. They are the 'experts', the 'digital natives' (Prensky, 2001); their ability to use computers and technology in general is regarded as 'natural' (Tapscott, 1998). This assumption has led to a rhetorical construction of the 'techno-savvy child' – the notion of children as a 'digital generation' that is somehow spontaneously competent in its relationships with technology (Buckingham, 2007: 16-17). On the other hand, children and young people (especially the former) are seen as vulnerable, needing protection. In this view, digital media are portrayed as a source of trouble, from which children must be protected at any cost: 'electronic media are seen to have singular power to exploit children's vulnerability, to undermine their individuality and to destroy their innocence' (Buckingham, 2000: 41).

Distinct views regarding children's and young people's digital media uses not only influence the way media regulation is established and how public policy[2] is defined, but they also influence the way research priorities are shaped. Moreover, different discourses construct distinct *objects* for research: 'they inform the questions we ask, the methods of investigation we adopt, and the criteria we use to define what counts as valid knowledge' (Buckingham, 2000: 104).

At the end of this brief discussion one fact has become clearer: we need further research on (methods to reveal) children's actual technology uses and experiences. Many assumptions about media effects are still not always based on profound research. To get a true answer to several of the questions being raised, we need to focus on researching *actual* uses and experiences as well as the contexts in which technology is adopted.

Research 'on' or 'with' children

Traditionally, the sociological studies of childhood and children's experiences have been inclined to research children using observation rather than participation, without the knowledge of those at the focus of observations (see Pole, 2007: 69). Such studies have often been school based (for example Hargreaves, 1967; Ball, 1967). More quantitative examples of children's studies frequently included proxy informants – such as parents or carers, teachers, educators – as reliable informants on children's experiences. In spite of the fact that this kind of research is cheaper and easier with regards to recruitment and ethical issues, it must be emphasised that it is regarded as being highly unreliable and even misleading in its attempt to depict children's experiences. Hence, it must be recognised that it is problematic, even if convenient, to work with adult-originated or official accounts of children's experiences – parental accounts of media use, school's provision of test scores (for example achievement, reading) or teachers' reports (for example of concentration, aggression, sociability) (Lobe et al, 2007) – without complementing them with alternative methods (van Evra, 2004), including children's accounts, as they may differ from those based on an adult's interpretation of a child's perspective.

In recent years we have seen an increased emphasis on the rights of children themselves (Morgan et al, 2002) and the need to give them a 'voice' in social research (Buckingham, 1993; Mahon et al, 1996; Morrow and Richards, 1996; Greig and Taylor, 1999). Those who research children have therefore looked towards ways of locating children's lives at the centre of the research process, strengthening the position of the child as an *active research participant* instead of a *passive research object* (Pole, 2007: 70). Such researchers regard the status of childhood as equal to any other stage in the life course.

This shift has been marked by the prepositional shift from working 'on' to working 'with' children (Lobe et al, 2007). Epistemologically, this is underpinned by recent sociological research of childhood that asserts the agency of children, albeit shaped and defined by their social and cultural contexts (cf James et al, 1998). The child-centred approach regards children as competent and reflexive in reporting their own experiences, giving them a voice and taking seriously what they say (Mayall, 1996). Researchers taking this view work 'with' and 'for' children rather than 'on' them at all levels of the research process – from designing the study, data collection to the data reporting. Such an approach has implications for the design of research with children, emphasising the importance of including everyday contexts within the scope of the research (and not, for instance, bringing children as 'subjects' into a laboratory or neglecting to note the characteristics of their household or neighbourhood when surveying children). It also tends to favour the qualitative over the quantitative (Lobe et al, 2007).

In stressing children's agency within a structured, often intrusive or highly determining, adult context, the new sociologists of childhood argue that children's lives are often lived in the interstices of adult spaces or timetables and that children may be expected to circumvent, evade or subvert adult expectations or norms as regards their behaviour. The researcher must thus design their methods in such a way that such micro-tactics of everyday life are recognised (de Certeau, 1984; Corsaro,

1997). Children are, after all, playful, sometimes silly or naughty, often serious and forthright. The point is for our research methods to find the meaning in their actions.

Last but not least, this child–centred approach also demands sensitivity to ethical issues (Morrow and Richards, 1996). The recruitment, sampling, data collection and analysis of data have to follow ethical standards. Normally, the first step would be to obtain informed consent from children by providing them with accurate information about the research, how the data will be anonymised and stored, as well as how the results will be disseminated. Complete anonymity needs to be guaranteed for children. They need to be aware at all times that they can voluntarily decide whether they wish to participate in the research or not (it is not up to their parents to decide). Reciprocity among a researcher and a child respondent needs to be assured (see Lobe et al, 2007). Finally, at the phase of data collection itself children need to be listened to closely and compassionately.

Methodological issues of researching children's digital uses and experiences

This section deals with the methodological issues regarding research on children's online and digital risks and opportunities. First, we discuss differences between adults and children that are methodologically relevant. Then, we specify in more detail which methods are most appropriate for researching children's media/internet use and experiences. Finally, we end by discussing the usefulness of mixed methods in studying children.

Each research project, whatever the participants' ages, starts with a specification of the research purpose that leads to a certain choice of method. Often, a choice of a particular theoretical framework goes hand in hand with a corresponding method (or methods in the case of triangulation of data) (Greene and Hogan, 2005: 16). From a perspective of the 'new sociology of childhood', for instance, methods that involve children as 'active' subjects will be preferred over methods that involve children as 'passive' objects.

In selecting the right methods, one might consider whether existing methods conceived for working with adults can also be used for working with children. To do this, methods should be evaluated against the children's level of understanding, knowledge, interests and particular location in the social world (Greene and Hill, 2005: 8). This exercise is more complex than a simple check of the method against what children of one chronological age should developmentally be able to do or understand. Children should be studied in context, so their interests and role within social constructs are also to be taken into account. Children are or have the potential to be active and conscious media users and should be treated as such in research.

When methods for adults are evaluated for their appropriateness to use with children, three differences between adults and children have to be taken into account: power hierarchies, participants' competencies and vulnerability. That said, in many areas we might conclude that there are likely to be more similarities between children and adults than differences, and indeed it might be more worthwhile to focus on differences between children. For instance, even within an equal chronological age, there are many differences among children, for example because of their gender or ethnic backgrounds.

When researching children's digital and online media use and experiences the first concern must be one of how questions are expressed. Children may use different terms to adults. Identifying these is not only vital to obtain valid research findings but also to provide a useful way in to children's own perspectives on media (Lobe et al, 2007). Second, when conducting studies on children's online risks, it has become apparent that the online risks of primary concern to children (for example bullying, viruses, spam, hoaxes) differ from those that concern adults (for example pornography, violence, paedophiles, 'race' hate). A possible negative consequence might be that an interview schedule could impose adult concerns on children and fail to discover their own concerns (Lobe et al, 2007).

The discussion of methods that are appropriate to research children's media/internet use and experiences starts by determining what kind of data one would like to obtain. There are three important research foci, each leading to a specific methodological approach. First, one might aim to understand children's online and digital subjective experiences. Second, the focus may be broader, with an aim of understanding children's experiences in context. Finally, one may wish to map children's online/digital access and use or document children's age-related competencies (Greene and Hogan, 2005).

Observations, interviews or more creative methods are most appropriate to *analyse children's subjective experiences with digital or online media*. If dynamics and experiences in a peer culture are concentrated on, focus groups may be more appropriate (Lobe et al, 2007). 'Experience' is an interpretative category, mediated through textual, discursive or visual accounts, and needs methods that grasp this multifaceted character in all its richness, individuality and meaning (Greene and Hogan, 2005). *When approaching children in their context*, ethnographic methods are preferred. Although ethnographic methods can give useful insights into children's everyday life, there is a drawback to naturalistic studies as well. Typically, such studies are characterised by less control, and it may be difficult to draw inferences from behaviours that occur in a particular context (Greene and Hogan, 2005: 97). *To map children's online and digital access and use*, quantitative methods such as standardised questionnaires are preferred. Moreover, measuring commonalities and differences in behaviour patterns also requires appropriate statistical methods (Greene and Hogan, 2005).

This concise methodological overview brings us back to whether one should adapt or extend existing methods of research to work with children (see Lobe et al, 2007). According to some researchers, children's vulnerability as research participants implies a need for specific methods. Others argue that there is no need for a specific set of methods to approach children, as instead they see children as competent and autonomous social actors. In determining how to treat child informants and in an attempt to find a middle way between these two extremes, a reflexive and self-critical approach is required of the researcher. In general, understanding children's (complex) experience, attitudes and behaviour requires a multiplicity of methodological approaches (Punch, 2002; Greene and Hogan, 2005).

As regards mixed methods, it seems almost intuitively appealing to imagine that a range of methodological strategies would capture a broader and deeper range of children's perceptions and experiences than reliance on a single technique (Darbyshire et al, 2005). Each method tends to provide only a partial account and may need to be supplemented by other methods. Further, using a variety of methods can itself stimulate and maintain the interest of the participant (Lobe, 2008). However, studies employing different methods are not per se preferable to those only relying on one method. Researchers should employ methods that enable them to solve the specific research problem most effectively, even if his can be done only by a single method. While mixing methods is not the only possible way to get the most out of a research project in which children are involved, it does promote a variety in approach by shifting the focus or introducing varied materials, which can help tackle children's limited concentration span. Not only are multiple methods preferable but so too are multiple interactions (Rogers et al, 2005).

Conclusion

The widespread acceptance of the United Nations (UN) Convention on the Rights of the Child and the 'new sociology of childhood' has led to a remarkable turning point. From that moment on, it has become more and more accepted and socially desirable to take children's voices and opinions seriously, seeing them as reliable people of value with their own rights. As a consequence, researchers have been challenged to find appropriate frameworks and methods to actively involve children in research projects. Because children's lives and experiences are so complex (mixed and) multidisciplinary approaches are preferred. To understand their world, no single theoretical or methodological approach should be dominant. Instead, the different approaches complement, build on or challenge each other.

When children are approached as unique individuals who are active agents, shaping their own lives and able to express their particular subjective experiences, qualitative research methods are most suitable. Moreover, if children are approached from an all-encompassing view, embedded in their socio-cultural context, ethnographic methods may be even more appropriate. In contrast, if the topic of research is focused on 'the child' (as far as this exists), or on a description of the parameters of children's experiences, then quantitative methods might be more appropriate. Typically, developmental psychology documenting children's age-related competencies or research projects that map children's online access and use rely on data that are obtained quantitatively.

To conclude this chapter, we would like to call for more research on methods that involve children. Far too often researchers do not go further than describing their method instead of also critically analysing it. Similarly, researchers tend to offer widely varying views on media effects that are not based on profound research revealing children's actual uses and experiences. Especially with the advent of new technologies, which adults did not grow up with and which allow children to be active 'prosumers' (professional consumers), good methods are crucial to understand these new experiences and to reveal the corresponding risks and opportunities.

Notes

[1] It is worth noting that children are increasingly becoming targets of marketing at a worldwide scale (especially as a result of multinational entertainment industries) and also at younger ages (or, to put it differently, they are becoming

older younger), which ultimately impacts on the way childhood is being constructed.

[2] In addition to the media, public policy may also be regarded as a major source of the social construction of childhood and youth, since it contributes to frame them in public discourse as policy targets that need particular attention, especially when they are regarded as problematic.

References

Ball, S.J. (1967) *Beachside comprehensive: A case study of secondary schooling*, Cambridge: Cambridge University Press.

Bennett, A. (2000) *Popular music and youth culture: Music, identity and place*, London: Macmillan.

Buckingham, D. (1993) *Reading audiences: Young people and the media*, Manchester: Manchester University Press.

Buckingham, D. (2000) *After the death of childhood. Growing up in the age of electronic media*, Cambridge: Polity.

Buckingham, D. (2007) *Beyond technology: Children's learning in the age of digital culture*, Cambridge: Polity.

Corsaro, W.A. (1997) *The sociology of childhood*, Thousand Oaks, CA: Pine Forge Press.

Darbyshire, P., MacDougall, C. and Schiller, W. (2005) 'Multiple methods in qualitative research with children: more insight or just more?', *Qualitative Research*, vol 5, no 4: 417–36.

de Certeau, M. (1984) *The practices of everyday life*, Los Angeles, CA: University of California Press.

Featherstone, M. (1995) *Undoing culture: Globalization, postmodernism and identity*, London: Sage Publications.

Greene, S. and Hogan, D. (2005) *Researching children's experience. Approaches and methods*, London: Sage Publications.

Greig, A. and Taylor, J. (1999) *Doing research with children*, London: Sage Publications.

Hargreaves, D.H. (1967) *Social relations in a secondary school*, London: Routledge and Kegan Paul.

James, A., Jenks, C. and Prout, A. (1998) *Theorizing childhood*, Cambridge: Cambridge University Press.

Lobe, B. (2008) *Integration of online research methods*, Ljubljana, Slovenia: Faculty of Social Sciences Press.

Lobe, B., Livingstone, S. and Haddon, L. (eds) (2007) *Researching children's experiences online across countries: Issues and problems in methodology*, London: London School of Economics and Political Science, EU Kids Online (Deliverable D4.1 methodological issues review for the EC Safer Internet Plus Programme).

Mahon, A., Glendinning, C., Clarke, K. and Craig, G. (1996) 'Researching children: methods and ethics', *Children & Society*, vol 10, no 2: 145-54.

May, C. (2002) *The information society. A sceptical view*, Cambridge: Polity.

Mayall, B. (1996) *Children, health and social order*, Buckingham: Open University Press.

Morgan, M., Gibbs, S., Maxwell, K. and Britten, N. (2002) 'Hearing children's voices: methodological issues in conducting focus groups with children aged 7-11', *Qualitative Research*, vol 2, no 1: 5-20.

Morrow, V. and Richards, M. (1996) 'The ethics of social research with children: an overview', *Children & Society*, vol 10, no 2: 90-105.

Pole, C. (2007) 'Researching children and fashion: an embodied ethnography', *Childhood*, vol 14, no 67: 67-84.

Prensky, M. (2001) 'Digital natives, digital immigrants', *On the Horizon*, vol 9, no 5: 1-2.

Punch, S. (2002) 'Research with children: the same or different from research with adults?', *Childhood*, vol 9, no 3: 321-41.

Robins, K. and Webster, F. (1999) *Times of the technoculture. From the information society to the virtual life*, London/New York, NY: Routledge.

Rogers, A.G., Casey, M., Ekert, J. and Holland, J. (2005) 'Interviewing children using an interpretive poetics', in S. Greene and D. Hogan (eds) *Researching children's experiences: Approaches and methods*, London: Sage Publications: 158-74.

Tapscott, D. (1998) *Growing up digital: The rise of the net generation*, New York, NY: McGraw-Hill.

van Evra, J. (2004) *Television and child development* (3rd edn), Mahwah, NJ: Lawrence Erlbaum Associates.

Webster, F. (1995) *Theories of the information society*, London: Routledge.

FOUR

Opportunities and pitfalls of cross-national research

Uwe Hasebrink, Kjartan Ólafsson and Václav Štětka

Looking beyond national borders for comparative purposes has a long tradition in the history of social science research, and can be traced back to early social scientists such as Max Weber and Émile Durkheim. And a discussion of the methodology of cross-national comparison is not an entirely new phenomenon (Rokkan, 1968). However, it has only been in the last couple of decades that cross-national (or cross-cultural) comparative research has really gained in popularity in the social sciences (Hoffmeyer-Zlotnik and Harkness, 2005). Among processes that have contributed to this trend, we can certainly name the gradual internationalisation of the academic community and the removal of political barriers as well as the digitalisation of communication. Hence, crossing traditional boundaries – geographical as well as social and cultural – has become easier. Funding bodies and policy makers have also been increasingly calling for comparative research, and this call seems to be readily accepted by researchers who find themselves initiating or invited to collaborate in multinational comparative projects (Livingstone, 2003).

The topic of children's use of online media demonstrates perhaps better than most other research topics the potential and pitfalls of cross-national comparative research. This chapter addresses some of the key theoretical and methodological questions related to cross-national comparative research, focusing in particular on the research field of (new) media and communication technologies. Following their presentation and some critical reflections in the first part of the chapter, these methodological considerations will then be applied to the topic of children's online behaviour and online risks and opportunities, taking the research conducted within the European Union (EU) Kids Online project as a concrete empirical example.

Existing research on children and new media: single countries dominate

As noted in Chapter Two of this volume, one of the steps taken in the EU Kids Online project involved mapping the available research on children's access to and use of the internet and related online and mobile technologies in the 21 countries participating in the project (for a description of the collection policy and key findings see Staksrud et al, 2009). Based on the sample of almost 400 studies collected and conducted in the years 2000-08, cross-national research does not seem to be the most common type of research. In fact, only about 8% of the studies cover more than one single country and a third of the 'multi-country' studies cover only two or three countries. Whether the data support the previously mentioned thesis that comparative research is increasing is a matter of definition, however. From Table 4.1 it is clear that multicountry studies have been growing in absolute number but so too have the single country studies, and as a result the multicountry studies constitute roughly the same proportion of studies each year between 2000 and 2008. There is also no clear indication that multicountry studies are growing in terms of the number of countries involved.

Thus, despite the growing number of comparative studies on children and new media, researchers certainly do not appear to be abandoning studies confined to only one country for studies covering more countries. When the single country studies are compared to the multicountry studies it is also interesting to note that there are many similarities between the groups. Both single country and multicountry studies focus on roughly the same age groups and use much the same methodology. In terms of topics researched, there is a tendency for multicountry studies to be more focused on topics related to risks (61% compared to 44%) and regulation (45% compared to 36%). The multicountry studies also have a slightly different funding structure: while none of the multicountry studies received funding from national regulators, 45% of them received all or part of their funding from the European Commission (EC). There might also be a link between the funding structure of the multicountry studies and their thematic focus, as the EC seems to be particularly interested in studies that explore the issues of risks (Stald and Haddon, 2008: 51).

Table 4.1. Number of studies conducted each year by number of countries involved

Year of data collection	Single country studies	Within multi-country		
		Multi-country studies	Covers two or three countries	Covers four or more countries
Before 2000	19	1	0	1
2000	17	3	1	2
2001	24	2	2	0
2002	44	5	1	4
2003	41	3	0	3
Total 2003 and before	145	14	4	10
As % of the total number of studies	*91.2*	*8.8*	*2.5*	*6.3*
2004	47	4	2	2
2005	59	7	2	5
2006	65	5	2	3
2007	42	2	0	2
2008	10	1	1	0
Total 2004 to 2008	223	19	7	12
As % of the total number of studies	*92.1*	*7.9*	*2.9*	*5.*

Source: EU Kids Online database, see www.eukidsonline.net

Doing comparative research: benefits and dilemmas

Given the increasing awareness of a need for more cross-national comparative research, it is perhaps interesting to note that this kind of research has not grown more rapidly, and has only just managed to keep up with the overall increase in studies on children and the internet. The most likely explanation is that doing cross-national comparative research is considerably more problematic than doing research that does not go beyond national or cultural borders in terms of data collection and interpretation. Putting it in mathematical language: if the problems facing researchers in a single country study are X, then the problems facing researchers in a multicountry setting are at least X *times* N, where N is the number of countries involved. Understandably, the larger the N, the more potential problems there are to deal with.

Cross-national comparative research has always entailed a variety of methodological problems regarding the quality and comparability of data that it is based on, especially in relation to country-specific meanings associated with issues or practices that are the subject of comparison. However, equally important to international comparisons are the differences in the social and political context of the research problem, for example in the academic and research traditions of the countries involved. These issues are particularly relevant when conducting research within the broad and diverse set of countries that were part of the EU Kids Online project.

Reasons for conducting comparative research are not difficult to enumerate. One of the most obvious concerns the question of universality and, simultaneously, uniqueness of findings based on nation-specific data, which cannot be answered unless we compare them with the data from other countries. Among other values of cross-national comparisons, broadening the research perspective and providing a 'fresh insight' into the issues examined within a particular national context are probably most often cited, implying that such an approach can reveal significant gaps in knowledge or point to new (and previously hidden) variables and factors influencing the phenomenon under scrutiny (Hantrais and Mangen, 1996; Livingstone, 2003).

Despite these self-evident advantages and benefits, cross-national research must cope with many methodological as well as practical challenges and pitfalls, causing some scholars to warn against injudicious and theoretically unfounded engagement in cross-country explorations. In enumerating the key methodological problems cross-national or cross-cultural collaborative research is facing, authors usually mention the selection of the research unit (which is typically the nation-state), the issues of sampling and comparability of data in the first place (Tilly, 1997), complemented by more practical issues such as variations in professional academic cultures and standards of writing and communication (Livingstone, 2003) – although they can also have serious methodological implications.

There is rarely a smooth, 'default' solution for any of the problems awaiting researchers at the start of a comparative research project. According to Else Øyen, 'there is no reason to believe there exists an easy and straightforward entry into comparative social research' (Øyen, 1990: 1). Possibly the only way forward is trying to learn from the examples – and mistakes – of others (Livingstone, 2003). In the following we describe and reflect on the comparative procedures of the EU Kids Online network in order to provide an example for future comparative projects.

Selecting countries for analysis

In the case of the EU Kids Online network, the EU Safer Internet Programme framed the research objectives as well as the organisational context. The EU's structure and its institutions are better thought of as being supranational than transnational. Many activities of the programme take place on the supranational level, aimed at informing the member states and their respective initiatives to promote a safer internet, and, as a rule, policies are developed on the EU level and on the level of the member states. The EC wants to acquire information about the commonalities and differences between the countries in order to appreciate the extent to which EC activities have to be adapted to specific national conditions. The member states want to gather as much information as possible about their own populations and beyond that they need comparative indicators that serve as a kind of benchmark and as such provide strong political arguments regarding the 'strengths' and 'weaknesses' of their respective countries. Such a framework predetermines a research design that takes countries as the unit of analysis.

Beyond this contextual argument for taking countries as the unit of analysis there is further support for this decision. First, the field of interest for this study is still substantially shaped by structures and procedures that are defined on the level of the nation states: information infrastructure, information and communication technology (ICT) regulation, educational policy and so on. Second, to a large extent the research community in Europe is structured along national borders or at least along language borders. The vast majority of research on children's online behaviour is based on samples that have been built on the national (or even regional or local) level, and is published in the language of the respective country and discussed in national forums (as noted above, only 8% of studies on children and new media cover more than one country).

With regard to the basic question of which countries should be included in the research, there was no theoretical argument for a selection of countries – in other words, countries were not chosen with respect to research questions or hypotheses. Ideally, in order to cover the EU as a whole, all EU member states as well as all candidate countries should have been included. In practice, the selection of countries to be included in the project was determined by three rather pragmatic factors: (a) the overall budget for the project setting a limit at about 20 countries; (b) the need to include 'larger' European countries; and (c) respected research centres with experience in children's online behaviour and in international projects.

Comparative procedures of the EU Kids Online network

When choosing the organisational structure of a cross-national research project there are two basic options. The first is a top-down approach where a single team of researchers collects data on all the countries involved and compares them according to a set of predefined criteria. The second one, which was used by the EU Kids Online network, is a more bottom-up approach, where research teams from all participating countries are involved and have the task of describing their respective countries. Following that, these descriptions are compared in a process of communicative validation. This approach requires a good deal of coordination work and, as a consequence, a substantial budget for travel expenses. However, the first option involving primary data collection in all participating countries is generally even more expensive. Given the fact that most research projects are organised on a national level and usually published in the national language, 'national correspondents' who are experts in the research area of interest are necessary to obtain a comprehensive and valid picture of the respective empirical evidence.

While this kind of approach seems to be straightforward, it is surrounded by serious challenges. The empirical evidence provided by national correspondents is far from an objective representation of the state of knowledge. Instead, it is inevitably a construction based on the correspondents' disciplinary perspective, as well as their academic and institutional networks. The EU Kids Online network included research teams with differing main disciplinary perspectives, ranging from communications, psychology and education to sociology. In addition, some teams had a purely academic background; others were more closely linked to public institutions, which serve as the national contacts of the EC Safer Internet Programme.

The situation is even more complex, since the different national teams are to a greater or lesser extent marked by research cultures and specific discourses about online safety prevalent in the respective countries. Bearing this in mind the EU Kids Online network dedicated a substantial amount of work to the analysis of the contexts of research on children and media. The results of that work revealed substantial differences among countries with regard to, for instance, financial and organisational resources for research, priorities as regards certain areas of research and methodological paradigms (Stald and Haddon, 2008). Issues of children's internet usage and online risks have been investigated with different thematic priorities, using different methods and from different theoretical perspectives. Figure 4.1 shows this logic of research adopted by the EU Kids Online network, consisting of three levels. The first level specifies the issues that researchers are interested in studying (in this case, online usage and risks). The second level represents the empirical evidence regarding online usage and risks, the amount of which depends on the research infrastructure of the country in question. How this empirical evidence is then interpreted on a third, cross-national comparative level, is again dependent on the individual researcher or research team that acts as a correspondent for that particular country.

Figure 4.1: Factors influencing national reports

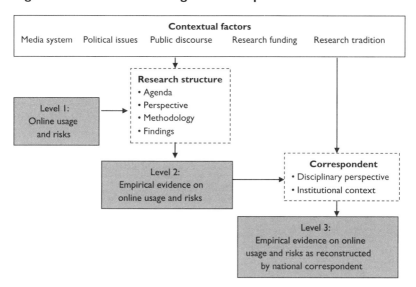

Realising the importance of common understandings in this process, the EU Kids Online network devoted a considerable amount of time and effort to discussing and developing a conceptual framework for the comparative process (Hasebrink et al, 2009). As a result all research teams had a shared understanding of the field of research and the relevant variables. Another important preparatory step was the collection and annotation of relevant studies in all participating countries (see Staksrud et al, 2009; and Chapter Two of this volume). These built the basis for the country reports (see below).

Before undertaking the main analysis, an exploratory comparison of three selected countries (Poland, Portugal and the UK) was conducted. The national teams from these countries wrote draft reports, and on this basis, a first comparative report was drafted (Hasebrink et al, 2007).

The respective experiences with this 'pilot' served as a basis for the full comparative analysis.

In this way, the EU Kids Online comparative approach was developed in accordance with two main objectives. First, on the basis of the indicators of children's and teenagers' online behaviour, classifications of countries were identified that represented differences and similarities between the countries on the level of aggregated individual behaviours, such as the incidence of online risk experienced by children and young people, or the incidence of online opportunities taken up by children and young people, or the nature and extent of parental activities that mediate children's online activities. Second, the EU Kids Online network identified European similarities and differences in macro-societal contextual factors: specifically (a) the media environment; (b) ICT regulation; (c) public discourse on children's internet use and possible risks of the internet; (d) general values and attitudes regarding education, childhood and technology; and (e) the educational system (see Figure 1.1 in Chapter One of this volume). Figure 4.2 provides an overview of the procedure that underlies the comparative analysis on the level of individual indicators. The four stages are explained in more detail below.

Figure 4.2: Overview of the procedures of the comparative analysis

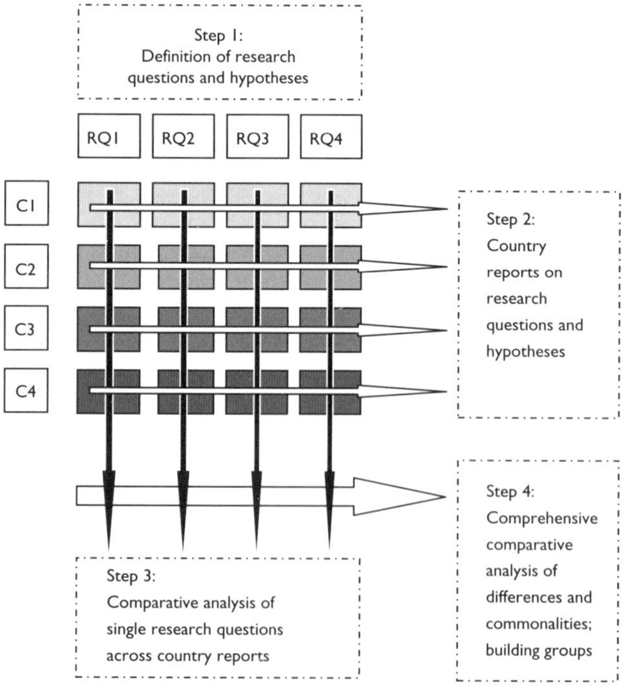

Stage 1: Definition of research questions and hypotheses

Based on the preparatory steps and discussions at a preparatory meeting, the coordinators developed a template for writing country reports, which included 12 research questions and 15 hypotheses. This also included a selection of those contextual factors that could possibly explain similarities and differences between countries.

Stage 2: Country reports

Teams in each country critically reviewed the available findings in their country that could be used to answer the research questions and to support or contradict hypotheses. By then addressing these research questions and hypotheses, each team sought to provide state-of-the-art information for their respective country. These country reports also included a discussion of the contextual factors. An important part of this stage was to discuss all draft reports collectively within the network, to allow for a critical reflection on the content.

Stage 3: Comparative analysis of single research questions

Selected members of the project team then conducted the comparative analysis of single research questions or hypotheses. They compiled all the empirical findings reported across the country reports, and checked in how many countries the specific hypothesis could be supported or had to be rejected. As a result of this stage, a summary of the relevant differences and commonalities among countries was produced. In addition, the authors responsible for this interim analysis proposed a classification of the countries according to contextual factors. In this stage there was also room for new hypotheses to be developed. The directly comparable data from the recent Eurobarometer survey (EC, 2006) allowed for investigation of some of the research questions at this stage. Although that particular dataset is based on parents' interviews and provides fairly superficial indicators for online risks and opportunities, it proved to be particularly fruitful because it allowed for an international comparison across all member states.

Stage 4: Comprehensive comparative analysis of differences and commonalities; building groups

The fourth and last stage was for the project coordinators to analyse the texts produced in the third stage to determine whether they provided evidence for clustering groups of countries according to differences and commonalities. Here the most important indicators were the usage of online media by children and the evidence for internet-related risks. These two indicators were then used for a classification of countries.

This last stage, comparing the commonalities and differences between countries, was complemented by a project meeting where all teams discussed the draft report and the respective classifications. As a process of communicative validation, the national teams were asked to comment on the attribution of their respective country to a specific group and to propose changes. This procedure resulted in a text that was regarded as a valid description of the empirical evidence.

The first level of comparison provides an overview of existing research on children's and teenagers' use of the internet and online-related opportunities and risks in Europe. Following the general model of the research field, the second part of the comparative analysis set out to define and collect relevant contextual factors or background variables, which helped to explain the similarities and differences between countries. The procedure followed the same principles as shown for the level of countries as contexts; it will therefore only be described briefly. Following the template that specified five main contextual factors (that is, media landscape, ICT regulation, public discourse, values and the educational system), the national correspondents wrote sections in the country reports, which were then analysed by selected members of the project team. Once again, the coordinators carried out the overall analysis, aiming to develop some classifications of countries on the basis of these contextual factors, which would help explain the differences and commonalities between the countries, as in the previous stage.

An additional approach has been followed by applying qualitative comparative analysis beyond these explorative approaches to explain differences and commonalities regarding children's online behaviours (see Rihoux, 2006, for the general approach, and Chapter Fourteen, this volume, for an application on the EU Kids Online data). This allows an analysis of contextual factors, which in combination are able to explain the differences and commonalities as they were observed in the first stage of the analysis.

Conclusion

As has been shown in the previous sections, the 21 national teams that comprise the EU Kids Online network have developed constructive working arrangements designed to capture both similarities and diversity across member states so as to facilitate the identification of common patterns, themes and best practice. This procedure allowed for a productive use of the twin dynamic of recognising differences and drawing out shared understandings. For those in similar or related domains who are contemplating the conduct of a cross-national analysis of similarities and differences in findings, we propose that our analytic framework and working methods can be of considerable value.

Specifically, our approach permitted a clear translation of three main rationales for cross-national research into an effective strategy for comparing countries on multiple dimensions, as organised through an explicit theoretical framework. First, the analysis could respect findings of both pan-European similarities and differences. Second, it could test specific hypotheses and also address open research questions. And third, it could situate each country in the context of the others, and it could situate the individual child in the context of national cultural factors.

On the other hand, the process was undoubtedly demanding in terms of research effort – both for each national research team and in terms of the management of and commitment to a highly collaborative and iterative working process. The analysis was also limited by the quality and extent of the available evidence base – the many gaps in the data and the many differences in definitions, samples and methods used for such core issues as online use and risk mean that all claims and conclusions must be treated as indicative rather than conclusive.

Simply put, some data were weaker than could be wished, some were absent and some were difficult to interpret. We proceeded, therefore, on the bold assumption that conducting comparisons is preferable to saying nothing about pan-European patterns, since some added value must surely be extracted from the many studies that have been conducted. But we did so with extreme caution, not least in order to stimulate more and better research in the future.

The hardest task, other than locating relevant data and negotiating its significance across the network, was in producing the country classifications. Some may argue that these are too reductive, turning differences in degree into absolute differences. But for theoretical and pragmatic reasons, we propose that country classifications are useful, providing a basis for discussing similarities and differences as well as focusing attention on policy priorities (notably, high-risk countries).

It is also noteworthy, if unsurprising, that although most available findings were national studies, for many purposes the comparative European data (mainly Eurobarometer, although other sources were also useful) provided the strongest basis for cross-national analysis. In terms of quality control, we have sought to explicate the basis for our claims and conclusions throughout, both for network members and others, by making it possible to trace the conclusions back to the country reports and the actual data sources. Thus, not only final reports but also country reports were made available at the project website (see www.lse.ac.uk/collections/EUKidsOnline/), thereby contributing to a better transparency of the entire research process, and enabling individual researchers to compare their contributions and to learn from each other's practices as well as mistakes.

Many comparative studies produce the empirical basis for cross-national comparisons but end their work at the stage of producing a series of country reports or country profiles, effectively leaving the task of identifying and explaining observed similarities and differences to the reader. We hope our present work can provide a model for the crucial stage of comparative analysis that can systematise and maximise the benefits of cross-national research. As the demand for pan-European comparative research (within the present EU borders or even going beyond them) will only grow in the coming years, so there will be a need for innovative, clear-cut and reliable comparative methodologies. Although far from ideal (as its still remaining weaknesses document), the example presented above might serve as an inspiration for future comparative efforts, both in the field of children and new media as well as in social science research in general.

References

EC (European Commission) (2006) *Eurobarometer survey on safer internet. Special Eurobarometer 250*, Brussels (http://ec.europa.eu/information_society/activities/sip/docs/eurobarometer/eurobarometer_2005_25_ms.pdf).

Hantrais, L. and Mangen, S. (1996) 'Method and management of cross-national social research', in L. Hantrais and S. Mangen (eds) *Cross-national research methods in the social sciences*, New York, NY and London: Pinter: 1-12.

Hasebrink, U., Livingstone, S., Haddon, L. and Ólafsson, K. (2009) *Comparing children's online opportunities and risks across Europe: Cross-national comparisons for EU Kids Online* (2nd edn), London: London School of Economics and Political Science, EU Kids Online (Deliverable D3.2 for the EC Safer Internet Plus Programme).

Hasebrink, U., Livingstone, S., Haddon, L., Kirwil, L. and Ponte, C. (2007) *Comparing children's online activities and risks across Europe. A preliminary report comparing findings for Poland, Portugal and UK*, London: London School of Economics and Political Science, EU Kids Online (Deliverable D3.1 for the EC Safer Internet Plus Programme).

Hoffmeyer-Zlotnik, J.H.P. and Harkness, J. (2005) 'Methodological aspects in cross-national research', *ZUMA-Nachrichten Spezial*, no 11.

Livingstone, S. (2003) 'On the challenges of cross-national comparative media research', *European Journal of Communication*, vol 18, no 4: 477-500.

Øyen, E. (1990) *Comparative methodology: theory and practice in international social research*, London: Sage.

Rihoux, B. (2006) 'Qualitative comparative analysis (QCA) and related systematic comparative methods: recent advances and remaining challenges for social science research', *International Sociology*, vol 21, no 5: 679-706.

Rokkan, S. (ed) (1968) *Comparative research across cultures and nations*, Paris: Mouton.

Staksrud, E., Livingstone, S., Haddon, L. and Ólafsson, K. (2009) *What do we know about children's use of online technologies? A report on data availability and research gaps in Europe* (2nd edn), London: London School of Economics and Political Science, EU Kids Online (Deliverable D1.1 for the EC Safer Internet Plus Programme).

Stald, G. and Haddon, L. (2008) *Cross-cultural contexts of research: Factors influencing the study of children and the internet in Europe*, London: London School of Economics and Political Science, EU Kids Online (Deliverable D3.2 for the EC Safer Internet Plus Programme).

Tilly, C. (1997) *Micro, macro, or megrim?*, New York, NY: Columbia University (www.asu.edu/clas/polisci/cqrm/papers/Tilly/TillyMicromacro.pdf).

FIVE

Cultures of research and policy in Europe

Leslie Haddon and Gitte Stald

Europe is traditionally regarded as a cultural entity with shared historical roots, values, systems and institutions. At a meta-level this provides a shared point of departure within and outside Europe. However, Kevin (2003: 2) notes that 'definitions of Europe cannot logically be confined to specific political, cultural, or geographic descriptions'. When considering the various levels on which Europe may be understood, one must note that the European Union (EU) is more integrated at the political and economic levels than in terms of culture and traditions. Bondebjerg and Golding discuss the elements of a perceived European common culture thus:

All accounts perceive a common heritage, in which democracy, Enlightenment values, science, reason, and individualism are infused in a potent brew which has a unique European flavour. To this heady mix is added a strong historical sense of roots in a common Greco-Roman tradition, together with a loose association of these values with something called "civilization". (2004: 12)

However, they also go on to point to the difficulties in grasping 'this protean myth of a European culture or identity', noting that there is also 'a discernible contradiction in the policy arena within Europe among the emerging panoply of European institutions and pan-national agencies' (Bondebjerg and Golding, 2004: 13).

Given the juxtaposition of a common European heritage, with tendencies towards the homogenisation of policy specifically with the EU, and diverse national institutions and cultural histories, there is always the question of how much is similar or different across Europe. This applies to the research undertaken in any field, including that on children's experience of the internet. How far are research contexts common across countries and how much is country-specific? Can an understanding of these research contexts account for differences in the research conducted cross-nationally? Where is it possible to make a comparative analysis? Why are different aspects of children and the internet researched, or not, in different European countries?

The challenge is to understand the social shaping of research. Admittedly, the nature of what research is conducted, and how it is conducted, partly reflects the interests and orientations of particular researchers or research teams. But the focus here is on the wider social factors that may influence this process – and whether they vary cross-nationally. Although there is an emerging body of cross-national research, as indicated in Chapters Two and Four of this volume, questions about the shaping of research, and its implications for policy, are rarely asked in general, let alone in relation to children and the internet. Hence, this chapter is conducted in the spirit captured by Jensen (2002: 273):

> Media studies, like their object of analysis, originate from a particular social and historical setting. Part of the relevance of media studies is that they may contribute to the social conditions under which communication will take place in the future. Like the media themselves, then, university departments and other research organizations may be understood theoretically as institutions-to-think-with, enabling (second-order) reflexivity about the role of media in society.

Our approach

This chapter seeks to explain the patterns of national research already reviewed in Chapter Two of this volume (and as detailed in Staksrud et al, 2009). For the present purposes, we have excluded multicountry studies, since our interest is in the national factors that influence research, although we do examine the role of the European Commission (EC) in funding research, especially in countries where research funding is scarce. Master's and PhD theses are also excluded from this discussion, although they are included in the EU Kids Online data repository in countries where empirical research is limited. A template for country reports was discussed within the EU Kids Online network, containing a range of questions regarding national contextual factors and histories. National teams then completed these structured reports, seeking out the appropriate information and discussing issues with colleagues where appropriate. There was a further division of labour whereby individuals and groups analysed particular questions across countries.

It is not always straightforward to divide up contextual factors. However, an initial distinction can be drawn between those developments in different societies that may have some influence on whether research takes place and those factors that are due to the nature and history of the particular national research community. The former include the spread of the internet itself as well as broader societal discourses about children and the internet, and here we look in particular at media representations. On a more detailed level, we asked whether there were debates about particular themes (for example the commercialisation of childhood) that appeared to have led to research focused on such topics. It seemed appropriate to ask about the role of particular agents, for example non-governmental organisations (NGOs), active in the field, as well as whether there was any evidence that political initiatives (widely defined) or even particular events seemed to have had some bearing on research.

Factors related to the nature and history of the national research communities included their relative sizes, whether the timing of their earliest research was important, whether the existence of particular disciplines encouraged certain research and whether existing data collection practices produced more or less research on children's experiences of the internet. There were questions about institutional processes, practices and tendencies, to see if they promoted or hindered research in this field. And last, but definitely not least, we examined the different sources of research funds available in the different countries.

Contextual material can appear in the form of numbers (about the rate of internet adoption) or in a form that lends itself to clustering countries (for example dates when certain research commenced). However, much of this material, for example about the nature of media coverage or the processes at work within an institution, can be relatively more discursive, more qualitative. Even this material can sometimes be ordered into typologies, and then one can look for systematic differences between groups of countries differentiated by some criteria. But this is not always possible. Sometimes the contributors to country reports added so many caveats that to neatly cluster countries would be unjustified. Sometimes only a few national teams could provide evidence while others thought that certain processes might occur, but it was difficult to provide examples.

For these reasons, two different logics were used related to two of Kohn's (1989) ways of conducting cross-national analysis (see also Livingstone, 2003). The idiographic approach treating nations as objects of study in their own right was adopted, this allowing for some country clustering to examine differences among (groups of) nations. Additionally, nations were, in effect, treated as contexts for study, meaning that feedback from different countries was pooled in order to investigate common factors at work across Europe that potentially shape the research process, while recognising that this might take slightly different guises in the different countries.

Societal influences on research

There is a fair correlation between internet adoption rates and the number of studies, but there were far more studies in the UK and Germany than the level of adoption would suggest. This reflects the fact that several processes influence the figures and one is the size of population, and with it the number of universities conducting research (see below). Hence, Figure 5.1 controls for population size, although that places counties like Iceland and Estonia as outliers partly because of their fewer inhabitants. However, it is clear that internet penetration correlates with the amount of research on children and the internet.

Figure 5.1: Total number of single country studies per million inhabitants (excluding Master's/PhD theses), by internet penetration in late 2008

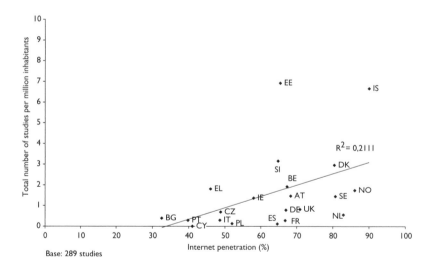

Base: 289 studies

To support the analysis of the role of media, the EU Kids Online team conducted a 14-country study involving a content analysis of press coverage, as reported in Chapter Thirteen of this volume. One key point to draw from this is that media coverage varies by country, and more specifically the balance of media coverage of the risks discussed in this volume also varies by country – with content, contact and conduct risks being emphasised to different degrees in different countries. The implication is that not only may the general public be sensitised to different risks in different countries – with implications for how they answer surveys – but so too might the different research communities (or their funders, or those instigating political activities in this field).

In addition, national teams in Belgium, Denmark, Germany, Italy, Ireland, the Netherlands and the UK reported detailed examples of academic research in general, as well as specific projects, being influenced by media coverage. For example, in the UK: 'The media picked up on the phenomenon of happy-slapping. Some NGO commissioned research probably followed from this. Certainly one cyberbullying study was commissioned by an NGO' (Stald and Haddon, 2008: 60). In the case of Germany: 'It seems that in the case of Happy Slapping and Cyber Bullying, research was influenced by the media coverage, because this phenomenon was firstly raised up by the media (by presenting isolated cases from other countries, eg Great Britain)' (Stald and Haddon, 2008: 60). And in the Netherlands: 'If at all, public discourse has only indirectly influenced research in the Netherlands. Discussions in newspapers and on television, in particular on online grooming and on internet addiction, have contributed to the rise of the Safer Internet Programme in the Netherlands and policy attention to these matters. As a result of this more research has been done' (Stald and Haddon, 2008: 60).

These examples suggest that media representations – including moral panics – might sometimes play some part in setting the research agenda or, at least, in stimulating the instigation of research. This in turn can contribute to producing different types of research in different countries (or can sometimes contribute to producing similar research, as in the German case above). More specific public discourses, such as debate about the commercialisation of childhood and children's rights, also vary by country. In the case of the commercialisation of childhood, there was some indication that in certain countries the debates, or lack of them, related to the amount of research on that issue. But this was less clear as regards children's rights, which appeared in general to attract less media attention.

Do national political initiatives, for example attempts to introduce the internet into schools or initiatives to train teachers in internet use promoting internet awareness, lead to research evaluating these schemes, and hence to introducing variation between countries? It certainly became clear that national governments are the most central actors in creating the climate for research into the area of children and the internet. Of the countries included in our analysis, about half reported such government-initiated research studies. Moreover, such government initiatives could also lead to an expansion of the data already collected as regards children's use of the internet. Related examples of agencies producing such initiatives included, occasionally, regional governments and regulators. Another important observation was that EC initiatives are pivotal to the conduct, financing and proliferation of funding research and played a major role in shaping the internationally comparative data that were available.

Various national teams also reported the activities of NGOs in keeping issues alive in the media and sensitising politicians – which may have indirectly influenced research. For example, in the case of Belgium:

> It is clear that they play an active role in keeping the issue of Internet safety of the children and safety awareness of children and parents in the public debate. For instance, the Bond (Flanders)/Ligue des Families (Wallonia), an organisation of family matters, frequently draws attention to this issue in their magazines, on their website and in their education initiatives for parents. As such, this NGO keeps the public and political world sensitive to this issue. (Stald and Haddon, 2008: 61)

There were some examples where NGOs even added to the national body of research themselves. For instance, in the UK: 'Apart from lobbying, a range of NGOs also conduct research. The children's charities are active in this area and regularly commission new research to draw attention to key challenges to children's safety from internet/ mobile technologies – examples include the recent bullying survey, the activities of Childnet International, Barnardo's research on child victims of online grooming, etc' (Stald and Haddon, 2008: 61).

Meanwhile, when asked whether any events had led to particular national studies, two types of event were identified as influencing research: particular one-off events and the cumulative or 'drip' effect of seeing the same type of event repeated over time. But, as with political initiatives, in the case of both NGOs and events it proved difficult to develop the comparative analysis further beyond demonstrating that, and sometimes how, such factors could play a role in the shaping of research.

Influence of national research communities on research

Does the overall amount of research there is in a country have any bearing on the amount of research specifically on children and the internet? The most easily available data available in all the countries that could act as a proxy for research volume was the number of universities. But even counting this institutional 'academic base' by no means proved to be a straightforward task. In France, for example, the 'Grandes Écoles' and 'Grands Établissements' are universities except in name, while in the UK London University is actually an umbrella organisation for several universities. Based partly on explanations from the EU Kids Online team, various adjustments of this kind were made to take into account the circumstances of particular countries.

As noted earlier, the academic base in European countries proved to be highly correlated to the population, although there were some notable exceptions even among the EU Kids Online countries; for example Estonia, Ireland and Bulgaria have a larger academic base relative to small populations, with Greece and Italy a slightly lower one. Of interest in this chapter, Figure 5.2 shows that the academic base is a fair but not a strong predictor of the number of studies on children's internet use in that country.

To investigate the effects of timing of research, the dates of the first national studies about the internet were assembled (as well as dates of

Figure 5.2: Number of single country studies, by number of universities

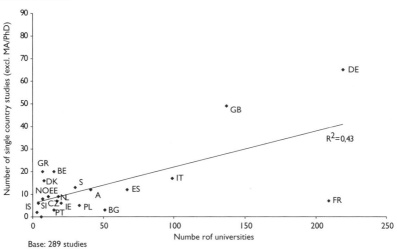

Base: 289 studies

the first studies of mass communications and mediated interpersonal communications, that is, telephony). As happened to a large extent with mass communications research, internet research followed the spread of the internet itself. Hence, in most European countries, internet studies originated in the 1990s with the emergence and burgeoning popularity of the internet. Many of the countries where research has only begun more recently – the Czech Republic, Cyprus, Belgium and Greece – have lower internet penetration rates, reflecting the fact that the market developed later. Thus there appears some understandable connection between the spread of the internet and the academic awareness of this as being an important and interesting area for research.

The next question was whether traditions of national disciplines had an influence on country research in this field. There were several problems here: many studies, especially more market-orientated research, did not fall easily into disciplines, some studies were interdisciplinary and some were difficult to categorise. Thus, this information had not been collected in the data repository. Nevertheless it became clear that education, psychology and sociology were important sources of studies. The next problem was that counting these departments would not differentiate countries for comparative purposes, since most universities in most participating countries had such departments. Hence, the focus turned to disciplines likely to conduct studies on children and the internet that were relatively new and still developing in some countries: media studies and communication studies.

Unfortunately, counting these proved even more problematic than counting universities. Many media studies and sometimes communications studies departments are very practically oriented, teaching production skills or journalism, rather than conducting research. While studies into media and communication research issues may exist, they may be researched and taught within sociology and social psychology departments. Where separate media and communications studies departments exist, their orientation depends on the larger faculty within which they are located. For example in Denmark, if they are located in the humanities, they have a more philosophical, literacy and aesthetic orientation, but within the social sciences, they are more empirically oriented. After making many adjustments at best we could say that some of those countries where media and communication studies are well established in universities appear to produce more studies on children and the internet – such as Belgium, Sweden and the UK. But given the issues outlined above, this had to be a very weak or 'soft' claim.

An area where one could make a stronger argument related to the general survey data of internet use in the population. Both in terms of the official government surveys, as shown in Table 5.1, but also non-government ones, there is a considerable national variation in the range of lower age limits of these surveys in different countries. This means there are more data on (younger) children available in some countries (for example Nordic ones) compared to others because they are captured in these general surveys.

Table 5.1: Lower age limits in government surveys of internet use by the general population

Lower age limit	Countries
16 year olds	Austria, Cyprus, Czech Republic, the UK
15 year olds	Belgium, Estonia, Ireland, Portugal, Spain
14 year olds	Germany
13 year olds	Greece
12 year olds	Bulgaria, France, the Netherlands
11 year olds	Italy
10 year olds	Slovenia
9 year olds	Norway, Sweden
7 year olds	Denmark

Turning to the practicalities of applying for research, there was some national variation in terms of whether there were stages that proposals had to go through or the degree to which they had to be checked. But ultimately the comments provided by the national teams suggested that this had little bearing on the amount of research in this field – ultimately more complicated procedures did not appear to be more restrictive. Nor did there appear to be ethical considerations that determined what could and could not be researched in countries. While there was national variation in the degree to which ethical guidelines were built into the research process, this was mainly made manifest at the level of institutional checks and rules relating, for example, to getting parental permission for child studies.

More generally, the majority of country reports mentioned growing institutional pressures to research and specifically to publish research. This relates to the opportunities for potential academic promotion, access to further funding and publishing as a general standard for measuring levels of research in departments. Hence, this pressure may potentially have contributed to the amount of research in this specific field as it influenced the amount of research in general. Varying by country, there is evidence of increasing demand at the political and the institutional level for cooperation between industry and academia, and variation in the degree to which these bodies approach each other, with, once again some suggestion that this could influence the amount and direction of research. Lastly, there is a tendency for research council funding to be increasingly directed towards strategic research, as exemplified in the case of Belgium:

> In Belgium, the public funding organisation Federal Science Policy has a research programme called "Future and Society" which explicitly invites researchers to do research on ICT. In Flanders, the Institute for the Promotion of Innovation by Science and Technology (IWT) is a funding organisation that focuses on stimulating and supporting technological and scientific innovation. ICT is one of the main research themes on which researchers are invited to submit research proposals. (Stald and Haddon, 2008: 44)

All of these developments have the potential to push research on children and the internet in certain directions, or to contribute to the variation in the amount and form of research within countries. However, that is the limit of what can be said here because it is difficult to get more fine-grained information that might actually demonstrate the detailed interaction of these factors. The participating national teams could comment on the various considerations that influenced their own research, but they were often 'outsiders' when looking at the research of their compatriots.

Finally, there is the issue of funding. Table 5.2 shows the typology of funding structures used to classify countries, taking into account the range of funding and relative predominance of public, academic and commercial sources. Apart from showing the specific issue of funding, Table 5.2 also illustrates the type of exploratory analysis frequently used with this contextual material.

Our hypothesis was that funding regimes would produce national differences, but in practice there was no clear correlation between the overall structure of funding and the total amount of research. In addition, while nations with diverse funding sources (the UK, Belgium, Germany and Sweden) were shown to produce research on a relatively wide range of topics, this can also occur for some countries with less diversity in funding. Perhaps surprisingly, the overall patterns of funding also seem to have little influence on which topics are researched in the

Table 5.2: Types of funding for research on children and the internet

Funding structure	Characteristics of funding	Countries
Predominance of public funding	Public funding dominates funding (more than 75%). Other forms of funding (commercial, non-profit or academic) play a minor role or do not exist at all.	Bulgaria, the Czech Republic, Denmark, Estonia, France, Greece, Iceland, Ireland, the Netherlands, Norway, Poland, Slovenia and Sweden
Predominantly public and academic funding	Public funding is the most important form of financing but it has a more modest role. Academic funding is important. Non-profit and commercial funding is rather low or does not exist.	Austria, Belgium, Cyprus, Portugal and Spain
Predominantly public and commercial funding	Besides public institutions, commercial companies and trade associations are important. Academic and non-profit funding are of little or no relevance.	Germany and Denmark
Hybrid funding structure	The percentage of public funding is at most 60%, public, commercial and academic funding play an important role.	UK and Italy

different countries. This is because the interests of specific funders of research differed between European countries. Public institutions like national or regional governments, ministries, regulation authorities or research councils in one country sometimes sought different kinds of data from their counterparts in others, while commercial companies, say, in Germany were sometimes interested in different aspects of children's online use than, say, in the UK.

However, moving the analysis away from the funding structures above to consider the role of different types of funder, several points can be made. There are a number of issues that are mainly addressed by public institutions or to a minor extent by academic funding: interpreting online content, identity play, social networking and learning online. Commercial funding is relatively important for research on concerns and frustrations, search strategies, privacy risks and online gaming. Studies on risks, that are of special interest for EU Kids Online, are most frequently financed by commercial and public institutions.

Conclusion

Methodologically, this part of the EU Kids Online project always faced constraints. The national teams had locations in various disciplines and had differing backgrounds from which to approach the task of addressing questions in their national reports. The accessibility of certain information in different countries also varied (for example depending on the size of the research community and whether that information was easily locatable). This, as noted, had a bearing on how far some paths of analysis could be followed. Nonetheless, the exercise, often involving considerable searching and consultation, produced a wealth of information for the project to begin to address the question of how contextual factors influence research and what different logics of analysis could be employed.

At a substantive level, this chapter has shown that, and sometimes how, different studies can be instigated by different stakeholders for a range of reasons, so that the activities and interests of industry, media, public, academics, government and NGOs may all contribute to the national pool of empirical research on children and the internet. Societal factors such as the degree of internet adoption overall played some role in influencing the variation in cross-national research, as did a range of characteristics of the national research community such as its size and the timing, or history, of internet studies, itself related to the development of the national internet market.

Returning to the quote earlier on in this chapter from Jensen, research environments are influenced by their cultural context, including, in the case of children and the internet, different national cultural values regarding risks. Yet this chapter provides at best a snapshot since the very factors that shape research may also change over time, in a complex interaction with the changing access to and use of new media, national cultural values and social conditions as well as academic institutional practices themselves, as captured in this observation: 'A study of changing media in Europe is also a study of changing Europe as societies are undergoing vital changes, as political associations and alliances, demographic structures, the worlds of work, leisure, domestic life, mobility, education, politics and communications themselves are all undergoing important transformations' (Bondebjerg and Golding, 2004: 7). Hence the need for policy makers in this field to be attentive not only to the development of new media like the internet but also to the changes in this broader social context, and how these are reflected in the research environment itself.

References

Bondebjerg, I.B. and Golding, P. (2004) *European culture and the media. Changing media, changing Europe, vol 1*, Bristol: Intellect.

Jensen, K.B. (ed) (2002) *A handbook of media and communication research*, London: Routledge.

Kevin, D. (2003) *Europe in the media. A comparison of reporting, representation, and rhetoric in national media systems in Europe*, London: Lawrence Erlbaum Associates.

Kohn, M.L. (1989) 'Introduction', in M.L. Kohn (ed) *Cross-national research in sociology*, Newbury Park, CA: Sage Publications.

Livingstone, S. (2003) 'On the challenges of cross-national comparative media research', *European Journal of Communication*, vol 18, no 4: 477-500.

Staksrud, E., Livingstone, S., Haddon, L. and Ólafsson, K. (2009) *What do we know about children's use of online technologies? A report on data availability and research gaps in Europe* (2nd edn), London: London School of Economics and Political Science, EU Kids Online (Deliverable D1.1 for the EC Safer Internet plus Programme).

Stald, G. and Haddon, L. (2008) *Cross-cultural contexts of research: Factors influencing the study of children and the internet in Europe*, London: London School of Economics and Political Science, *EU Kids Online (Deliverable D3.2 for the EC Safer Internet plus Programme)*.

Section II
Going online: new opportunities?

SIX

Opportunities and benefits online

Veronika Kalmus, Pille Runnel and Andra Siibak

The internet and other online technologies provide children across Europe with a range of opportunities and benefits. The main opportunities can be classified into four categories: education, learning and digital literacy; participation and civic engagement; creativity and self-expression; and identity and social connection (Livingstone and Haddon, 2009; and see Chapter One, this volume). Research evidence suggests that adults and children agree that children use the internet mostly as an educational resource, for entertainment, games and fun, for searching for global information and for social networking and sharing experiences with distant others (Hasebrink et al, 2009).

The question about children's opportunities and benefits online can be theoretically contextualised by the notions of *structure* and *agency*. Structure refers to *rules and resources*, which are 'always both enabling and constraining, in virtue of the inherent relation between structure and agency' (Giddens, 1984: 169). Rules and resources related to children's internet use include parental guidance, rules and restrictions, material resources for using the internet at home and at school (for example broadband connection, a child's own computer), the availability of time to be spent online and so on. Meanwhile, the concept of agency has been associated with a long list of terms including freedom, creativity, self-hood, choice, motivation, will, initiative and so on (see Emirbayer and Mische, 1998), where 'agency refers not to the intentions people have in doing things but to their capability of doing those things in the first place' (Giddens, 1984: 9).

Online opportunities are themselves interconnected and they all depend on children's agency and literacies. The significance of the internet for participatory activities lies in the shift from the 'traditional' public sphere to everyday active participation in a networked, highly heterogeneous and open public sphere (Burgess, 2007). But making use of any online opportunities connected to participation and civic engagement largely relies on communicative competencies in general and digital skills in particular. Hence, digital literacy can be seen as an essential competency important for democratic practices (Dahlgren,

2006). Digital literacy is also linked to participation through user creativity, that is, through various practices involving online content creation. Moreover, such creativity is essentially social as it needs individuals to be capable of using, transforming and extending information in a way that enables other individuals acting in the social field to recognise and acquire the information (Csíkszentmihályi, 1996). The internet as an interpersonal medium is, therefore, also relevant to social connection and identity because it provides opportunities to meet other people and to communicate online.

Children's engagement in online activities takes place in a broader context of domestic, familial, social, cultural, political and economic factors (Hasebrink et al, 2009). International research (for example Alakeson, 2003; see also Chapter Nine, this volume) has reported significant differences in digital inclusion both cross-nationally and within particular countries. Most notably, inequalities in socio-economic status (SES) have consequences for children's online opportunities, where higher status parents with more resources are more likely than those of lower status to provide their children with home access to the internet (Livingstone and Haddon, 2009).

Livingstone and Helsper (2007) have proposed a continuum of digital inclusion with gradations from non-use through low use to more frequent use. They suggest that 'going online is a staged process, with systematic differences between those who take up more and those who take up fewer opportunities' (2007: 683). On the first stage, children use the internet mainly for information seeking, either for school or in general. Stage 2 adds in online games and email. In stage 3 children also start using the internet for goals such as instant messaging and downloading music. Stage 4 includes a diversity of additional uses including interactive and creative activities. This study found that most activities online become more common with age as children seem to climb a ladder of online opportunities (Livingstone and Helsper, 2007)

In this chapter we focus on different types of online opportunities taken up by children across Europe. We draw on Livingstone and Helsper (2007) to apply the gradations in digital inclusion on a cross-national level. We also analyse how some structural aspects are connected to children's online activities.

Gradations in taking up online opportunities

In this section we take a closer look at what opportunities children take up online. To answer this question we combine the findings of studies carried out in the European Union (EU) Kids Online network countries with a more detailed analysis of the Mediappro survey covering eight European countries (Mediappro, 2006). We selected the Mediappro database because it is one of very few cross-national surveys focusing on the appropriation and use of digital media by children and because it provides some relevant indicators of the structural aspects influencing those practices.

In Table 6.1 the Mediappro countries are arranged by their decreasing scores on the (horizontal) index of versatility of internet use while online opportunities are ordered according to the frequency of their take-up, as seen in the final column. The opportunities taken up by at least half of the respondents in each country are in bold. The pattern emerging is, in a number of aspects, similar to the gradation of digital inclusion shown by Livingstone and Helsper (2007). Some differences and exceptions exist, however.

School-favoured uses

Stage 1, like step 1 in Livingstone and Helsper (2007), centres on information seeking and educational use. Most young internet users in all Mediappro countries have taken up these opportunities. In the context of contemporary schooling and curricula, which foster using the internet for study-related activities, we may term this stage of taking up online opportunities *school-favoured uses*. The internet, quite obviously, has turned into a new type of educational medium, also offering stimulating resources to those children who would otherwise remain rather passive users. One qualification to the use of this label relates to the fact that pan-European research (see Hasebrink et al, 2009) concludes that children themselves associate the use of the internet more with edutainment, where children report that they search for information they themselves perceive as interesting and fun.

Popular uses

Stage 2 adds in four activities related to communication and entertainment (see Table 6.1). These opportunities are taken up by 60%-70% of children in most of the Mediappro countries. In the majority of the EU Kids Online network countries, young people value the internet mainly for providing them with various environments for communication and networking (Hasebrink et al, 2009). Thus, we may term this stage of taking up online opportunities *popular uses*. Compared to the findings by Livingstone and Helsper (2007), based on UK data

Table 6.1: Online opportunities in the MEDIAPPRO countries (taken up at least 'sometimes', %)

		Estonia	UK	Poland	Denmark	Portugal	Belgium	France	Greece	Average
Index of use versatility (mean)		6.49	5.92	5.71	5.58	5.45	4.90	4.88	4.73	5.44
Opportunities										
Stage 1	Uses search engines	90	98	91	92	95	95	94	81	91
	Uses for school work (at school)	80	91	81	92	84	85	86	76	84
Stage 2	Uses instant messenger	88	78	75	87	77	81	69	39	71
	Listens to music, radio	87	68	67	69	70	58	57	70	66
	Sends and reads emails	69	81	62	66	69	74	67	46	65
	Downloads music, movies, software, video games	73	60	67	50	60	58	49	65	60
Stage 3	Watches videos, television	71	47	53	52	64	46	46	58	53
	Plays games online	56	67	57	52	50	33	31	76	51
Stage 4	Goes to a chat room	33	20	34	26	38	28	32	41	32
	Has a blog or personal web page	30	35	29	21	26	38	30	25	29
	Fills out surveys, enters competitions	44	22	24	29	16	25	23	19	25
	Buys things	10	45	28	20	11	9	28	10	19
	Makes phone calls	28	11	30	15	11	14	15	8	16

Note. The sample base are 11- to 18-year-old children who were studying in typical schools in each country in autumn 2005 and had used the internet (N = 4558, 96% of population). Online activities were measured on a 5-point scale (1 – 'never' ... 5 – 'very often'). The index of use versatility is based on eleven indicators; being engaged in each activity at least 'sometimes' added one point to the index. The opportunities taken up by at least 50% of children in the respective country are in bold.

from spring 2004, using instant messaging tools and downloading music and other files had become remarkably more widespread among European children by autumn 2005, bringing them into the category of popular use rather than more advanced use.

Studies in Belgium (Depandelaere et al, 2006), the Netherlands (Valkenburg et al, 2005) and Austria (Rathmoser, 2008) indicate that the use of instant messaging and social networking sites could be regarded as a new opportunity for the social development of adolescents. These tools are seen as especially useful for community building among peers, for expanding social contacts and preparing for relationships, not to mention offering new opportunities for shy children to overcome their social fears (Valkenburg et al, 2005). Furthermore, children use instant messaging not only for communicating with their friends and making appointments but also for sharing photographs and music files or information about schoolwork (Depandelaere et al, 2006). Thus, the huge popularity of this application can be explained by the universality of the medium.

Resource-bound uses

Stage 3 adds in two entertainment-related opportunities – watching videos, movies and television programmes and playing games online – which demand more resources such as a high-speed broadband connection and the opportunity to spend more time online. We may therefore term this stage of taking up online opportunities *resource-bound uses*. Slightly more than half of children in the Mediappro sample are engaged in those activities, with significant differences between the countries, especially in terms of the frequency of playing games (see Table 6.1).

Playing online games is also one of the most favourite entertainment-related opportunities that the studies in the EU Kids Online data repository. The practice is especially popular among children in Iceland (81% of young internet users; see Ólafsson and Jónsson, 2008), the UK (70%; see Livingstone and Bober, 2004), the Czech Republic (57%; see Štětka, 2008) and Italy (55%; see Eurispes Telefono Azzurro, 2006). Although many adults may perceive playing computer games as a waste of time, researchers in the EU Kids Online network have suggested that one should view the activity as being a 'motivational step on the way to "approved" activities' (Hasebrink et al, 2009: 48). Findings from the Mediappro survey confirm this perspective, since 50% of the children claimed that playing computer games led them to use the internet to get additional information, 32% said that the activity led them to use the internet to meet other players and 28% had met new friends through online gaming. Therefore children's engagement in computer games also provides them with opportunities related to learning and social connection.

Advanced uses

Stage 4 adds a range of interactive and creative activities, consistent with step 4 as described by Livingstone and Helsper (2007). These are practised by less than half of children in all Mediappro countries (see Table 6.1) and may be called *advanced uses*. At this stage, considerable cross-cultural differences exist, particularly in regard to children's economic participation (buying things online). With regard to blogging and making homepages, the Mediappro findings are in line with the trend emerging from studies in the EU Kids Online data repository, according to which creativity-related opportunities tend to be more often taken up by those children in the high and medium internet use countries (for example Belgium, France, the UK, Denmark and Estonia; see Hasebrink et al, 2009). Our previous analysis has shown that while basic technical skills are indispensable, children's individual agency, creativity and their order of priorities as shown by time allocation are even more crucial in shaping their involvement in online content creation (Kalmus et al, 2009a).

Climbing the ladder of online opportunities

The Mediappro data support the claim by Livingstone and Helsper (2007) that as they grow older children climb a ladder of online opportunities. Most activities online become more common with advancing age and older children are also more versatile internet users than younger ones (see also Chapter Eight, this volume, for age differences). However, some exceptions to this general tendency exist. Playing games actually becomes less common as children get older while there are no significant differences between age groups with regard to watching videos and television online, going to a chat room and blogging and creating homepages. The exceptionality of creative activities is very clearly revealed by the data from an Estonian survey of schoolchildren in 2007: children are less active in creating content online as they grow older (Kalmus et al, 2009b). The same data indicate that in older age groups the motivation to create one's own homepage notably diminishes.

Thus, we may postulate that in addition to the tendency for children to climb a ladder of online opportunities, their priorities when taking up different opportunities alter as they become older. We may assume that such changes are partly caused by the developmental effect, that is, older pupils just grow out of the habit of playing games online, turning their attention to other activities. In other words, older children tend to use their free time as a scarce resource for taking up somewhat different opportunities than younger children. In the case of content creation, the lack of age differences or greater passivity of older children in some countries (for example Estonia) may also stem from the cohort effect, that is, the fact that the older age group first acquired the internet at a later age (cf Livingstone and Helsper, 2007), which has resulted in their lower computer skills restricting their ability, for example, to create homepages.

Resources and rules

In order to explain the main trends and exceptions in the take-up of online opportunities at a cross-cultural level, we analyse the distribution of resources for using the internet and parental rules in the Mediappro countries. Table 6.2 reveals that children's online activities tend to be more versatile in those countries where the material resources for using the internet (either a broadband connection at home or an internet-connected computer in the child's bedroom or both) are more widespread, that is, in Denmark, Estonia, the UK and Poland. Thus, the availability of a high-speed connection and the chance to use the internet in the privacy of one's bedroom (presumably for quite long periods of time) increase the probability that children take up more online opportunities.

Parental rules also have an effect on the take-up of online opportunities. Table 6.3 shows the correlations between the frequency of online activity and the frequency of a parental ban on that same activity, as perceived by children in the Mediappro countries. The significant negative correlations suggest that instituting such rules is, to some extent, effective.

Consistent with the findings by Livingstone and Helsper (2008) concerning the parental mediation of UK children's internet use, children in the Mediappro countries take their parents' rules seriously in relation to downloading material, instant messaging, sending and reading emails and talking in chat rooms. Parental rules do not appear to be as effective in the case of playing games online. In fact in Denmark, those children who were banned more frequently from playing online

Table 6.2: Resources for using the internet in the MEDIAPPRO countries (%)

	Estonia	UK	Poland	Denmark	Portugal	Belgium	France	Greece	Average
Index of use versatility (mean)	**6.49**	**5.92**	**5.71**	**5.58**	5.45	4.90	4.88	4.73	5.44
Resources									
Broadband connection at home	**75**	**65**	40	**76**	52	52	58	21	54
Internet-connected computer in the child's bedroom	**52**	34	**51**	**59**	43	32	35	49	44

Note: The sample base is 11- to 18-year-old children who were studying in typical schools in each country in the autumn of 2005 and who had used the internet (N = 4558, 96% of population). The mean values and percentages notably above the sample average are in bold.

Table 6. 3. Correlations between activities and parental rule banning those activities in the MEDIAPPRO countries

Activities	Estonia	UK	Poland	Denmark	Portugal	Belgium	France	Greece	Average
Down-loading music or movies	−.14**	−.19**	−.25**	−.18**	−	−.23**	−.28**	−.14**	−.22**
Instant messaging	−.12*	−.18**	−.26**	−.19**	−.12*	−.21**	−.19**	−	−.19**
Email	−	−	−.20**	−	−	−.18**	−.23**	−	−.12**
Talking in a chat room	.11*	−.17**	−	−	−	−.21**	−.14**	−.15**	−.11**
Playing games online	−	−	−	.12**	−	−	−	−	−

Note: The sample base is 11- to 18-year-old children who were studying in typical schools in each country in the autumn of 2005 and who had used the internet (N = 4558, 96% of population) * p < 0.05, ** p < 0.01.

games tended to engage in this activity more actively. In general, parental bans seem to be more effective in Belgium, France, Poland and the UK (see also Chapters Fourteen and Sixteen, this volume, regarding parental mediation).

Conclusion

Although the take-up of online opportunities by children across European countries varies in its detail, overall it follows a general pattern, according to which the advancing experience in internet use as children grow older and their changing priorities and motivations lead to a greater variation of online activities. Taking up online opportunities can therefore be seen in terms of a gradation in digital inclusion (cf Livingstone and Helsper, 2007), where advancing stages imply increasing user agency, and this is a pattern that applies across countries. Our cross-national analysis also showed that the versatility of taking up online opportunities is related to structural aspects such as material resources for using the internet at home.

The main question for discussion is whether and how taking up online opportunities is important for or beneficial to children. Our analysis showed that the most frequent activities – seeking information and educational use – stem in part from the internet being a new kind of educational medium favoured by school. That said, these activities, although obviously important in terms of obtaining general knowledge and digital literacies, are just one aspect of user agency.

At the next stage, taking up opportunities related to communication and entertainment foregrounds children's motivations related to sociability, facilitating community building and expanding relationships with peers. Moreover, those highly popular activities are a source of excitement and fun for many children.

Entertainment-related opportunities entering in the third stage – watching videos and television and playing games online – require considerable resources, particularly time, and are often in the focus of parental mediation. Their role in children's development, however, is ambiguous. For instance, we saw that when placed on the 'ladder of online opportunities' gamers can be interpreted as constituting a source of motivation for moving towards more 'approved' uses of the internet. We have yet to learn how to apply entertainment-related opportunities effectively in education.

The most complex stage, which also includes blogging and creating homepages, has only been reached by a minority of young internet users across European countries. Many of those interactive and creative opportunities involve forms of social participation, potentially leading to civic engagement. It is important to note that the take-up of these opportunities does not entail significant additional internet resources, but instead depends mostly on user agency – motivation, creativity and setting one's priorities. Furthermore, previous research has indicated that blogging and creating homepages can both contribute to the development of advanced digital literacies – active engagement in those practices is related to taking a responsible attitude towards one's own postings as well as towards the content of online comments in general (Kalmus et al, 2009a). Thus, media education could turn more attention to fostering children's creative activities in less stuctured online environments such as blogs and homepages.

Our analysis showed that parental restrictions have some effect on children's take-up of online opportunities across countries. However, as several entertainment and communication-related activities can lead to the take-up of more 'approved' opportunities, the utility of restricting applications such as online games or instant messaging becomes questionable. Rather, parents and teachers should pay more attention to teaching children how to make informed choices online.

Although this chapter has pooled such evidence as is available, the EU Kids Online network has shown that there is still little cross-nationally comparable evidence regarding the incidence and take-up of online opportunities by children (Livingstone and Haddon, 2009). Current knowledge is mostly based on the data from studies carried out at different points of time in various countries where variation in research methods can be an obstacle to making trustworthy comparisons. Up to now, the Mediappro project remains one of very few studies that provides simultaneous cross-national observations. Thus, more quantitative and qualitative research is needed to get more insights into how children take up and benefit from different online opportunities, especially online content creation and civic participation.

Acknowledgements

The Mediappro research project and the EU Kids Online thematic network were funded by the European Commission Safer Internet Programme. The preparation of this chapter was supported by research grant no. 6968, financed by the Estonian Science Foundation; the project no. SF0180017s07 was financed by the Estonian Governmental Scientific Research Support Scheme.

References

Alakeson, V. (2003) *Inclusion in the information society: A case study with AOL Europe: Final report*, London: Forum for the Future (www.forumforthefuture.org/files/DigitaleuropeInclusioncasestudy.pdf).

Burgess, J. (2007) 'Vernacular creativity and new media', Unpublished doctoral dissertation, Queensland University of Technology, Australia (http://eprints.qut.edu.au/10076/1/Burgess_PhD_FINAL.pdf).

Csíkszentmihályi, M. (1996) *Creativity: Flow and the psychology of discovery and invention*, New York, NY: HarperCollins Publishers.

Dahlgren, P. (2006) 'Civic participation and practices: beyond "deliberative democracy"', in N. Carpentier, P. Pruulmann-Vengerfeldt, K. Nordenstreng, M. Hartmann, P. Vihalemm and B. Cammaerts (eds) *Researching media, democracy and participation*, Tartu, Estonia: Tartu University Press: 23-34.

Depandelaere, M., Gabriels B., Huylenbroeck J., Jonckheere L., Jutten S. et al (2006) *Kamedi@leon: I love media: De invloed van nieuwe media op de identiteitsvorming bij jongeren* (Kamedi@leon: I love media: The impact of new media on the identity-building of young people), Gent: Graffiti Jeugddienst ism UGent (Ghent: Graffiti Youth Service in cooperation with the University of Ghent) (www.apestaartjaren. be/sites/default/files/kamedialeon.doc). Report in Flemish.

Emirbayer, M. and Mische, A. (1998) 'What is agency?', *The American Journal of Sociology*, vol 103, no 4: 962-1023.

Eurispes Telefono Azzurro (2006) *Seventh report on childhood and youth*, Rome: Eurispes.

Giddens, A. (1984) *The constitution of society: Outline of the theory of structuration*, Cambridge: Polity Press.

Hasebrink, U., Livingstone, S., Haddon, L. and Ólafsson, K. (2009) *Comparing children's online opportunities and risks across Europe: Cross-national comparisons for EU Kids Online* (2nd edn), London: London School of Economics and Political Science, EU Kids Online (Deliverable D3.2 for the EC Safer Internet Plus Programme).

Kalmus, V., Pruulmann-Vengerfeldt, P., Runnel, P. and Siibak, A. (2009a) 'Mapping the terrain of "Generation C": places and practices of online content creation among Estonian teenagers', *Journal of Computer-Mediated Communication*, vol 14, no 4.

Kalmus, V., Pruulmann-Vengerfeldt, P., Runnel, P. and Siibak, A. (2009b) 'Online content creation practices of Estonian schoolchildren in a comparative perspective', *Journal of Children and Media*, vol 3, no 4.

Livingstone, S. and Bober, M. (2004) *UK children go online: Surveying the experiences of young people and their parents* (www.york.ac.uk/res/e-society/projects/1/UKCGOsurveyexec.pdf).

Livingstone, S. and Haddon, L. (2009) *EU Kids Online: Final report*, London: London School of Economics and Political Science, EU Kids Online (Deliverable D6.5 for the EC Safer Internet Plus Programme).

Livingstone, S. and Helsper, E.J. (2007) 'Gradations in digital inclusion: children, young people and the digital divide', *New Media & Society*, vol 9, no 4: 671-96.

Livingstone, S. and Helsper, E.J. (2008) 'Parental mediation of children's internet use', *Journal of Broadcasting & Electronic Media*, vol 52, no 4: 581-99.

Mediappro (2006) *The appropriation of new media by youth*, A European research project, Brussels: Chaptal Communication with the Support of the European Commission/Safer Internet Action Plan.

Ólafsson, K. and Jónsson, G.K. (2008) 'National report for Iceland', in U. Hasebrink, S. Livingstone, L. Haddon and K. Ólafsson (2009) *Comparing children's online opportunities and risks across Europe: Cross-national comparisons for EU Kids Online* (2nd edn), London: London School of Economics and Political Science, EU Kids Online (Deliverable D3.2 for the EC Safer Internet Plus Programme) (www.lse.ac.uk/collections/EUKidsOnline/Reports/WP3NationalReportIceland.pdf).

Rathmoser, M. (2008) 'National report for Austria', in U. Hasebrink, S. Livingstone, L. Haddon and K. Ólafsson (2009) *Comparing children's online opportunities and risks across Europe: Cross-national comparisons for EU Kids Online* (2nd edn), London: London School of Economics and Political Science, EU Kids Online (Deliverable D3.2 for the EC Safer Internet Plus Programme) (www.lse.ac.uk/collections/EUKidsOnline/Reports/WP3NationalReportAustria.pdf).

Štětka, V. (2008) 'National report for the Czech Republic', in U. Hasebrink, S. Livingstone, L. Haddon and K. Ólafsson (2009) *Comparing children's online opportunities and risks across Europe: Cross-national comparisons for EU Kids Online* (2nd edn), London: London School of Economics and Political Science, EU Kids Online (Deliverable D3.2 for the EC Safer Internet Plus Programme) (www.lse.ac.uk/collections/EUKidsOnline/Reports/WP3NationalReportCzech.pdf).

Valkenburg, P.M., Schouten, A.P. and Peter, J. (2005) 'Adolescents' identity experiments on the internet', *New Media & Society*, vol 7, no 3: 383-402.

SEVEN

Adolescents and social network sites: identity, friendships and privacy

Jochen Peter, Patti M. Valkenburg and Cédric Fluckiger

In the past five years, many European teenagers have started to use social networking sites such as MySpace, Facebook and Bebo. Social networking sites can be defined as 'web-based services that allow individuals to (1) construct a public or semi-public profile within a bounded system; (2) articulate a list of other users with whom they share a connection; and (3) view and traverse their list of connections and those made by others within the system' (boyd and Ellison, 2007: 211). While the specific social networking sites that are most popular among teenagers differ across European countries, their most important common aim is to enable teenagers to communicate with other people from their extended social network. Unlike earlier web-based social applications, such as chat rooms, social networking sites encourage the activation of latent ties that already exist offline rather than the creation of new, purely online-based ties (Haythornwaite, 2005; Valkenburg et al, 2006; Ellison et al, 2007).

Although the nature of social networking sites contradicts popular concerns about the lonely adolescent who connects online with strangers, public responses to adolescents' use of social networking sites have been critical. The 'MySpace generation', it has been suggested, is narcissistically obsessed with digital self-presentation, prefers the quantity of friendships over their quality, and lacks any sense of privacy in publicly disclosing intimate information (for a summary of the critique, see Hinduja and Patchin, 2008; Livingstone, 2008). Although these concerns resemble anxieties that seem to emerge around each new technology (McRobbie and Thornton, 1995), they do point to three important aspects of adolescents' use of social networking sites: (a) identity construction; (b) friendships; and (c) privacy.

Identity construction, the development of stable and fulfilling friendships and the ability to disclose private information in appropriate ways and settings are important developmental tasks in adolescence.

However, despite the significance of these developmental tasks and their potential relation to adolescents' use of social networking sites, research on the issue is still scarce and scattered. This chapter therefore systematises and reviews the available literature, trying to answer the question of how adolescents' use of social networking sites shapes, and is shaped by, the three developmental tasks just mentioned. To contextualise the literature, it is necessary to give a brief account of what is known about European adolescents' use of social networking sites and parents' concerns about their children's activities on these sites.

Use of social network sites and parental concern

Given the novelty of social networking sites, the rapid change of users' online preferences and differences in research activities in European countries, cross-nationally comparable, up-to-date data on adolescents' use of these sites are hard to obtain. Hence we rely on recent commercial data derived from measurements of internet traffic (comScore, 2009). To map parents' concern about their children's activities on social networking sites, we draw on latest Eurobarometer (EC, 2008) data.

Figure 7.1: Use of social network sites (SNS) in Europe and parental concern

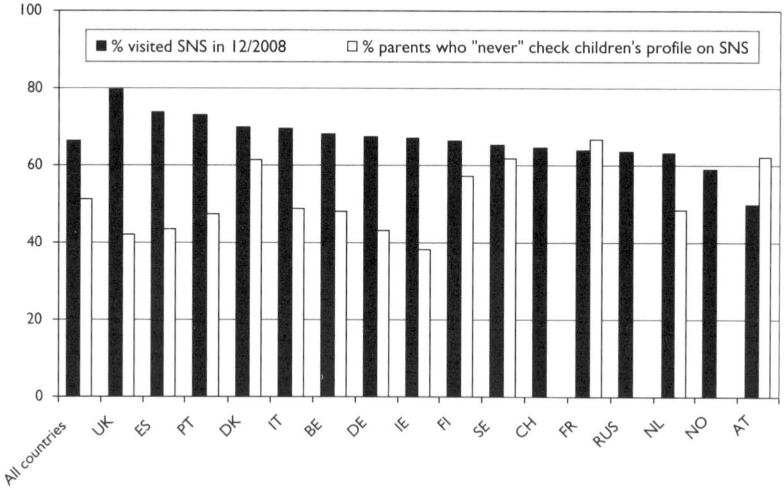

Note: Data are taken from comScore (2009) for the black bars, and from Eurobarometer (2008) for the white bars. Parental concern data were not available for Switzerland (CH), Russia (RUS) and Norway (NO).

Base: (comScore) Internet traffic of 282.7 million EU users aged 15 or over who went online in December 2008 (Eurobarometer, N = 12,803 parents in 27 EU member states).

The black bars in Figure 7.1 show, for 16 European countries, the percentage of internet users *aged 15 or older* who visited a social networking site in December 2008. The white bars indicate the percentage of parents who said in 2008 that they had *never* checked whether their child had a profile on such a site. Across all countries, 66% of all internet users aged 15 and older visited a social networking site in December 2008. Overall, then, the majority of young internet users are active on these sites. There are, however, some striking country differences. In the UK (80%), Spain (74%) and Portugal (73%), about three quarters of young internet users are users of social networking sites. By contrast, in the Netherlands (63%), Norway (59%) and Austria (50%), less than two thirds of young internet users visit these sites.

Parental concern about their children's activities on social networking sites seems to be less marked than the massive use of these sites would suggest. As Figure 7.1 shows, more than 50% of European parents have never checked whether their children have a profile on any one of these sites. In Denmark (61%), Finland (57%) and Sweden (62%), as well as in France (67%) and Austria (62%), these figures are even higher. In contrast, Irish, German and Spanish parents seem to be somewhat more concerned about their children's activities on social networking sites, given that 'only' about four in ten parents have never checked whether their children have profiles. Although a general pattern does not emerge, it seems that parents in Nordic countries (that is, Denmark, Finland and Sweden) are generally less worried than other European parents about what their children do on these sites.

In sum, the available data on adolescents' use of social networking sites show that their use is not limited to particular European countries – all across Europe this has become a ubiquitous phenomenon among people aged 15 years and older, with the majority of internet users being active on such sites. European parents, by and large, do not seem overly concerned about their children's use of social networking sites. The widespread use of social networking sites, along with a relative autonomy from parental control, constitute important conditions for adolescents' identity construction, their development of friendships and the exploration of the public–private boundaries of the self.

Identity construction

Scholars agree that at least five characteristics of social networking sites facilitate adolescents' identity construction (Hinduja and Patchin, 2008; Lewis et al, 2008; Manago et al, 2008; Zhao et al, 2008; Livingstone and Brake, in press). First, the easy *accessibility* of these sites makes them convenient venues for adolescents' identity exploration. Second, the *user-friendliness* of social networking sites enables adolescents to quickly create a standardised profile of themselves. At the same time, most sites allow for the personalisation of the profile through the uploading of user-generated content, such as private photographs or messages. Third, although some social networking sites include synchronous internet applications, such as instant messaging, the predominantly asynchronous character of these sites ensures a greater *controllability of self-presentation*. This controllability is further enhanced by the various ways in which content can be reassembled or manipulated. Fourth, the greater control over one's self-presentation is complemented by social networking sites' options for *network management*. By adjusting their private settings to particular groups of viewers of the profile, users of the sites can target different groups of their network with different pieces of information about themselves. Concurrently, the feedback from others may provide adolescents with information relevant to the verification and validation of the identities they present on the sites. Finally, the *reduced auditory and visual cues* that typify communication through social networking sites may encourage adolescents to present information that, in face-to-face communication, may be inappropriate and embarrassing. In sum, these sites are easy, efficient and powerful tools for adolescents' identity construction.

Whereas several studies have investigated young people's self-presentation in chat rooms and on personal websites (Döring, 2002; Valkenburg et al, 2005; Subrahmanyam et al, 2006), research on adolescents' identity construction is still in its infancy. However, existing research agrees on a number of general features of how adolescents construct their identity on social networking sites. First, identity constructions take place along a continuum of implicit and explicit identity claims (Zhao et al, 2008). Implicit identity claims are mainly visual and portray the self as a social actor, notably in its connection with peers, for example by posting party pictures ('relational self'). Explicit identity claims, in contrast, are largely narrative descriptions and portray the self as an individual actor ('individual self'), for example, when adolescents describe on social networking sites who they are. In the middle of this continuum, a mixture of implicit and explicit identity claims is made, which are partly enumerative, showing the self of consumption preferences and tastes ('cultural self'). Typical expressions of the cultural self are references to favourite music styles, music artists or brands.

Of all identity claims, implicit claims – and thus the portrayals of the relational self – occur most often (van Cleemput, 2008; Zhao et al, 2008). In addition, developmental changes underlie the identity claims of adolescents. Whereas younger adolescents tend to present their cultural selves, older adolescents and emerging adults emphasise more strongly their relational selves (Fluckiger, 2008; Livingstone, 2008). In doing so, adolescents increasingly try to lead independent cultural and social lives from their parents. The identity claims made on social networking sites thus also express adolescents' emancipation from parental control.

Second, as the portrayal of the relational self dominates profiles, it is not surprising that identity construction on these sites is also partly social identity construction entailing the internalisation of attributes and the status of a group by self-categorisation processes (Hogg, 2003). Various scholars have pointed out that profiles on social networking sites are often place-markers in a social group rather than genuine self-portrayals (Fluckiger, 2008; Livingstone 2008). Identity-related information is thus often used to reinforce or improve one's standing in a group. Important in this process is the use of insider jokes (Livingstone, 2008; Manago et al, 2008), which, being inaccessible to out-group members, reaffirms one's position within the in-group and, eventually, one's relational self.

A third feature of identity construction on social networking sites is the dominance of social popularity claims in profiles (Fluckiger, 2008; Livingstone, 2008; Manago et al, 2008; van Cleemput, 2008; Zhao et al, 2008). Adolescents predominantly present themselves as individuals worth having friendships with. To illustrate this quality, they compete with others over the size of their friend network or make public the private posts of friends. Similarly, they emphasise traits that show their sociability, for example their open-mindedness, thoughtfulness, optimism and spontaneity (Zhao et al, 2008).

A fourth feature of identity construction involves the role of feedback on social networking sites for self-verification. While identity construction on these sites entails to some extent the presentation of idealised parts of the self, the positive feedback of others endows this self-presentation with social legitimacy (Fluckiger, 2008; Livingstone, 2008; Manago et al, 2008; van Cleemput, 2008). Adolescents thus gain important information about how their desired identities resonate with others. This self-verification is all the more important because the contacts on social networking sites rarely emerge from virtual ties, but are rooted in face-to-face relationships (boyd and Ellison, 2007; Fluckiger, 2008). Overall, if the response to adolescents' identity construction is positive, it seems to increase their self-esteem, while negative responses harm adolescents' self-esteem (Valkenburg et al,

2006). Negative responses are often elicited by the presentation of over-idealised or inauthentic identities. Self-presentation on social networking sites is generally judged according to its veracity and authenticity, and violations of these criteria are typically punished in the form of negative comments (Manago et al, 2008; van Cleemput, 2008).

A final feature of identity construction on social networking sites is its intertwining with expressions of adolescents' lifestyles. The very choice of a social networking site in itself involves considerations about how to express a particular lifestyle (Livingstone, 2008). Similarly, adolescents carefully craft their cultural selves by displaying their affinity with, or aversion to, particular subcultures (van Cleemput, 2008). Specifically, adolescents use their consumption preferences and tastes for cultural products, such as films, music and books, to locate their identities in a cultural space (Fluckiger, 2008).

In sum, social networking sites provide adolescents with an easy and attractive opportunity to construct their identities. Although adolescents can emphasise different aspects of their self – the relational, the cultural and the individual self – these sites are dominated by identity claims that show adolescents in relation to others. On social networking sites, identity construction is a social construction. Identity exists only in its interpersonal relations: it is modelled for others and legitimised or sanctioned by others.

Friendships

Recent research has reliably shown that the use of social internet applications such as instant messaging enhances adolescents' social connectedness (for a review, see Valkenburg and Peter, 2009). However, as far as social networking sites are concerned, we are only starting to understand their implications for the quantity and quality of adolescents' friendships. In terms of the *quantity* of friendships on social networking sites, it is important to note that, generally, adolescents' use of these sites is motivated by their wish to stay in touch with their networks of friends (Fluckiger, 2006; Ellison et al, 2007; Lenhart and Madden, 2007). However, this does not preclude the possibility that latent or remote ties are activated or new friendships formed. For example, researchers have found that if adolescents used social networking sites more frequently, they were more likely to establish new friendships (Valkenburg et al, 2006). Similarly, when researchers traced how the number of friends of users of these sites developed over the course of one year, they found a significant increase (Steinfield et al, 2008). These findings suggest that the use of social networking sites augments the quantity of adolescents' friendships.

In terms of the *quality* of adolescents' friendships on social networking sites, research has mainly concentrated on the development of adolescents' social capital. Broadly defined, social capital refers to the resources people accumulate through their relationships (Coleman, 1988). Putnam (2000) further distinguishes between bridging and bonding social capital. Bridging social capital encompasses weak connections between people. These connections may provide useful information, but lack emotional depth. Bonding social capital, in contrast, refers to emotionally close relationships, as they can typically be found between close friends. Both cross-sectional and longitudinal research has shown that the use of social networking sites increases bridging social capital (Ellison et al, 2007; Steinfield et al, 2008; Subrahmanyam et al, 2008), being particularly useful for establishing and maintaining 'lightweight contact with a broad set of acquaintances' (Steinfield et al, 2008: 443). Interestingly, users low in self-esteem benefit most from social networking sites: they were consistently found to accumulate more bridging social capital than users high in self-esteem (Ellison et al, 2007; Steinfield et al, 2008).

There is also some first evidence that the use of social networking sites is associated with greater bonding social capital (Ellison et al, 2007). However, there are two caveats to this finding. First, the causal relationship between the use of social networking sites and bonding social capital is currently unclear. It may be (a) that the use of these sites increases bonding social capital; (b) that bonding social capital increases the use of social networking sites; or (c) that both influences occur simultaneously. Second, the use of social networking sites explains the accumulation of bonding social capital less well than the accumulation of bridging social capital (Ellison et al, 2007). Thus, the affordances of social networking sites seem to encourage the formation of loose connections but appear less suitable for creating the emotionally close relationships typical of bonding social capital.

In sum, social networking sites seem to do well at helping adolescents maintain and extend their social network. There also seems to be a poor-get-richer effect: individuals with a low self-esteem make more friends than individuals with a high self-esteem. Although the use of these sites is related to closer, more emotional relationships, most users of social networking sites seem to establish and maintain less involving, loose connections on such sites.

Privacy

Worries about adolescents' lack of concern about privacy on social networking sites figure highly in the public debates about the dangers of such sites. However, research on this issue is not only scarce, but also comes to contradictory conclusions. For example, after an analysis of 4,000 Facebook profiles in 2005, Gross and Acquisti (2005) concluded: 'Based on the information they provide online, users expose themselves to various physical and cyber risks, and make it extremely easy for third parties to create digital dossiers of their behaviour' (2005: 79). More specifically, Gross and Acquisti pointed out that few users took advantage of the more limiting privacy settings and willingly accepted the default settings, which maximise the users' visibility to others. In contrast, a 2006 study of Facebook profiles found that 40% of adolescent users restricted access to their profiles (Hinduja and Patchin, 2008). Of those whose profiles were visible to anyone, less than 10% listed their full name. However, as Hinduja and Patchin explicitly noted, 'it is very possible to locate … youth using the little information they provide on this site' (2008: 138).

The results from analyses of profiles on social network sites are not fully consistent with findings from survey or interview-based research. For example, in a survey study conducted in 2006, 66% of adolescents reported that they limited others' access to their profiles on websites (Lenhart and Madden, 2007). Similarly, after open-ended interviews with 16 teenagers conducted in 2007, Livingstone (2008) emphasised that 'it would be mistaken to conclude that teenagers are unconcerned about their privacy' (2008: 404).

At least three reasons may account for these diverging research findings. First, given the rapid transformations of use and users of social networking sites in the past years, sensitivity to privacy issues may have increased significantly, particularly among adolescents. In 2005, when Gross and Acquisti (2005) carried out their study, Facebook was still limited to university networks in which privacy may not have been such a concern (boyd and Ellison, 2007). With the wider spread of social networking sites, however, the protection of privacy has become more important. Second, different study designs may account for the contradictory findings. In interviews (for example in the studies by Lenhart and Madden [2007] and by Livingstone [2008]), the majority of respondents may give the socially desirable answer that they protect their profiles, while analyses of the profiles may show that, in fact, only a minority protects their profiles (see studies by Gross and Acquisti [2005] and Hinduja and Patchin [2008]).

A final reason for the discrepancy between what adolescents say about privacy and what is publicly accessible on their profiles may come from the mismatch between the privacy wishes of users and the operation of privacy settings on the sites. As Livingstone (2008) has pointed out, users have difficulty in translating the gradation of friendship levels into adequate privacy settings. The often binary distinction required between private and public does not reflect the different types of friendships adolescents have. As a result, they may be forced to display some information although they consider it private, or to withhold information they might wish to share with a broader audience.

In sum, research into adolescents' privacy on social networking sites is still in a nascent state. Our lack of knowledge partly results from the rapid changes in the affordances and use of these sites with which academic research has difficulty keeping pace. At the same time, however, it seems that not enough attention has been paid to theoretically interesting and practically relevant questions. For example, a recent study has demonstrated that users of social networking sites are more likely to have a private profile if their friends have private profiles, if they are more active on the sites, if they are female and if they prefer only music that is very popular (Lewis et al, 2008). While this study is certainly a step in the right direction, future research should focus on a theoretical framework that explains the link more coherently between privacy on social networking sites and users' motives and characteristics.

Conclusion

While some media have diagnosed the emergence of a narcissistic, exhibitionist 'MySpace generation', with superficial social ties, by and large research does not support this negative view of the users of social networking sites. Although adolescents' identity construction is necessarily about the 'me', it is a heavily social enterprise in which identities are co-constructed with others. Similarly, there is currently no reason to assume that relationships on these sites, loose though they may be, displace emotionally close relationships. Finally, many adolescents seem to be aware of privacy issues on social networking sites although the technical affordances of these sites may not provide them with the fine-tuned possibilities they would prefer in order to display information of varying degrees of sensitivity.

Research thus provides first insights in how adolescents' use of social networking sites shapes, and is shaped by, developmental tasks in adolescence. However, there are several challenges that need to be addressed in future research. First, we need more research among adolescents. Most research focuses on emerging adults, but important identity developments take place before the age of 18. Second, existing research lacks an explicit developmental focus. It is unclear how adolescents' use of social networking sites changes with their development. Also, it is unclear how adolescents' use differs from adults' use of these sites. Third, while several of the questions posed aim at causality problems, internally valid designs are missing, a recent longitudinal study by Steinfield et al (2008) notwithstanding. Finally, we need more theoretically coherent work. Many of the studies refer to theories that were developed for other purposes. However, what future research on social networking sites needs is theory building that is genuinely related to these sites and explains how and why these sites affect crucial developmental tasks in adolescence.

References

boyd, d.m. and Ellison, N.B. (2007) 'Social network sites: definition, history, and scholarship', *Journal of Computer-Mediated Communication*, vol 13, no 1: 210-30.

Coleman, J.S. (1988) 'Social capital in the creation of human capital', *American Journal of Sociology*, vol 94: S95-S120.

comScore (2009) *Tuenti most popular social networking site in Spain* (www.comscore.com/press/release.asp?press=2733).

Döring, N. (2002) 'Personal home pages on the web: a review of research', *Journal of Computer-Mediated Communication*, vol 7, no 3.

Ellison, N.B., Steinfield, C. and Lampe, C. (2007) 'The benefits of Facebook "friends": social capital and college students' use of online social network sites', *Journal of Computer-Mediated Communication*, vol 12, no 4: 1143-68.

EC (European Commission) (2008) *Towards a safer use of the internet for children in the EU – A parents' perspective, Analytical report*, Flash Eurobarometer Series # 248, conducted by The Gallup Organisation, Hungary, Luxembourg: EC (http://ec.europa.eu/information_society/activities/sip/docs/eurobarometer/annexesanalyticalreport_2008.pdf).

Fluckiger, C. (2006) 'La sociabilité juvénile instrumentée. L'appropriation des blogs dans un groupe de collégiens', *Réseaux*, vol 138: 111-38.

Fluckiger, C. (2008) 'Teens and blogs network: an online community emerging from a teenage gang', Paper presented at the AOIR Internet Research 9.0 conference: 'Rethinking Community, Rethinking Place', Copenhagen, Denmark, 15 October.

Gross, R. and Acquisti, A. (2005) 'Information revelation and privacy in online social networks (The Facebook case)', Paper presented at the ACM Workshop on Privacy in the Electronic Society (WPES), Alexandria, VA, 7 November.

Haythornwaite, C. (2005) 'Social networks and internet connectivity effects', *Information, Communication, and Society*, vol 8, no 2: 125-47.

Hinduja, S. and Patchin, J. W. (2008) 'Personal information of adolescents on the internet: a quantitative content analysis of MySpace', *Journal of Adolescence*, vol 31, no 1: 125-46.

Hogg, M.A. (2003) 'Social identity', in M.R. Leary and J.P. Tangney (eds) *Handbook of self and identity*, New York, NY: Guilford Press: 462-79.

Lenhart, A. and Madden, M. (2007) *Social networking websites and teens: An overview*, Pew Internet and American Life Project (www.pewinternet. org/Reports/2007/Social-Networking-Websites-and-Teens.aspx).

Lewis, K., Kaufman, J. and Christakis, N. (2008) 'The taste for privacy: an analysis of college student privacy settings in an online social network', *Journal of Computer-Mediated Communication*, vol 14, no 1: 79-100.

Livingstone, S. (2008) 'Taking risky opportunities in youthful content creation: teenagers' use of social networking sites for intimacy, privacy and self-expression', *New Media & Society*, vol 10, no 3: 393-411.

Livingstone, S. and Brake, D. (in press) 'On the rapid rise of social networking sites: new findings and policy implications', *Children & Society*.

McRobbie, A. and Thornton, S.L. (1995) 'Rethinking moral panic for multi-mediated social worlds', *British Journal of Sociology*, vol 46, no 4: 559-74.

Manago, A.M., Graham, M.B., Greenfield, P.M. and Salimkhan, G. (2008) 'Self-presentation and gender on MySpace', *Journal of Applied Developmental Psychology*, vol 29, no 6: 446-58.

Putnam, R. (2000) *Bowling alone: The collapse and revival of American community*, New York, NY: Simon & Schuster.

Steinfield, C., Ellison, N.B. and Lampe, C. (2008) 'Social capital, self-esteem, and use of online social network sites: a longitudinal analysis', *Journal of Applied Developmental Psychology*, vol 29, no 6: 434-45.

Subrahmanyam, K., Smahel, D. and Greenfield, P.M. (2006) 'Connecting developmental constructions to the internet: identity presentation and sexual exploration in online teen chat rooms', *Developmental Psychology*, vol 42, no 3: 395-406.

Subrahmanyam, K., Reich, S.M., Waechter, N. and Espinoza, G. (2008) 'Online and offline social networks: use of social networking sites by emerging adults', *Journal of Applied Developmental Psychology*, vol 29, no 6: 420-33.

Valkenburg, P.M. and Peter, J. (2009) 'Social consequences of the internet for adolescents: a decade of research', *Current Directions in Psychological Science*, vol 18, no 1: 1-5.

Valkenburg, P.M., Peter, J. and Schouten, A.P. (2006) 'Friend networking sites and their relationship to adolescents' well-being and social self-esteem', *Cyberpsychology & Behavior*, vol 9, no 5: 584-90.

Valkenburg, P.M., Schouten, A.P. and Peter, J. (2005) 'Adolescents' identity experiments on the internet', *New Media & Society*, vol 7, no 3: 383-402.

van Cleemput, K. (2008) 'Self presentation by Flemish adolescents on profile sites', *Tijdschrift Voor Communicatiewetenschap*, vol 36, no 4: 253-69.

Zhao, S.Y., Grasmuck, S. and Martin, J. (2008) 'Identity construction on Facebook: digital empowerment in anchored relationships', *Computers in Human Behavior*, vol 24, no 5: 1816-36.

EIGHT

Young people online: gender and age influences

Helen McQuillan and Leen d'Haenens

Setting the scene

Digital technologies and their use among children and young people in Europe have become increasingly more complex and pervasive (Livingstone and Bovill, 2001; Larsson, 2003; Lenhart, 2005). Numerous studies show that young people are far from homogeneous, yet age and gender continue to be particularly strong predictors of patterns of use (Wartella et al, 2000). Age differences are usually supposed to be linear: with age one tends to engage in more online opportunities and in more risky behaviour. Gender differences are commonly supposed to be strong but unpredictable (Weiser, 2000). The gender picture becomes more complex when one compares young children with teenagers as to their experience of online opportunities and risks, also taking into account cultural differences between countries. Because of these complexities, in this chapter gender and age-based practices are interpreted within a theoretical framework that incorporates the study of the digital divide, the uses-and-gratifications theory and gender socialisation theory.

Defining the digital divide as binary is not a useful approach: one is not either in or out, digitally included or excluded. Hence, it makes much more sense to map a continuum of use with gradations in digital inclusion, from non-use through low use to more frequent use. Substantial differences in adoption styles and online attitudes are due to socio-demographics as well as psychological factors (Broos and Roe, 2006). Van Dijk (2006) questions which inequalities the digital divide concept actually refers to, making distinctions between different kinds of digital divide (material, motivational, skills and usage) and the importance of potentially missing out on technologically mediated opportunities in terms of life chances, resources, participation and capabilities. Livingstone and Helper's (2007) *ladder of online opportunities* is put forward as a useful analytical tool for exploring variations in the breadth and depth of digital technologies' use. While the gender divide in access has closed in North America and north-western Europe, gender gaps in usage persist. Obviously, none of this evidence is static: it is therefore crucial to see how digital media applications change over time as well as users' expectations and interests.

Digital technologies are usually used to gratify certain needs or wants. The uses-and-gratifications research tradition focuses on factors influencing motives for use and outcomes from people's media-related behaviour (Newhagen and Rafaeli, 1996). Merging traditional and interactive media platforms have facilitated different kinds of synchronous user experiences. Nevertheless, investigations of motivational access and online skills, choice of applications and diversity or lack of these among young people in Europe remain relatively scarce. Hence, attempts to identify and understand differential adoption styles and patterns of use constitute a fruitful strand of research (Johnsson-Smaragdi, 2001).

Childhood socialisation emphasises the transmission of social and cultural norms during childhood and adolescence within society's three major socialising agencies: family, school and peer groups. Norms are set for age and gender, influencing peer group and young people's behaviour and conformity.

Aims and scope

Van Dijk (2006: 229) warns about 'notoriously unreliable' cross-country statistics on uses of digital technologies due to shifting definitions. For North America, the surveys of the Pew Internet and American Life Project (2001-07) (see www.pewinternet.org/) and the UCLA Internet Reports (2000-09) (see www.worldinternetproject.net) are among the most reliable sources for measures of the use of digital technologies. For Europe, the Eurobarometer surveys (EC, 2005, 2007, 2008), due to their level of detail, often prove to be the most reliable sources, but although they include the time spent on several digital platforms and applications they fail to provide an insight into the motivations for use and gratifications sought and obtained. This chapter, aimed at providing insights into both usage patterns and indications of motivations for using digital technologies, draws on cross-national empirical data from a range of sources (Hasebrink et al, 2009).

Mapping these cross-national data and comparing young people's internet use across Europe is far from being an easy job. Blumler et al (1992) extended an invitation to researchers to conduct cross-cultural studies to determine whether media uses and gratifications were universal and whether they had different functions in different societies. We accept their invitation in this chapter and focus on both commonalities and differences in the integration of digital technologies into European young people's daily lives and youth cultures. In particular, we ask: to what extent do age and gender differences emerge as critical factors explaining differential adoption and use in terms of motivational access, defined as a varying readiness to engage in different types of online risks as well as online opportunities? In what ways are skills to embrace online opportunities and to cope with online risks influenced by age and gender differences? We are also interested in examining whether these differences are just part of life's rich tapestry or whether they can be considered inequalities that require policy intervention.

Access and use

Internet use among children in the EU27 is commonplace and growing continually. Eurobarometer research on the safer internet (EC, 2005, 2008) reports an increase in the overall percentage of internet users (aged 6-17) within a three-year period, from 68% in 2005 to 75% in 2008, mostly attributable to an increase in internet use by younger children aged between 6 and 13. Internet use by children is dependent on age and the general pace of internet diffusion in the country under study. The proportion of children online in a country increases for each year of a child's age, but now appears to plateau already by the age of 10 or 11, at which point a ceiling is reached in the proportion of children online (Hasebrink et al, 2009). Significantly higher rates of access and use are evident for all age groups in countries that have implemented information society policies with an emphasis on high home and school access. However, average internet use figures for young people mask considerable variance between countries, ranging from a low of 47% in Italy to a high of 94% in Finland. In addition, greater increases in internet use are evident in the recent entrants to the European Union (EU) in Central and Eastern Europe. This reminds us of cross-cultural differences and indicates a digital divide between countries.

The Flash Eurobarometer (EC, 2008) survey on parents' perceptions of their children's internet use reports that home and school remain the most common sites for internet access, the EU27 figures for home and school internet access being 65% and 57% respectively. An emerging pattern is the growth in young people's personal computer ownership. More than a third (34%) of young people have their own computer and the trend towards solitary internet use and the growing bedroom culture reported in the Eurobarometer survey (EC, 2005) continues. Again, there is considerable variance in this phenomenon across Europe. For example despite relatively high (88%) home internet use by young people in Ireland, only 9% have their own computer. This compares with two thirds (67%) of young people in Denmark.

While gaps between European countries persist, a positive trend is the shrinking gender difference in young people's internet use across Europe, with girls' use now slightly higher than boys' use (76% versus 74%). Only in the 6- to 7-year-old age group is girls' internet use lower than boys' use (46% versus 48%). According to the Flash Eurobarometer (EC, 2008), boys (35%) and girls (34%) were almost equally likely to have a personal computer. Overall there is equality of internet access for boys and girls, indicating a positive trend as a result of schools' and parents' investment in information and communication technologies (ICTs) for their children.

While the gender gap in internet access has diminished, researchers note that more subtle gender differences in online activities of young people are emerging (Lenhart, 2005; Livingstone et al, 2005). Small but persistent differences are evident in terms of time spent by boys online, the number of places they access the internet from and their access to a computer and internet in their bedrooms, compared with girls. Evidence across Europe also points to different online experiences, preferences and practices for girls and boys, which in turn impact on skills sets.

Skills and confidence

Internet confidence is related to frequency of use, which in turn impacts on skills, self-perceptions of skills and effective and beneficial use of the internet. Gender is commonly reported as a significant variable with respect to self-perceived skills and expertise (Hargittai and Shafer, 2006), with boys expressing higher self-perception of ICT expertise. Eleven of the 21 countries participating in the EU Kids Online network reported on gender differences in internet skills. With the exception of the UK, in countries where young people self-report and self-evaluate their internet skills (Austria, Bulgaria, the Netherlands, Sweden, Estonia, France, Poland, Italy, Germany and Bulgaria), boys tend to rate themselves higher than girls, describe themselves as more expert and claim to have more technical or advanced skills.

Eurobarometer (EC, 2007) reports that self-learning is claimed by all the young research participants, where observation, games, chat and instant messaging were the most cited means of learning to use the internet. Learning at school is secondary, often because, as pointed out in the Mediappro (2006) study, school ICT activity and teaching mainly covers basic, functional applications, rather than creative or interactive ICT use. Informal learning and skills acquisition were not investigated in the EU Kids Online research analysis, so hypotheses about any greater levels of skills for boys are difficult to prove or disprove. Evidence suggests that boys and girls may be developing different skills sets based on their actual different activities and, as explained by the uses-and-gratifications research tradition, on different motivational factors for use, presumably rooted in different subjective expectations about the utility and value of internet access and use.

We explore these skills using the 'ladder of online opportunities' approach of Livingstone and Helsper (2007), who propose a graduated sequence of activities from information searching to interactive communication and gaming, to more creative uses. Adopting this framework to examine young people's internet use across Europe, we can observe some common trends regarding age, gender and breadth of online activities. Relationships exist between age and frequency of use; age and skills; age and confidence; age and knowledge of risks; and age and risk-taking behaviour. These all suggest more limited online opportunities for younger age groups. Younger children are subject to more parental control, spend less time on the internet and have more limited use than older children. However, as children go online from an earlier age, childhood socialisation increasingly involves computer use, internet use and gaming as leisure activities, for both boys and girls.

Breadth and depth of young people's online opportunities

The breadth and depth of young people's internet use is increasing as new internet applications and faster connection speeds offer new opportunities. Characterising and measuring the quality of internet use is difficult, but cross-national research comparison suggests that the benefits of internet use depend on age, gender, social class, time, expertise and breadth of opportunity. How far up the ladder of opportunity young people venture is dependent on motivations, skills and confidence, as well as on demographic characteristics. In general, children progress up the ladder as they get older and while boys and girls enjoy many similar activities, there are some common gender differences.

Looking for information on subjects that are of interest or browsing for fun is the most widespread use of the internet for all ages and for both sexes (EC, 2007). Cross-national comparison of EU Kids Online data revealed gender differences in internet searching among older age groups in most countries, but these were not uniform. Although in Bulgaria, Germany, Italy, Spain, the Netherlands and the UK girls are more likely than boys to search for information on the internet for educational purposes, this appears a more popular activity for boys in Norway, Sweden and Greece, indicating cross-cultural differences.

Communicating with friends via email and chat rooms is becoming an equally important online activity for teenage boys and girls, although younger European boys (in the 12-14 age bracket) are less likely than their female counterparts to use email (EC, 2007). Individual country data supports this finding. For example, German research (JIM, 2007) notes similarities in boys' and girls' communication practices, incorporating email (58% of boys; 61% of girls), instant messaging (75% of boys; 68% of girls) and chat (30% boys and girls). Similarly, research in Norway (SAFT, 2006) reports almost equal numbers of boys and girls chatting online (47% of boys; 48% of girls) and using instant messaging (32% of boys; 30% of girls). Email is also popular with both, although slightly more popular with girls (44% of boys; 50% of girls). Email and chat are also common activities for young people in Poland, involving slightly more boys (44%) than girls (40%). Email is also a popular activity for young people in Portugal, although more popular with boys than girls (64% versus 52%). Email, chat and instant messaging activities are increasing across Europe for both sexes. Results from the 'Teens and ICT: Risks and Opportunities' (TIRO) research project in Belgium (Pauwels and Bauwens, 2008) explores young people's motives for going online and concludes that, among 12 to 18 year olds, girls' main use of the internet is for social contact (61%), whereas boys see the internet mainly as a leisure activity (43%). This evidence, notwithstanding the lack of uniformity, tends to show us that although gender gaps are closing, girls seem to be somewhat more attuned to the internet's communicative aspects, and boys more toward its use for gaming and entertainment.

Many positive aspects of game playing are reported, including social interaction, rich learning environments and experiences (Hasebrink et al, 2009). Although traditionally targeted at boys, a greater number of computer games aimed specifically at girls may have contributed to some increase in the popularity of game playing among girls. However, research data from all countries participating in the EU Kids

Online network indicate that computer and online gaming remain predominantly male–dominated activities.

Metton (2006) observed gender differences among French youth in terms of frequency of game playing and attitudes to gaming. More than four times as many boys as girls (44% versus 9%) play games on a daily basis; 59% of boys say they love playing computer games, compared to 21% of girls. German research (JIM, 2007), which investigated online and multiuser gaming, reported significant gender differences in play (24% of boys versus 4% of girls). Research in Greece (EC, 2007) also indicates that online gaming appeals mainly to older boys, rather than girls. Similarly, in Portugal, almost half of male youth play online games, compared with a third of girls (49% versus 33%). Polish data also demonstrates a considerable gender gap, with twice as many boy gamers as girls (71% versus 35%).

Computer gaming increasingly involves downloading, a further step on the ladder of online opportunities. Music and video downloads are also becoming popular activities, particularly for older children. The Mediappro (2006) collaborative research between nine European countries reported that downloading material from the internet is widely practised, including the illegal downloading of music. French research for this study reported that twice as many boys than girls download content from the internet and they access more video clips. In Portugal downloading music is more popular with boys than girls (26% boys versus 11% girls), as is downloading software (16% boys versus 5% girls). Similarly in Sweden, boys are more active downloaders of music, games, software and films. A different pattern emerges in Greece where music, video and film downloading are more common activities for girls (EC, Greece, 2007).

More creative users of the internet, referred to by Livingstone and Helsper (2007) as 'all rounders', engage in blogging, website development and other modes of media production. The Eurobarometer survey (EC, 2007) suggests that creating blogs and homepages and posting texts, photographs and music on the internet are predominantly older children's activities, for girls in particular. Online content creation is a relatively new phenomenon, supported by the development and promotion of Web 2.0 applications, encouraging young people's more interactive contribution to the internet. Mediappro (2006) suggests that these activities are at an early stage, but more recent Estonian research (Kalmus et al, in press) points to distinct gender differences also emerging in this area. These data indicate that girls are more likely than boys to publish personal information (50% girls versus 17% boys), post photographs they have taken (79% girls versus 46% boys) or self-publish texts and poetry (29% girls versus 11% boys). Girls are less likely to publish videos on their homepages (40% girls versus 53% boys). Findings across Europe are not uniform: whereas in Cyprus and Iceland blogging is more popular with girls, the trend is reversed in Sweden, Italy and the UK.

French research (Pasquier, 2005) indicates that older children are less interested in extending their social networks and use online communication to support existing friendships and peer networks. However, girls are more likely to use the internet to maintain rather than extend existing social networks. In Ireland, twice as many boys as girls (16% versus 7%) use social networking sites to make new friends. Ofcom (Office of Communications) (2008) research in the UK indicates that social networking sites have higher social currency with girls than boys (aged 12-15). While 30% of boys and girls have one profile or page, 30% of girls have two or more sites, compared with 18% of boys. Girls are also more likely than boys to visit these sites several times a week, and to have set access settings to 'friends only' (58% of girls use this setting, compared with 48% of boys).

The findings above illustrate more diversity than uniformity in young people's internet use across Europe and indicate the need to be cautious about interpreting these differences as inequalities. Different preferences and choices of internet activities, as well as different motivations for going online, are providing a range of opportunities for boys and girls – with breadth and depth increasing with age. In the light of the above, a more appropriate term might be 'digital diversity' – representing choices as well as constraints – perhaps more influenced by age, socio-economic status (SES), social norms and cultural values than gender.

Conclusion

In this chapter we explored key findings on internet practices among young people across Europe with a specific focus on gender and age, and the interaction between these two factors. We drew on three theoretical options: uses-and-gratifications (focusing on individual choice), the digital divide (focusing on structural constraints) and childhood socialisation (examining how children negotiate the choices and constraints differently over time).

Do these help us make sense of the various data across Europe on gender differences and similarities in young people's internet use? Given the uneven distribution of studies across Europe and the considerable variability in the quality of the available research, this is a difficult task. Is there a common youth culture in Europe that cuts across age and gender lines when it comes to digital technology use patterns and the strategies used to embrace online opportunities and to cope with online risks? Findings suggest that youth digital media culture incorporates similar broad activities and common risks across Europe. Overall, as time goes by and digital technologies become more pervasive, commonalities tend to prevail over differences or divides. But what this brief *tour d'horizon* does indicate is that young people are far from homogeneous and the opportunities provided by new media technologies applications are expanding year after year, leading to greater digital diversity.

To what extent do age and gender differences emerge as critical factors explaining differential adoption and use in terms of motivational access, defined as a varying readiness to engage in different types of online risks as well as online opportunities? Age is a critical explanatory factor, where breadth of activity is linked to age, given more constraints on younger people's use, more concerns and awareness about internet risk and safety and more parental supervision. As children grow older and move up the ladder of online opportunities, usage is more likely to be linked to choices rather than constraints, influenced by opportunities to communicate with peers online and more communal and social aspects of internet use. Gaming is the single area where gender differences persist, common to all countries. While different genres appeal to boys and girls, girl gamers have become a significant market segment.

In what ways are skills to embrace online opportunities and to cope with online risks influenced by age and gender differences? Different activities result in differential exposure to risks and different skills sets. The more limited internet use of younger people exposes them to less risk. Findings across Europe on gender differences in skills are inconclusive, but need to be tracked more closely as media literacy skills increasingly become essential life skills.

Researchers and policy makers tend to be more concerned about digital divides and internet risks than opportunities and digital diversity. We continue to have little insight into the benefits that internet use brings to young people, or whether these are different for boys and girls. Compared to some studies that make universalistic claims about gender, the mixed evidence provided by cross-cultural studies provides a more nuanced picture. Comparative, longitudinal studies studying the breadth and depth of young people's online opportunities will help us understand the complexities and diversity of experiences. Complementary to this quantitative research, we identify a real need for more qualitative research contributions that allow young people to speak in their own voices – reflecting diversity, choices and constraints.

References

Blumler, J.G., McLeod, J.M. and Rosengren, K.E. (1992) 'An introduction to comparative communication research', in J.G. Blumler, J.M. McLeod and K.E. Rosengren (eds) *Comparatively speaking: Communication and culture across space and time*, Newbury Park, CA: Sage Publications: 3-18.

Broos, A. and Roe, K. (2006) 'The digital divide in the playstation generation: self-efficacy, locus of control and ICT adoption among adolescents', *Poetics*, vol 34, nos 4-5: 306-17.

EC (European Commission) (2005) *Eurobarometer survey on safer internet*, Luxembourg: EC.

EC (2007) *Safer internet for children: Qualitative study in 29 European countries*, Luxembourg: EC (Directorate-General for Information Society and Media).

EC (2008) *Towards a safer use of the internet for children in the EU – A parents' perspective, Analytical report*, Flash Eurobarometer Series # 248, conducted by The Gallup Organisation, Hungary, Luxembourg: EC (http://ec.europa.eu/information_society/activities/sip/docs/eurobarometer/analyticalreport_2008.pdf).

Hargittai, E. and Shafer, S. (2006) 'Differences in actual and perceived online skills: the role of gender', *Social Science Quarterly*, vol 87, no 2: 432-48.

Hasebrink, U., Livingstone, S., Haddon, L. and Ólafsson, K. (2009) *Comparing children's online opportunities and risks across Europe: Cross-national comparisons for EU Kids Online* (2nd edn), London: London School of Economics and Political Science, EU Kids Online (Deliverable D3.2 for the EC Safer Internet Plus Programme).

JIM (2007) *JIM-Studie 2005. Jugend, Information (Multi-Media). Basisuntersuchung zum Medienumgang 12- bis 19-Jähriger*, Stuttgart: Medienpädagogischer Forschungsverbund Südwest.

Johnsson-Smaragdi, U. (2001) 'Media use styles among the young', in S. Livingstone and M. Bovill (eds) *Children and their changing media environment: A European comparative study*, Hillsdale, NJ: Lawrence Erlbaum Associates: 131-41.

Kalmus, P., Pruulmann-Vengerfeldt, P., Runnel, P. and Siibak, A. (in press) 'Online content creation practices of Estonian school children in comparative perspective', *Journal of Children and Media*.

Larsson, K. (2003) 'Children's on-line life – and what parents believe: a survey in five countries', in C. von Feilitzen and U. Carlsson (eds) *Promote or protect? Perspectives on media literacy and media regulations*, Gothenburg, Sweden: Nordicom: 113-20.

Lenhart, A. (2005) *Protecting teens online*, Washington, DC: Pew Internet and American Life Project (www.pewinternet.org/Reports/2005/Protecting-Teens-Online.aspx).

Livingstone, S. and Bovill, M. (eds) (2001) *Children and their changing media environment: A European comparative study*, Hillsdale, NJ: Lawrence Erlbaum Associates.

Livingstone, S. and Helsper, E.J. (2007) 'Gradations in digital inclusion: children, young people and the digital divide', *New Media & Society*, vol 9, no 4: 671-96.

Livingstone, L., Bober, M. and Helsper, J. (2005) 'Active participation or just more information? Young people's take-up of opportunities to act and interact on the internet', *Information, Communication & Society*, vol 8, no 3: 287-314.

Mediappro (2006) *The appropriation of new media by youth*, A European research project, Brussels: Chaptal Communication with the Support of the European Commission/Safer Internet Action Plan.

Metton, C. (2006) *Devenir grand. Le rôle des technologies de la communication dans la socialisation des collégiens*. Paris: EHESS.

Newhagen, J.E. and Rafaeli, S. (1996) 'Why communication researchers should study the internet: a dialogue', *Journal of Communication*, vol 46, no 1: 4-13.

Ofcom (2008) *Media literacy audit: Report on UK children's media literacy*, London: Ofcom.

Pasquier, D. (2005) *Cultures lycéennes. La tyrannie de la majorité*, Paris: Editions Autrement.

Pauwels, C. and Bauwens, J. (2008) *Teens and ICT: Risks and Opportunities (TIRO), Final report* (www.belspo.be/belspo/fedra/TA/synTA08_en.pdf).

SAFT (Safety, Awareness, Facts and Tools) Project (2006) *SAFT 2006 Parent and Children Survey. 2004-2006*, Norwegian Action Plan for Children, Youth and the Internet and the European Commission Safer Internet Action Plan, Norwegian Media Authority.

van Dijk, J. (2006) 'Digital divide research, achievements and shortcomings', *Poetics*, vol 34, nos 4-5: 221-35.

Wartella, E.A., O'Keefe, B. and Scantlin, R. (2000) *Children and interactive media: A compendium of current research and directions for the future*, New York, NY: Markle Foundation.

Weiser, E.B. (2000) 'Gender differences in internet use patterns and internet application preferences', *CyberPsychology and Behavior*, vol 3, no 2: 167-77.

NINE

Digital divides

*Panayiota Tsatsou, Pille Pruulmann-Vengerfeldt
and Maria Francesca Murru*

Digital divides: beyond access and usage

Since the mid-1990s there has been an increasing interest in the nature and extent of digital divides, and in academic circles the term itself has gradually given way to that of 'digital inclusion'. In the mid-1990s the 'digital divide' has been seen in terms of a dichotomy between the 'information haves' and the 'information have-nots' (Wresch, 1996), or, in economic terms, the 'information poor' and the 'information rich' (Webster, 1995). One of the first theorisations of digital divides was based on diffusion theory (Rogers, 1995). It argued that the acquisition of and access to computers and internet equipment is a fundamental criterion for overcoming gaps and inequalities. This understanding of digital divides has been criticised for presenting a limited conceptualisation of the phenomenon, as access to information and communication technologies (ICTs) cannot be considered sufficient for overcoming exclusion from new digital opportunities (Selwyn, 2003, 2004a, 2004b; Warschauser, 2003; Bradbrook and Fisher, 2004). Carpentier (2003) analyses the discourses of academics and politicians concerning digital divides, concluding that three main lines of criticism apply: (1) a limited focus on access instead of kinds of use; (2) an over-simplified dichotomy between 'haves' and 'have-nots'; and (3) a lack of clarity due to the application of the 'digital divide' concept to a wide variety of activities.

After 2000, scholars such as Norris (2001) presented a more complex picture of digital divides, discarding the dichotomy between haves and have-nots and at the same time taking into account the quality and efficiency of the use of digital technologies. The literature increasingly allowed more elaborated positions, suggesting a 'thicker description of the various shades of information and telecommunications inequalities' (Wilhelm, 2000: 69-70). Social, cultural and educational parameters influence the capability of the individual to make effective use of digital technologies through requisite skills, knowledge and support (van Dijk, 2006). Material resources and economic capacity, socialisation into the dominant culture, technical skills and awareness of the prevalent techno-culture, as well as social networks, are all forces shaping digital divides (Selwyn, 2004a). Policy strategies and regulatory practices also significantly influence the nature of digital divides in specific national and regional contexts (Tsatsou, 2008). Thus, digital divides are not an individual problem alone, as they result from contextual and social resources shaping the particular information environment (Pruulmann-Vengerfeldt, 2006). At the same time, we can no longer argue about an unbridgeable gap between 'users' and 'non-users', as relative and gradual differences derive from structural inequalities in the skills and usage of the new ICTs (Hacker and van Dijk, 2003). As a result, the term 'digital inclusion' has been used to discuss how ICTs and digital technologies have the potential to lead to new forms of social inclusion and exclusion depending on how they are taken advantage of in terms of quality, breadth, duration and efficiency of use (Livingstone, 2002; Selwyn, 2004a). This raises issues of levels and quality of use, as well as attitudes towards digital technologies, going beyond the number of people who have access to these technologies.

The next section discusses conceptualisations of childhood in terms of digital rights, empowerment and learning expectations, looking at mediating factors shaping the ways in which children engage with ICTs.

Children and digital divides: the 'digital generation', digital literacy and research today

Research on digital divides among children is relatively scarce and researchers have only recently addressed the multiple stratifications in children and young people's access to and use of the internet (Peter and Valkenburg, 2006; Livingstone and Helsper, 2007). These reveal that, counter to wishful expectations, the internet does not work as a naturally equalising and empowering force. At the same time, the focus has shifted towards specific internet uses and towards the promotion of digital literacy to enable and encourage beneficial uses and to discourage potentially harmful ones.

The lack of attention given to digital divides among children is partly linked to an optimism surrounding so-called 'digital generations'. Tapscott (1998) has emblematically argued the rhetoric that associates childhood with a cyberlibertarianist ideology. According to Tapscott, a generational gap exists between technophobic, inflexible and conservative adults and their intuitive, spontaneous and playful children who, thanks to intrinsically democratic network technologies, reveal themselves as more and more creative and autonomous. However, empirical evidence points to a highly differentiated usage pattern among children and young people, even where most have equal access to the internet. It is precisely at the levels of skills and usage that digital differentiations occur beyond internet access, revealing the recursive and stratified nature of the digital divide phenomenon.

Several studies have highlighted the correlation between the kind of use and opportunities taken up on the internet by children and their unequal access to socio-economic, cognitive and cultural resources (Peter and Valkenburg, 2006; Livingstone and Helsper, 2007). Whether differences are codified in terms of the prevalence of entertainment versus information and social usage (Peter and Valkenburg, 2006), or in terms of a continuum from basic users to the interactive and creative 'all rounders' (Livingstone and Helsper, 2007: 684), research clearly reveals the direct and indirect role of socio-economic background, along with other mediating factors such as gender, age, usage experiences and skills. Livingstone and Helsper's idea of a staged process of going online (2007: 683) takes into account the mediating factors shaping children's engagement with ICTs and it distinguishes between the various forms of access and usage according to the variety of capitals that children have at their disposal. The latter significantly influence the ability, willingness and effectiveness of children in using ICTs and the internet in particular, while disparities in the distribution of cultural, social, economic and technological capital entail respective forms of divides.

In order to capture the irregular degrees of inclusion/exclusion in the information society, research in recent years has attempted to reframe the notion of ICT access through the concept of media literacy. According to Warschauser (2002), the effective appropriation of the media is fully realised only through the engagement in 'meaningful social practices', whether in terms of interpersonal communication, access to institutional information or processing that information through innovative social discourses. In this broader sense then, the cultural and symbolic integration of ICTs becomes a process very similar to that of 'literacy', which is described as 'mastery over the processes by means of which culturally significant information is coded' (Warschauser, 2002: 6).

The concept of media literacy has been characterised by heterogeneous and sometimes controversial meanings, becoming trickier when applied to the competencies and skills activated in internet use (Livingstone, 2004). Internet use should be regarded as an enriched and 'thick' platform of multimedia practices, displaying a vast array of opportunities in the political domain, in the highly competitive knowledge economy and in the field of cultural expression and personal fulfilment (Livingstone, 2004). Consequently, the research agenda on digital divides among children integrates the technological dimension of ICT access within the complex frame of educational and cultural policies. According to Buckingham (2000), media literacy should not be an educational strategy that aims to protect children from media influence or to convey the same critical perspective of adults. On the contrary, the purpose should be to enable their rights to social participation, giving them the necessary tools to contribute as free citizens to the 'means and substance of cultural expression' (Buckingham, 2000: 206). As a result, rather than framing all the hopes of social changes in an essentialist and sentimentalist conceptualisation of digital childhoods, this approach envisages children's experience with ICTs as a 'right' that should be protected and actualised.

How much digital divides matter for children in Europe: empirical evidence and implications

This section presents the findings of the Eurobarometer 2008 survey (EC, 2008) and a rich cross-cultural analysis of European data conducted by the EU Kids Online network (Hasebrink et al, 2009). First we look at geographical aspects, referring to divides within and between countries in Europe. Then we consider how restrictions on access, lack of interest and less effective use underline the necessity of examining the role of socio-economic inequalities. Third, we take into consideration the suggestion that there is a generation gap in technology use and we look at children's versus parents' internet adoption in Europe. Other parameters, such as gender, are framed in terms of inequalities in other chapters of this volume (see in particular Chapter Eight, this volume).

Geography of divides in Europe: beyond the North–South divide?

The EU Kids Online researchers have argued that cross-national data concerning children's access to the internet provides an incomplete and fragmented picture of the extent to which access inequalities are still significant in Europe (Hasebrink et al, 2009). On the other hand, the Eurobarometer 2008 survey (EC, 2008) highlights significant variations between countries (see Figure 9.1). As the comparative EU Kids Online report concluded (Hasebrink et al, 2009), although internet access has increased across Europe, differences are still significant between as well as within countries.

As regards internet usage, national data and the Eurobarometer 2008 survey essentially provide a typology of countries in Europe with high, medium and low usage:

- Group 1: countries with high internet usage, namely countries where more than 85% of children use the internet – Denmark, Estonia, Finland, the Netherlands, Sweden, the UK, Poland, Slovenia and Norway.
- Group 2: countries with medium internet usage, namely countries where between 65% and 85% of children use the internet – Austria, Belgium, Bulgaria, Czech Republic, France, Germany, Ireland, Iceland, Portugal and Spain.
- Group 3: countries with low internet usage, namely counties where less than 65% of children use the internet – Italy, Cyprus and Greece.

Figure 9.1: Children's internet usage in Europe, by country

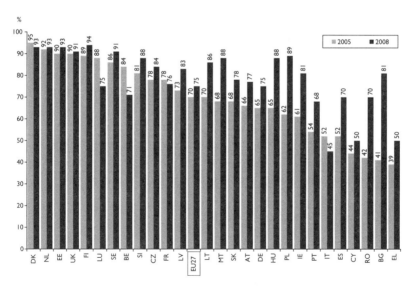

Base: All children aged 6-17, as reported by their parent/carer

Source: EC (2006, 2008)

In the EU25, 68% of children (6 to 17 years old) used the internet in 2005/06 and three quarters (75%) in the EU27 were users in 2008. The number of children using the internet varies significantly across Europe. According to the three groups of countries identified, all countries except for Italy, Greece and Cyprus had more than 65% internet use in 2008, while an exceptionally rapid increase in internet use has occurred in East European and Balkan countries (for example Bulgaria). In countries where internet penetration had been high among children since early in the decade, such as France, Luxembourg and Belgium, internet penetration had changed less significantly by 2008.

The gaps in internet use in Europe have decreased, but they still exist, with Southern European countries lagging behind countries in Western and Central Europe. Although Figure 9.1 shows change since 2005/06, the Eurobarometer 2008 survey confirms the conclusion of the EU Kids Online comparative study of earlier research that digital divides remain in Europe (Hasebrink et al, 2009).

Last, as far as qualitative aspects of digital divides are concerned, the EU Kids Online country comparison proposes a classification of internet opportunities for children that resembles the earlier-described staged concept of internet use from basic to participatory (Livingstone and Helsper, 2007). These opportunities present the child as recipient, participant or an actor and differentiate the online providers' motives in terms of education, participation, creativity and identity construction and maintenance (Hasebrink et al, 2009). The comparison of national and cross-national research leads to the conclusion that children in most European countries use the internet for entertainment and educational purposes, while social networking and communication is a key online activity for about half of the countries in Europe (Hasebrink et al, 2009). To a lesser extent, children use the internet for searching global information, although there is insufficient research regarding online opportunities for children in specific geographic areas and with regard to specific types of online opportunity (Hasebrink et al, 2009).

Digital and socio-economic divides

A large part of the digital divide research has been devoted to the tracking of digital inequalities according to pre-existing social stratifications, marked by socio-demographic variables such as income, age, gender, education and ethnicity. In almost all cases, these studies have confirmed the diffusionist assumptions about adopters' ideal types (Rogers, 1995). This shows that in the majority of countries studied, individuals who first access ICTs also have higher incomes, occupational status and levels of education. Although these studies have clearly demonstrated that a link exists between social inclusion and digital engagement, there remains a debate about the extent, the permanence and the causality of this correlation. If we look at the latest empirical data available in Europe and collected by EU Kids Online, we find that in almost all countries a large volume of evidence supports the existence of a correlation between households' socio-economic status (SES) and children's access to the internet. That connection is corroborated by the last two Eurobarometer surveys (EC, 2006, 2008). More specifically, data on parents' occupation (Figure 9.2) show that children living in higher-status families are more likely to use the internet.

Figure 9.2: Parents' social status and children's internet use (%)

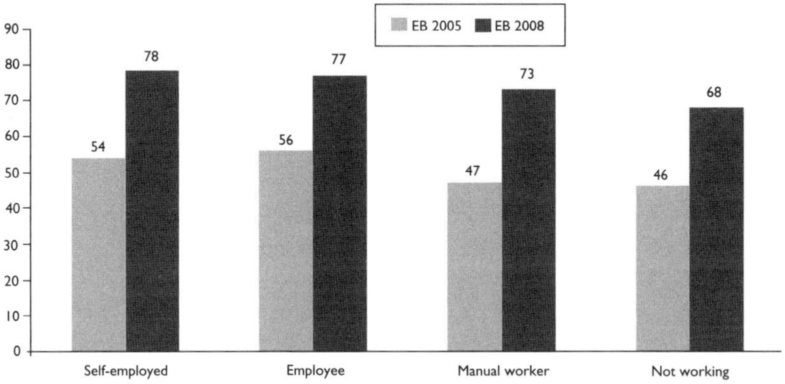

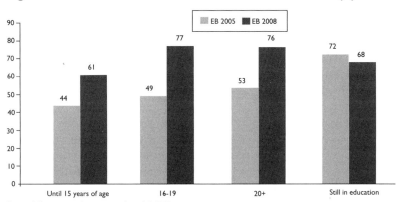

Base: All respondents; total n=12,803

Similarly, data on parents' education (Figure 9.3) show that children having better-educated parents are more likely to use the internet.

Figure 9.3: Parents' education and children's internet use (%)

Base: All respondents; total n=12,803

The general argument about the role of socio-economic indicators starts to fade as we move the focus towards specific aspects of internet usage. Surveys in France (Pasquier, 2005) and the UK (Livingstone and Helsper, 2007) show that SES differences in amount of use disappear if children with equal home access are compared. Similar results are found in Sweden and Estonia (MMM Project, 2005). In contrast, research conducted in Iceland and Norway reports that children having parents with higher education and/or of higher class use the computer more often than other children (Hasebrink et al, 2009).

At the same time, one must keep in mind the fact that while the different socio-economic background of parents may no longer influence the amount of time and frequency of children's internet usage, they may strongly influence the activities of children when actually surfing the net. With regard to the number and types of online opportunities taken up, although evidence is lacking in several countries, available data show a correspondence between particular internet uses and the SES of a child's family that merit further exploration. Especially in Spain, France, the Netherlands, the UK and Sweden, the majority of studies support the hypothesis that while children from working-class families use the internet for leisure, downloading content and entertainment, children from middle-class families also tend to use it for education, information and civic participation purposes (Hasebrink et al, 2009).

Adult–child digital divide

As mentioned earlier, young people who have grown up with the everyday presence of ICTs are often labelled as belonging to a 'digital generation'. However, any optimism about this generation, with expectations of a forthcoming paradigmatic shift in terms of its changing perspectives, attitudes and practices towards new technologies, needs to be viewed critically. For instance, Herring (2008) stresses that differences are increasingly less in terms of whether the younger or older generation members are digitally connected, and more in terms of what do they do online. From that perspective any generation gap looks quite different. The Eurobarometer 2008 survey (EC, 2008) enables a basic comparison of the proportions of parents and children who are connected. Of all parents in the survey, 16% have never used the internet – parents appear significantly more likely to use the internet than non-parents, as 44% of all 16 to 74 year olds in the EU27 classed themselves as non-users (Eurostat, 2008). Of all the children aged 6-17, 24% are not using the internet, according to their parents. Figure 9.4

shows that across Europe children of parents who are more frequent internet users tend to be more frequent users themselves. However, it should be noted that more than half of the children whose parents do not use the internet nonetheless use it themselves. This indicates that although parental experience in internet use may support children using the technology, additional socialising factors such as schools, peer groups and public opinion can be sufficient to enable and encourage children's internet use. Nevertheless, parents' attitudes may well strongly influence children's use, especially those who are younger, as parents have the strongest influence on how pre-teens spend their resources (time, money and so on).

Figure 9.4: Parent–child internet use in Europe (%)

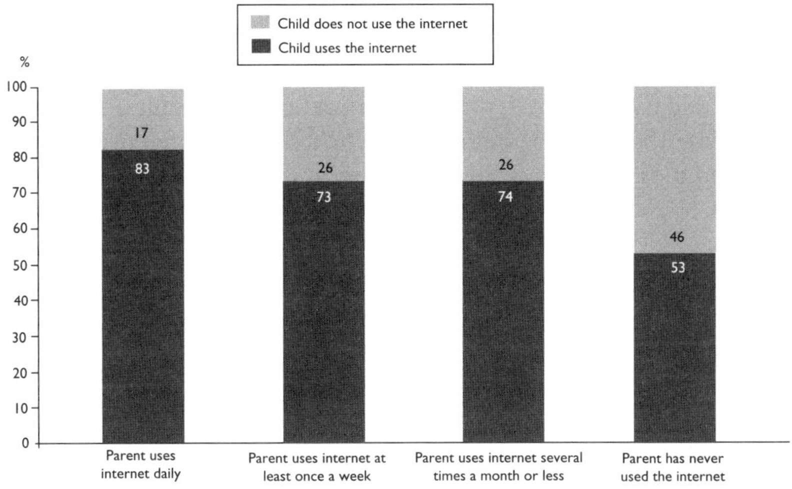

Base: All respondents; total n=12,803

Figure 9.5 also presents an interesting picture of generational differences. The age when the average European internet use among children reaches the same level as their parents is around 12. From age 16 onwards more children use the internet than their parents.

There are clear generational tendencies supporting the idea that general use of the new technologies among children matches or surpasses their parents' from the age of 12 onwards. At the same time, the limits of these data do not allow us to speculate about the richness and variety of such uses when comparing children and parents. Looking only at Estonia as a case study (Pruulmann-Vengerfeldt et al, 2008; Runnel et al, 2009), we can see that there are clear differences

Figure 9.5: Does the child/parent use the internet? (%)

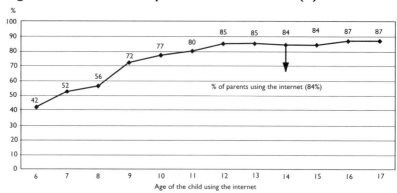

Base: All respondents; total n=12,803

between uses. One could argue that children's use – although richer in communicational and entertainment-related aspects – is still much poorer and narrower than that of the more advanced adult uses. At the same time, there are obviously adults who are very limited in their use, focusing mostly on single services – most children have more variety in their internet uses and also greater skills than these adults.

Conclusion

On the one hand, it is not easy to assess how much and what kinds of continuing divides really matter and for whom. This chapter has used the EU Kids Online data collection and Eurobarometer 2008 (EC, 2008) as the key empirical reference points, but neither source provides sufficient data to examine the issues in as much detail as the authors would like. The empirical evidence collected by EU Kids Online is rather fragmented and the contradictory nature of many findings makes comparative analysis a difficult task. The scope of generalisations is often limited by the fact that parameters used for measuring various indicators (for example SES, type of internet use and opportunities for children) vary between countries.

On the other hand, this chapter has reached some conclusions about the extent and nature of digital divides among children in Europe today. Although gaps in internet access and use have decreased in Europe, they still exist. Differences are significant between countries as well as within countries in Europe, with Southern Europe in particular lagging behind. Socio-economic factors still influence the degree of internet access for children and young people in Europe. Although this influence starts to fade as we move the focus towards specific aspects of internet usage, such as frequency and amount of use, evidence in some countries supports a correlation between socio-economic indicators and the online opportunities taken up by children. Finally, as regards 'digital generation' and 'generational gaps', empirical research in Europe has shown that although a lack of parental internet experience may inhibit children from using internet technologies, additional socialising factors such as schools, peer groups and public opinion can be enough to enable a child to take up internet use.

The contribution of this chapter lies in the provision of up-to-date data about the current picture of digital divides among children in Europe today, linking this to what research and literature in the field have reported. Nevertheless, more in-depth comparative analysis of the available empirical evidence has to be pursued, so that a more insightful picture of digital divides among children in Europe can be provided.

References

Bradbrook, G. and Fisher, J. (2004) 'Digital equality: reviewing digital inclusion activity and mapping the way forwards' (www.citizensonline.org.uk/site/media/documents/939_DigitalEquality1.pdf).

Buckingham, D. (2000) *After the death of childhood. Growing up in the age of electronic media*, Cambridge: Polity.

Carpentier, N. (2003) 'Access and participation in the discourse of the digital divide: the European perspective at/on the WSIS', in J. Servaes (ed) *The European Information Society: A reality check*, Bristol: Intellect: 99-120.

EC (European Commission) (2006) *Safer internet*, Special Eurobarometer 250/Wave 64.4 – Safe internet for children, Luxembourg: EC.

EC (European Commission) (2008) *Towards a safer use of the internet for children in the EU – A parents' perspective, Analytical report*, Flash Eurobarometer Series # 248, conducted by The Gallup Organisation, Hungary, Luxembourg: EC (http://ec.europa.eu/information_society/activities/sip/docs/eurobarometer/analyticalreport_2008.pdf).

Eurostat (2008) *Individuals regularly using the internet, by gender and type of connection* (http://epp.eurostat.ec.europa.eu/portal/page/portal/product_details/dataset?p_product_code=TIN00061).

Hacker, K. and van Dijk, J. (2003) 'The digital divide as a complex and dynamic phenomenon', *The Information Society*, vol 19, no 4: 315-26.

Hasebrink, U., Livingstone, S., Haddon, L. and Ólafsson, K. (2009) *Comparing children's online opportunities and risks across Europe: Cross-national comparisons for EU Kids Online* (2nd edn), London: London School of Economics and Political Science, EU Kids Online (Deliverable D3.2 for the EC Safer Internet Plus Programme).

Herring, S. (2008) 'Questioning the generational divide: technological exoticism and adult construction of online youth identity', in D. Buckingham (ed) *Youth, identity, and digital media*, Cambridge, MA: MIT Press: 71-94.

Livingstone, S. (2002) *Young people and new media*, London: Sage Publications.

Livingstone, S. (2004) 'Media literacy and the challenge of new information and communication technologies', *Communication Review*, vol 1, no 7: 3-14.

Livingstone, S. and Helsper, E.J. (2007) 'Gradations in digital inclusion: children, young people and the digital divide', *New Media & Society*, vol 9, no 4: 671-96.

MMM Project (2005) *Mina. Maailm. Meedia (Me. The world. The media)*, Tartu, Estonia: University of Tartu.

Norris, P. (2001) *Digital divide: Civic engagement, information poverty, and the internet worldwide*, Cambridge: Cambridge University Press.

Pasquier, D. (2005) *Cultures lycéennes. La tyrannie de la majorité*, Paris: Editions Autrement.

Peter, J. and Valkenburg, P.M. (2006) 'Adolescents' internet use: testing the "disappearing digital divide" versus the "emerging digital differentiation" approach', *Poetics*, vol 34, nos 4/5: 293-305.

Pruulmann-Vengerfeldt, P. (2006) *Information technology users and uses within the different layers of the information environment in Estonia*, University of Tartu, Estonia: Tartu University Press.

Pruulmann-Vengerfeldt, P., Kalmus, V. and Runnel, P. (2008) 'Creating content or creating hype: practices of online content creation and consumption in Estonia', *Cyberpsychology: Journal of Psychosocial Research on Cyberspace*, vol 2, no 1, online.

Runnel, P., Pruulmann-Vengerfeldt, P. and Reinsalu, K. (2009) 'The Estonian tiger leap from post-communism to the information society: from policy to practices', *Journal of Baltic Studies*, vol 40, no 1: 29-51.

Rogers, E.M. (1995) *Diffusion of innovations* (vol 4), New York, NY: Free Press.

Selwyn, N. (2003) 'Apart from technology: understanding people's non-use of information and communication technologies in everyday life', *Technology in Society*, vol 25, no 1: 99-116.

Selwyn, N. (2004a) 'Reconsidering political and popular understandings of the digital divide', *New Media & Society*, vol 6, no 3: 341-62.

Selwyn, N. (2004b) 'Technology and social inclusion', *British Journal of Educational Technology*, vol 35, no 1: 127-27.

Tapscott, D. (1998) *Growing up digital: The rise of the net generation*, New York, NY: McGraw-Hill.

Tsatsou, P. (2008) 'Digital divides and the role of policy and regulation: a qualitative study', in C. Avgerou, M.L. Smith and P.v.d. Besselaar (eds) *Social dimensions of information and communication technology policy*, New York: Springer Publishers: 141-60.

van Dijk, J. (2006) 'Digital divide research, achievements and shortcomings', *Poetics*, vol 34, nos 4-5: 221-35.

Webster, F. (1995) *Theories of the information society*, London: Routledge.

Warschauser, M. (2002) 'Reconceptualizing the digital divide', *First Monday*, vol 7, no 7 (http://firstmonday.org/htbin/cgiwrap/bin/ojs/index.php/fm/article/viewArticle/967/888).

Warschauser, M. (2003) *Technology and social inclusion: Rethinking the digital divide*, Cambridge; MA: The MIT Press.

Wilhelm, A. (2000) *Democracy in the digital age: Challenges to political life in cyberspace*, New York, NY and London: Routledge.

Wresch, W. (1996) *Disconnected: Haves and have-nots in the information age*, Brunswick; NJ: Rutgers University Press.

Section III
Going online: new risks?

TEN

Risky contacts

Marika Hanne Lüders, Petter Bae Brandtzæg and Elza Dunkels

Introduction

One of the anxieties regarding children's internet use relates to the potential for risky contacts (see, for example, EC, 2008). This chapter critically reviews the latest findings and theories on children's risky contacts with adults and children – grooming, harassment and meetings – in order to identify who is really at risk from what. Two primary types of risks will be discussed: children and young people as victims of aggressive communication and as victims of sexually oriented communication. This discussion will expand our current understanding of both media and social psychological dimensions of the misuse and abuse of the internet, which in turn can enable industry, policy makers and future generations to approach and develop an online environment that poses fewer dangers.

The specific characteristics of online communication that appear to lower thresholds to find, contact and interact with others have led to perceptions that dangerous encounters are likely. Media panics similarly emphasise the dangers represented by adults with intentions of deceiving children and young people online (Weathers, 2008). Whereas this is indeed a risk, with potentially grave and tragic outcomes, research shows that children and young people are quick to emphasise that they are aware of ill-intended adults online, and that they take action to prevent such contact (Dunkels, 2008). However, research concerning what counter-strategies are actually helpful is conspicuous by its absence. Children may be regarded as native users of contemporary technology, but there is little research on the effectiveness of their often self-taught strategies to avoid online victimisation. Young people who are at risk of meeting adults typically already face serious problems offline (Shannon, 2007), and often they are not being deceived (Ybarra et al, 2007). The most likely scenario is that a sexual predator takes advantage of the fact that a child discloses vulnerability online. The predator offers to be an understanding and supporting adult and starts building a manipulative relationship with the child. When this process, called *grooming*, is completed, the potential victim often readily travels to meet the predator, even if aware of the adult's sexual intentions.

Concept of risk

It is important to consider the conditions for, and the concept of, risk. Risk is both an objective reality and a social construct, which means that the notion of risk may vary between cultures and between countries. To some extent there exist globally accepted risks – such as sexual victimisation, physical and psychological abuse. However, there are other incidents that may be regarded as risks by some and not by others – for example discussing personal matters with strangers. Risky behaviour is like other forms of social behaviour, regulated by socially accepted and situational relevant norms. Moreover, there is a difference between risk as a probability of harm and harm itself. Risky behaviour does not necessarily lead to actual harm. The challenge is thus to identify the kind of risky behaviour that moves beyond 'normal' risk taking, while at the same time acknowledging that what is considered normal is not a constant measure across cultures and countries. What nevertheless appears to be universal is how users adapt and often liberalise their self-performances in online social spaces. Hence, in looking for the causes of risks and in order to prevent risky encounters, we should concentrate on the conditions of mediated communication that might facilitate risky behaviour, both from the perspective of harm doer and victim.

In European countries, young people are typically warned about the dangers of giving away personal information (such as name, photographs and contact information), and the importance of anonymity as a safeguard to avoid risky contacts. This is, for example, the primary message from Insafe, the network of national nodes that coordinates internet safety awareness in Europe (Insafe, 2005). Many European countries publish similar advice to children and parents on the national Insafe websites. The UK, Slovenia, Norway, Germany and Denmark are among those that use wordings like 'never give out personal information' (Safe.si, 2009). Other countries such as Finland, Cyprus, Sweden and Ireland focus on caution rather than prohibition: 'avoid giving out personal information' (Cyberethics, 2008). Many of these tips for safe internet use have been reproduced, in some cases with minor changes, from those formulated in the late 1990s, even though young people's internet use has gone through major changes since that time. One significant change is the explosion in the use of social media such as photograph and video-sharing sites and social networking sites. The problem seen from the point of view of young people themselves is that the risks of revealing personal information online are perceived as unlikely to become reality, whereas the social and personal advantages of having a disclosed online presence are validated every day (Lüders, 2009: in press). It is quite likely that years of internet safety advice have made a positive difference in young people's online behaviour. However, it is evident that children compare safety advice with personal experience (Dunkels, 2007), and there is reason to believe that they may be pushing the boundaries for online conduct as they become more experienced.

A question is, consequently, to what degree disclosure of identity traits is associated with risky encounters. This chapter reviews theories as well as recent European studies regarding risky contacts in order to assess constructive safety guidelines for young people. Of particular importance is the dimension of an anonymous versus a disclosed online presence, due to an increasingly information-rich, visible and participatory media environment.

Evidence of risks

Low, mid and high-risk countries in Europe

The EU Kids Online project has, based on an extensive review of studies conducted in 21 European countries between 2000 and 2008, identified indications of risky encounters (Hasebrink et al, 2009). Low-, mid- and high-risk countries emerged based on the percentage of children who claimed to have (a) received unwanted sexual comments online; (b) met online contacts offline; and/or (c) been bullied, harassed or stalked online. The results cannot be reliably compared, as they derive from different surveys in different languages, conducted at different times, but they nevertheless give some indication of the extent of risky encounters among young Europeans. One of the low-risk countries in Europe is Ireland, where all three above parameters are low. This is in stark contrast to the high-risk country Poland, where more than half of children and young people claim to have received unwanted sexual comments and to have been bullied, harassed and stalked online (Hasebrink, et al, 2009). However, it is difficult to assess a pattern between widespread internet usage and risky behaviour. For example, the internet and broadband diffusion is considerably lower in high-risk Poland compared to the low and mid-risk countries of Norway, the UK and Sweden (Hasebrink et al, 2009).

Interpreting these statistics is difficult, as they cover more than risky contacts. Sexually oriented conversations include dating, flirting and sexual (voluntary) experimentation between peers, hence not only contact between adults and children. Nor is meeting online contacts offline necessarily risky. Young people often get in touch online based on shared interests and values, learn to know each other online and eventually arrange an offline meeting (Lüders, 2009). The percentage of young people who have met online contacts offline says close to nothing about the actual risks involved. In a Swedish survey (Medierådet, 2006), 9% of the respondents had met an online contact offline. However, none of these respondents experienced the meeting as unpleasant; rather the most common response was that the meeting had been fun. A challenge for future research is hence to examine under what circumstances meeting online contacts is associated with risks.

Additional challenges with assessing risks

Whereas the EU Kids Online review gives some indication about the extent of risky encounters among young Europeans, research is still scarce in a European context. Recent US studies also highlight the lack of research with regard to online harassment and sexual solicitation (for example Kowalski and Limber, 2007; Hinduja and Patchin, 2008; Ybarra and Mitchell, 2008). According to Kowalski and Limber (2007), only a handful of studies focus on this problem and the scant research is inconclusive (2007: 23). Ybarra and Mitchell (2008) found that 15% of the 10 to 15 year olds surveyed reported unwanted sexual solicitation online, and 4% reported such incidents while using online social networking sites specifically.

It is also important to consider the relation between online and offline situations. Are more people harassed online than offline, and how is the harassment experienced? The question of online and offline is also relevant for sexually oriented communication: how do children and young people cope when experiencing unwanted sexual suggestions? Research findings suggest that the majority of young people disregard the attempts, rejecting further online contact (Hasebrink et al, 2009). Young people who are vulnerable to online risks typically engage in a pattern of different kinds of online risky behaviour, such as knowingly chatting with unknown others, visiting sex sites and talking about sex online with others (Ybarra et al, 2007). Yet these children are typically also experiencing problems in offline contexts (sexual abuse, parental conflict and offline interpersonal victimisation) (Ybarra et al, 2007). These children are at risk even if they initially present themselves anonymously online. Whereas the offline contexts of young people are hence crucial to identify those who are at risk, few studies pay attention to the children's lives offline (Livingstone and Haddon, 2008: 320).

A final problem with assessing evidence of risks is the considerable methodological challenges relating to attempts to measure the level and magnitude of risks among young people. Both harassment and bullying are defined in many ways. Quantitative surveys often lack the standardised measurements that could distinguish milder forms of harassment from bullying, or problematic sexual abuse incidents from sexually rude comments or hostility. Identifying who the victims are, older versus younger, is also difficult because of the environment of anonymity online. Qualitative as well as quantitative studies also face huge ethical obstacles in approaching children with these kinds of issues, and might easily either oversimplify issues or make the situation even worse by suggesting wrong interpretations.

Anonymous or accountable?

Whereas anonymity is stressed in the current safety guidelines for children and young people, the relationship between anonymity and undesired behaviour and contact is not clear-cut. For example, when the commercial web was still young, anonymity rather than disclosure was often regarded as problematic. Anonymous beings were regarded as more likely to behave irresponsibly online. Moreover, the development towards richer social media (with photographs and videos becoming prevalent) seems to make anonymous self-presentations less likely. More recently, researchers have also shifted their attention to self-presentations in less anonymous online environments (Zhao et al, 2008).

Anonymous and deindividuated behaviour

The impact on risks caused by anonymity versus non-anonymity online should be seen both in relation to media richness theory and the theory of deindividuation. According to media richness theory, media differ in the amount of information they can transmit. The features of a medium and the quality of communication the medium affords rank different media from richest to leanest according to their capability to provide immediate feedback, to transmit verbal and non-verbal communication cues and to provide a sense of personalisation and visibility (Daft and Lengel, 1986). This is also in accordance with social presence theory, which hypothesises that communication media vary in their degree of social presence, and that these variations are important in determining the content of the communication (Kaare et al, 2007). Media that provide a greater level of visual anonymity have been found to be related to a reduced fear of criticism and increased risk taking (Christopherson, 2006). Consequently, different media platforms in terms of information richness may cause various outcomes related to risks online, often explained by increased levels of deindividuation. Deindividuation refers to a special individual state in which there is less concern about normative standards, self-presentation and the later consequences of one's behaviours (Zimbardo, 1969). Face-to-face is regarded as the richest communication form, where people feel more accountable for their actions because of their lack of anonymity. Similarly, Douglas and McGarty (2001) studied how people communicated anonymously via the internet. They found that people who felt their identities were concealed showed a greater tendency to exchange 'flaming behaviour', which includes sending hostile and threatening messages to others online.

Consequently, with references to deindividuation theory, claims have been made that online behaviour becomes socially deregulated under conditions of anonymity and group immersion, as a result of reduced self-awareness (see Spears et al, 2002). This would suggest that common safety guidelines for young people online are flawed, and that anonymity rather than disclosure of information is the real problem, since usual inhibitions will be lowered, thus arguably increasing the likelihood of impulsive behaviour such as harassment, flaming and sexual disclosure.

The deindividuation claims have later been countered by a number of studies proposing a social identity model of deindividuation effects, arguing that there is no strong evidence for counter-normative behaviour under conditions of anonymity, and stronger evidence of conformity to group norms (Spears et al, 2002; Tanis and Postmes, 2005, 2007). But research findings are varied, several of which continue to support a correlation between anonymity and socially undesired behaviour. A survey by Chiou (2006) with 1,347 participants ranging from 16 to 23 years old, found that participants, especially young men, were much more likely to engage in sharing and responding to sexual topics over the internet when they knew their identities were concealed. Furthermore, this study found that the greater the anonymity people perceived, the greater the intent for sexual disclosure. Anonymity was hence found to lead to less inhibited, and often socially unacceptable, behaviours (Chiou, 2006). Similarly, Brandtzæg et al (submitted) found that girls aged 14-16 years were particularly likely to indulge in risky and uninhibited behaviour on social networking sites when the users were acting anonymously. One explanation is that young people online communicate unrestrainedly when they are anonymous, because they feel safer. At the same time this can cause frustration and low trust between users, because they are uncertain if the other user is being truthful concerning their identity.

One concern is that unrestricted communication and presentation (due to anonymity) might more easily facilitate contact with paedophiles and others (Ybarra and Mitchell, 2008). The experiences from the participants in Brandtzæg et al's study indicate exceptionally uninhibited behaviour online, where some young people get in touch with (what are perceived to be) sex-oriented older men, not because they have revealed their own personal information, but because of the anonymity provided by the environment. This parallels social psychological research in the last few decades that has identified anonymity and the lack of self-awareness as two of the most important conditions that may lead to the state of deindividuation. Finally, whereas social ties may be initiated anonymously, anonymity does not prevent risky encounters between children and ill-intended adults. Mediated communication takes place in interplay and in incremental steps: from initial and often anonymous encounters in online chats or social networking sites, to mobile phones and face-to-face contacts.

Recognisable and hence less risky behaviour?

We appear to have reached a conclusion where anonymity, that is, withholding references to one's offline self, is not likely to decrease harassment and unwanted sexually oriented communication. We also see that for social reasons anonymity is becoming a less attractive strategy for young Europeans. Rather, in many online environments young people take on a recognisable profile, posting personal information such as their first name, hometown and portrait photographs. This is also related to how the participatory web has become much more multimodal or rich in the last few years. In media-rich online environments, the main challenge for young people is to learn how to navigate and play safely in complex networked public venues. When this challenge is reflected in policy aims to augment young people's network competence and awareness, such aims must evolve beyond the crude advice of 'avoid giving out personal information'. As online performances are fundamentally integrated into offline lives, and with many connections between practices in various modes of socialising, being completely anonymous online is often not an alternative. The fundamental purpose is sharing experiences and feelings with real friends. Having a recognisable presence is therefore necessary.

However, even if complete anonymity is not regarded as desirable by young people, a number of alternative strategies for accountable online action are available and pursued. According to a US study, 66% of teenagers with online profiles restrict public access to their profiles (Lenhart and Madden, 2007). Of those with profiles visible to anyone online, only a small minority post their first and last name. Young people with restricted access to their profiles generally also allow themselves to post more personal information (Lenhart and Madden, 2007). They consequently choose to restrict access rather than to be anonymous (for example on Facebook). In secluded networked spaces, young people may also become more open with regard to everyday life and personal emotions (Lüders, 2007). Such tendencies reflect actions in offline worlds where people enact roles according to contexts. The difference is that online environments are more difficult to handle, and, as Livingstone (2008) has shown, young people may find it hard to manage the privacy settings of popular social networking sites such as Facebook. Moreover, the effectiveness of a restricted access safety strategy is uncertain, and it is possible that this strategy provides users with an exaggerated sense of safety.

Conclusion

European and US studies provide some indication of the levels of risk that children and young people take online. There seem to be significant differences between countries, although the reasons for these differences cannot easily be explained. Generally, very few children and young people are deceived into meeting ill-intended adults offline, and young people take precautions to prevent such encounters. Aggressive communication among peers is common, and it is difficult to take precautions to prevent being harassed, stalked or bullied online. Contrary to public internet safety advice, however, anonymity appears to be unsuccessful in preventing sexual communication, and it appears to increase the likelihood of young people harassing peers.

Recommendations for policy and the ICT industry

Four safety recommendations for policy making and the ICT industry are derived from the discussions presented in this chapter.

First, insisting that young people remain anonymous online is not a universally useful strategy. Guidelines should hence be more nuanced, taking into account the social media environment of young people. Anonymity may in fact cause harm in terms of increased sexual solicitation or increased levels of harassment. Harm doers act more aggressively when anonymous, while potential victims act in a more uninhibited fashion because of loss of self-awareness. Anonymity is hence no guarantee of online safety among young people. Moreover, online anonymity is likely to be connected to a deindividuation effect, lowering the threshold for harassment and bullying.

Second, the safety provided by privacy preferences in common social media services (from email to social networking sites) should be carefully evaluated. Industry must take into account privacy and identity when designing for social interaction, and facilitate easy access to and control of privacy preferences. Moreover, information about privacy must be available in a vernacular form, and children and youth must be able to assess for whom their personal content is available when they choose to restrict access to friends only. Enabling safe interaction between young people online, while at the same time acknowledging that they might prefer to be recognisable, might require systems for name and age verification. The ICT industry must therefore create better tools for handling privacy and online environments that allow users to ensure privacy easily.

Third, internet safety concerns the norms that children and young people meet in how they should approach and use online services. The messages provided by policy makers and the internet industry should be consistent when discussing net-etiquette and the norms related to desired behaviour. Openness concerning the user's identity as applied in Facebook may be a good approach to making children more self-aware online, increasing the likelihood of accountable behaviour and thus increasing the threshold for aggressive communication among peers. Social life online should be characterised by the same social norms as offline.

Fourth, special attention should be directed to particularly vulnerable children and young people. Ybarra and Mitchell (2008) conclude that instead of focusing on particular technologies, security measures should be directed towards children's behaviour against each other and children's general well-being, taking into account their psycho-social status. The challenge is therefore to identify the children most in need of positive networks, and social and psychological support. These children are the most vulnerable to online solicitation and victimisation, and if we can identify them, society's resources can be distributed to benefit them the most.

References

Brandtzæg, P.B., Staksrud, E., Hagen, I. and Wold, T. (submitted) 'Children's experiences of cyberbullying in different technological platforms', *Journal of Children and Media*.

Chiou, W.B. (2006) 'Adolescents' sexual self-disclosure on the internet: deindividuation and self-impression', *Adolescence*, vol 41, no 163: 547-61.

Christopherson, K. (2007) 'The positive and negative implications of anonymity in internet social interactions', *Computers in Human Behavior*, vol 23, no 6: 3038-56.

Cyberethics (2008) 'Tips for teenagers' (www.cyberethics.info/cyethics2/page.php?pageID=32).

Daft, R.L. and Lengel, R.H. (1986) 'Organizational information requirements, media richness and structural design', *Management Science*, vol 32, no 5: 554-71.

Douglas, K.M. and McGarty, C. (2001) 'Identifiability and self-presentation', *British Journal of Social Psychology*, vol 40, no 3: 399-416.

Dunkels, E. (2007) 'Bridging the distance: children's strategies on the internet', PhD thesis, Umeå, Sweden: Umeå University.

Dunkels, E. (2008) 'Children's strategies on the internet', *Critical Studies in Education*, vol 49, no 2: 171-84.

EC (European Commission) (2008) *Towards a safer use of the internet for children in the EU – A parents' perspective, Analytical report*, Flash Eurobarometer Series # 248, conducted by The Gallup Organisation, Hungary, Luxembourg: EC (http://ec.europa.eu/information_society/activities/sip/docs/eurobarometer/analyticalreport_2008.pdf).

Hasebrink, U., Livingstone, S., Haddon, L. and Ólafsson, K. (2009) *Comparing children's online opportunities and risks across Europe: Cross-national comparisons for EU Kids Online* (2nd edn), London: London School of Economics and Political Science, EU Kids Online (Deliverable D3.2 for the EC Safer Internet Plus Programme).

Hinduja, S. and Patchin, J. (2008) 'Personal information of adolescents on the internet: a quantitative content analysis of MySpace', *Journal of Adolescence*, vol 31, no 1: 125-46.

Insafe (2005) *How can I chat safely?* (www.saferinternet.org/ww/en/pub/insafe/safety_issues/faqs/chat.htm).

Kaare, B.H., Brandtzæg, P.B., Endestad, T. and Heim, J. (2007) 'In the borderland between family orientation and peer-culture', *New Media & Society*, vol 9, no 4: 603-24.

Kowalski, R.M. and Limber, S.P. (2007) 'Electronic bullying among middle school students', *The Journal of Adolescent Health*, vol 41, no 6: 22-30.

Lenhart, A. and Madden, M. (2007) *Teens, privacy and online social networks*, Pew Internet and American Life Project (www.pewinternet.org/Reports/2007/Teens-Privacy-and-Online-Social-Networks.aspx).

Livingstone, S. (2008) 'Taking risky opportunities in youthful content creation: teenagers' use of social networking sites for intimacy, privacy and self-expression', *New Media & Society*, vol 10, no 3: 393-411.

Livingstone, S. and Haddon, L. (2008) 'Risky experiences for children online', *Children & Society*, vol 22, no 4: 314-23.

Lüders, M. (2007) 'Being in mediated spaces. An enquiry into personal media practices', PhD thesis, Oslo, Norway: University of Oslo.

Lüders, M. (2009: in press) 'Why and how online sociability became part and parcel of teenage life', in R. Burnett, M. Consalvo and C. Ess (eds) *The handbook of internet studies*, Oxford: Blackwell.

Lüders, M. (2009) 'Becoming more like friends: a qualitative study of personal media and social life', *Nordicom Review*, vol 30, no 1: 201-216.

Medierådet (2006) *Ungar & Medier 2006* [*Youth & media*], Stockholm, Sweden: Medierådet.

Safe.si (2009) '10 things that I must know about internet safety' (http://english.safe.si/index.php?fl=0&p1=774&p2=776&p3=780&id=780).

Shannon, D. (2007) *Vuxnas sexuella kontakter med barn via internet* [*Adults' online sexual contacts with children*], Stockholm: Brottsförebyggande rådet.

Spears, R., Postmes, T., Lea, M. and Wolbert, A. (2002) 'When are net effects gross products? The power of influence and the influence of power in computer-mediated communication', *Journal of Social Issues*, vol 58, no 1: 91-107.

Tanis, M. and Postmes, T. (2005) 'Short communication. A social identity approach to trust', *European Journal of Social Psychology*, vol 35: 413-24.

Tanis, M. and Postmes, T. (2007) 'Two faces of anonymity: paradoxical effects of cues to identity in CMC', *Computers in Human Behavior*, vol 23, no 2: 955-70.

Weathers, H. (2008) 'The innocent victim, 12, of an internet paedophile describes: "the abduction that ruined my life"', *Daily Mail* (http://tinyurl.com/c5otal).

Ybarra, M.L. and Mitchell, K.J. (2008) 'How risky are social networking sites? A comparison of places online where youth sexual solicitation and harassment occurs', *Paediatrics*, vol 121, no 2: 350-8.

Ybarra, M.L., Mitchell, K.J., Finkelhor, D. and Wolak, J. (2007) 'Internet prevention messages: targeting the right online behaviors', *Archives of Pediatrics & Adolescent Medicine*, vol 161, no 2: 138-45.

Zhao, S.Y., Grasmuck, S. and Martin, J. (2008) 'Identity construction on Facebook: digital empowerment in anchored relationships', *Computers in Human Behavior*, vol 24, no 5: 1816-36.

Zimbardo, P.G. (1969) 'The human choice: individuation, reason, and order vs deindividuation, impulse and chaos', in W.J. Arnold and D. Levine (eds) *Nebraska Symposium on Motivation*, vol 17: 237-307, Lincoln, NE: University of Nebraska Press.

ELEVEN

Inappropriate content

Thomas Wold, Elena Aristodemou, Elza Dunkels
and Yiannis Laouris

Introduction

Use of the internet and its associated services is becoming an increasingly popular pastime, particularly among children and young people, but despite the many benefits offered there are also risks which they must be made aware of. The possibility that children could encounter inappropriate content online receives less public attention than the risk that they may make risky contact with people met online, and the range of content that is of potential concern is vast, including pornography, racist material, violent and gruesome content, self-harm sites (including pro-anorexia and pro-suicide sites), commercially exploitative material and more. The European Commission (EC) supports Safer Internet hotlines throughout Europe where people can anonymously report what they perceive as illegal or disturbing content (EC, 2009). Thirty-four hotlines across the globe are members of the International Association of Internet Hotlines see (www.inhope.org).

This chapter focuses on children and young people's access to inappropriate content online. The term 'inappropriate content' is not a well-defined term and one can find variations across generations and across countries and cultures. Content that seems inappropriate from an adult's perspective may not be perceived in the same way by children and young people. Furthermore, cultural differences may influence how we understand and categorise different types of content. This blurry middle ground can contain sexual content, for example, as it is hard to achieve consensus on what is pornography and what is sexual information or portrayal. On the other hand, certain content is universally classified as inappropriate for children in all cultures – for example the depiction of graphic violence or sexual abuse, and encouragement to harm one's self or others. Furthermore, some content can be classified as illegal (thus inappropriate), such as violent or sexual acts against children, and the promotion of racism and xenophobia.

The EU Kids Online network categorised the different types of inappropriate content and risks that children can encounter online (Hasebrink et al, 2009), as presented in Chapter One (this volume). The classification is based on the role of the child (as recipient, as participant or as actor) and the motives of the provider (commercial, aggressive, sexual and values-related). The aim of this chapter is to provide a description of the empirical evidence available within the EU Kids Online network, and where appropriate within the wider literature, regarding inappropriate material encountered by children online. The review focuses on (a) pornographic, violent and gruesome content; (b) racist material; and (c) self-harm-related material. We consider country, socio-economic and age differences in likelihood of access and in coping strategies used by children.

Access to pornographic, violent and gruesome content

Pornography is widely available on the internet and one will almost inevitably encounter such content while surfing. Child pornography in particular has important implications and is considered one of the most serious crimes on the net. Even possession of child pornographic material is illegal in most countries and is severely punished. Websites containing violent and gruesome content are also widely available online and children run a high risk of accessing them accidentally. Sexual content, like pornographic or otherwise unwelcome sexual depictions, might cause harm to children or lead them to personal contact with potentially dangerous strangers. Similarly, aggressive content, like violent and gruesome material, might cause harm, anxiety and aggressiveness towards children.

In Europe, four out of ten teenagers report having encountered pornographic, unwelcome sexual content or violent, gruesome content. Table 11.1 reports the percentages for countries for which data was available (Hasebrink et al, 2009).

However, interpretation of the above data should be attempted with caution, because such broad statistics combine many different elements. For example, Italy appears to have low risk on both types of content, but this may be partly because the samples surveyed were younger (7 to 11 year olds). Nonetheless, this meta-analysis of European data makes it evident that online risks are considerable and they justifiably attract public concern and policy attention. A US study, which attempted to determine the prevalence of 'displayed risk behaviour' from the self-reported 18-year-old adolescents' publicly accessible MySpace web

Table 11.1: Percentages of children and teenagers that have seen sexual and violent content online per country

Country	Sexual content (age)		Violent and gruesome content (age)	
Poland	80%	(Teenagers)	51%	(12–17)
United Kingdom	57%	(9–19)	31%	(9–19)
Iceland	54%	(9–16)	35%	(9–16)
Austria	50%	(10–15)	15%	(10–15)
Norway	47%	(9–16)	29%	(9–16)
The Netherlands	46%	(13–18)	39%	(13–18)
Belgium	40%	(9–12)	40%	(9–12)
Ireland	37%	(9–16)	90%	(12–20)
Sweden	37%	(13–16)	26%	(9–16)
France	33%	(12–17)	No data available	
Denmark	29%	(9–16)	35%	(9–16)
Italy	25%	(7–11)	25%	(7–11)

Source: Hasebrink et al (2009)

profiles, revealed that 54% of the profiles contained risk behaviour whereas 24% referenced sexual behaviours (Moreno et al, 2009). The authors defined 'displayed risk behaviour' as information they disclose on their public profiles regarding their sexual behaviours and references to alcohol, substance use and violence. It was hypothesised that children who displayed risk behaviour would be more at risk of encountering inappropriate content (Moreno et al, 2009). Although there are large cross-national variations, content risks are very widespread – with 'seeing pornography' the second most common risk in Europe and 'seeing violent or gruesome content' the third most common risk. 'Giving out personal information' is the most common risk, but there is considerable cross-national variation (Hasebrink et al, 2009). For instance, in a recent report it is stated to be the fourth most common risk (Taraszow et al, 2009: in press). However, in Chapter Ten of this volume Marika Lüders, Petter Bae Brandtzæg and Elza Dunkels argue that anonymity may also be harmful, and so giving out personal information may not always constitute a risk. For example, Sweden has high internet penetration, but only average risk, which may be due to young people having an effective level of safety awareness.

In some cases young people may be considered potential voluntary consumers of pornography. However, many children also complain about pornographic advertisements and see themselves as victims of the marketing of pornography (Dunkels, 2008). This is yet another example of how the perspectives of adults and children can differ.

Racist content

Within the context of EU Kids Online, racist content has been classified as a potential risk for children, but the collection of findings from its 21 country members revealed little research data about it. In the UK, 11% of 9 to 19 year olds have seen racist or hateful material online (Livingstone and Bober, 2005), and in Norway, 40% of 8 to 18 year olds have by chance visited web pages with hateful content, while 22% have done so on purpose (Medietilsynet, 2008). It seems that many studies put violent and hateful or racist content in the same category, and although racist content is often both hateful and violent, it would be desirable to see more studies that address racist content more specifically. As of now there is a big gap in our understanding of the likelihood that children will encounter such material. It is evident, however, that such content exists extensively on the net and children run a significant risk of accessing it.

Self-harm, pro-ana and pro-mia content[1]

Self-harm websites refer to websites that aim to 'help' people either harm themselves or maintain their unhealthy state of being, but so far they have received little academic attention. These websites offer detailed information about the subject, provide communication with other sufferers and describe ways and methods of injuring or killing oneself. They include blogs, discussion forums and chat rooms, thus serving as a resource of support for suffering people. Pro-suicide websites have been subjected to heavy criticism from both the mass media and clinical literature (Baker and Fortune, 2008). Researchers reported that they encourage harmful behaviours and that such encouragement would likely lead to influencing prone individuals to self-harm (Thompson, 1999; Mehlum, 2000; Becker, 2004). Moreover, clinicians report that the internet has a major impact on the lives, treatment and recovery of people who are self-mutilating but have no suicidal tendencies (Whitlock et al, 2007). The distinction between self-injury and suicide websites is that research on the latter suggests that visiting them is harmful (Biddle et al, 2008), whereas self-injury websites have been found to sometimes show positive effects on self-injurious people by helping them reduce those behaviours (Murray and Fox, 2006). What is still lacking from the literature, however, is the impact that viewing such websites might have on younger children and teenagers.

Pro-anorexia websites are websites that take a positive stance toward anorexia. They present it as a lifestyle rather than an illness (Bardone-Cone and Cass, 2007). These pro-eating disorder websites are usually similar in content and offer advice on losing weight, giving tips on how to keep the disorder a secret from the surrounding world (Wilson et al, 2006). Many of those sites also offer information on medication that can help achieve and maintain weight loss (Fox et al, 2005). Only a few of those present anorexia and bulimia as serious disorders and show the consequences that they impose on health (Lipczynska, 2007). There are also forums for those who suffer from or have recovered from these illnesses.

Peebles et al (2006) studied the differences among children and adolescents with eating disorders. Their findings revealed that children lose weight more easily than adolescents during their formative years. Thus they are at a higher risk of damage in their growth than adolescents (Peebles et al, 2006). Studies revealed that parents of adolescents with eating disorders were mostly unaware of their child's usage of pro-eating disorder websites (Wilson et al, 2006). However, we must be careful not to evaluate these sites only on a superficial level. Although there are only a few studies that focus on the young users' perspectives of self-harm sites, these studies also portray the sites as places where young people can vent their feelings. There seems to be a lot of friendship, support and discussion of emotional matters in these forums (Palmgren, 2007; Day and Keys, 2008). Furthermore, we do not know that the patterns of influence that have been found for traditional media would be the same in an environment of mainly user-generated content. If we approach self-harm sites from the young sufferers' perspective, one possible conclusion is that in general an offline intervention is needed in the lives of these young people. Until they can obtain proper medical and psychological treatment for their condition the self-harm sites can in some cases function as a support, however unhealthy they may seem to the outside world.

Gender and age differences in access to inappropriate content

Teenagers are exposed to a range of inappropriate content online, and this raises many questions. How do teenagers cope with this, in what ways are they affected by it and are some more vulnerable than others?

Empirical data collected through the EU Kids Online network indicate that there are gender differences in the range and type of children's online uses (Hasebrink et al, 2009; see also Chapter Eight of this volume). In general, boys spend more time on the internet, are involved in a wider range of online activities and have different preferences from girls, particularly in types of downloads and gaming activities. Girls are more likely to search for information for educational purposes, boys for entertainment purposes, although there is evidence that this gap is disappearing (Gross, 2004). If this is the case, this also makes them differently exposed to content risks. For instance, according to the same report, in Norway, 15% of boys and 3% of girls aged 9-16 watch pornography on the internet, and there are clear empirical indications from France, Germany, Ireland, Norway, Poland and the UK that boys are more likely than girls to visit websites with violent or hateful material. Although boys are more likely than girls to visit pornographic websites, both accidentally and purposefully, it is also quite common for girls to have seen erotic images or nudity online. Findings from Poland indicate that girls are more likely to be exposed to erotic material in emails and chat rooms. The EU Kids Online report also found that girls are more likely than boys to be shocked, upset or to feel discomfort because of encountering sexual images on the internet. By contrast there is a literature that suggests boys' tendency to seek out violent and pornographic material is merely a part of adolescent curiosity and an urge to claim increasing autonomy by challenging adult-imposed boundaries.

There is not much empirical data on age and exposure to risk, but it seems evident that as children grow older, they are exposed to a greater amount and range of online risks (Hasebrink et al, 2009), including exposure to inappropriate content. This can partly be seen as adolescent curiosity and a desire to push boundaries. It is also evident that older teenagers have a more varied usage of online media and cover more internet territory, and hence are more exposed to potential risk. Whether this means they are more vulnerable remains uncertain: internet-related skills increase with age, and it seems plausible that this includes the ability to protect oneself from online risks. The report by Hasebrink et al concludes that we should not be too complacent about these skills, as many adolescents 'forget' to take the necessary precautions and have unpleasant experiences on the internet. A further review of the evidence concluded that 'little is known on how teenagers cope with online risks' (Staksrud and Livingstone, 2009: 3).

Socio-economic status (SES) differences

Although findings are scarce, the evidence points to a correlation between SES and exposure to risk. Most of the findings reported in Hasebrink et al (2009) concern content and contact risk, and in general, it seems that children from lower-class families are more exposed to risk online, even though they have relatively less access than higher SES groups. In Spain, Germany and France, there is evidence that children from working-class families are more likely to encounter, receive or view pornographic or violent material, either on their email, web browser or mobile phone. In Spain, only 3% of young people from the higher social group stated that they had received violent content through the internet, as opposed to 60% of young people with a lower social status. Similarly, 4% of young people from the higher social group accidentally accessed pornographic pages, while 26% of those with a high social status and 61% of those with a lower social status did so. There is a similar picture concerning receiving pornographic pages through the internet or mobile phone; this is least common among the higher social group. In Germany, less educated teenagers viewed violent video films on the mobile phone to a larger extent than better educated teenagers. We can therefore conclude that those who belong to higher SES groups are generally exposed to fewest risks, middle SES groups experience more risk and lowest SES groups experience the most risks.

Why is the correlation between SES and risk so strong? When we look at access, there is also a strong correlation, with children and young people from higher SES groups having better access at home than children and people from lower SES groups. Increased access and increased opportunities also increases risks, so one would think that children with better access would also encounter more risks. This is not the case, however. It seems plausible that parents are differentially resourced to manage online risk exposure, and that children are already differently at risk. For instance, we find that higher SES families have more rules concerning media use, and parents in higher SES families monitor their children's internet use to a higher extent than parents in lower SES groups (Hasebrink et al, 2009). We also know that children from lower SES groups are more likely to have access to computers in their bedroom than higher SES groups (Downey et al, 2007), making monitoring more difficult.

Cultural preferences might differ between different SES groups. It might be that families within the lower SES groups have a higher preference for graphic violence and explicit sexual content than families of higher SES groups. In relation to this, one might also wonder if higher SES children are less likely to admit watching such content in surveys compared to lower SES groups, where they might be more likely to brag about such experiences.

Coping with risk

How do children and young people respond when exposed to violent, pornographic and self-harm material? Some findings suggest that such risks as children do encounter may be brushed off, or disregarded, by the majority of young people (Hasebrink et al, 2009), but can children be asked to self-report harm with reliable results? Can they be harmed in ways they cannot describe when asked by a researcher? Many studies report that only a small minority tell an adult if they see violence, pornography or hateful content online, but they often tell about such experiences on their profiles on social networking sites (Moreno at el, 2009). Nevertheless it appears that children are developing their own strategies to respond to online risks. Whether these strategies are effective or not remains unknown. On a European level, 31% of parents say that their child has encountered harmful content on the internet, and 66% say that their child knows what to do in such situations (Hasebrink et al, 2009). There are limited data on what children and young people do and how they react when they come across violent, pornographic or hateful web pages. When children are asked about such incidents, they typically report that they ignored the material encountered or that they did not think much of it. They also often report that they never visited that particular page again. A minority report feeling upset by the content, and a few said they thought it was funny or cool (Staksrud and Livingstone, 2009). There is a possibility that children under-report negative online experiences, partly because they want to seem older and more mature than they really are, and partly because they might worry about parents then restricting their use.

Very few children and adolescents tell their parents about negative online experiences (Hasebrink et al, 2009), which supports the latter assumption. Dunkels (2008) claims that some of her informants would never tell their parents or teachers if something distressing happened on the internet, because they were afraid that they would no longer be allowed to access the internet. We might also keep in mind that it might feel embarrassing for a child or teenager to discuss such topics with their parents, and that it is quite common for children at a certain age to keep secrets from their parents. All in all, we should not be surprised that young people prefer to discuss this with their peers rather than parents or teachers.

Conclusion

It is evident that older teenagers encounter more online risks than younger children (Hasebrink et al, 2009), although the question of how younger children cope with online risk remains little researched. Boys appear more likely than girls to seek out offensive or violent content, to access pornographic content or to be sent links to pornographic websites, but girls appear more likely to be upset by offensive, violent or pornographic material. Livingstone points out that public policy regarding children and the internet has been influenced by three important factors: the extraordinary speed of the development and use of the internet, the 'cultural fear of the new' causing media panics and the 'reverse generation gap' where children can be seen as exceeding adults in their knowledge development (Livingstone, 2009).

Awareness of risk does not necessarily reduce risky encounters, and we need more research on children's coping strategies and consequences. In Chapter Sixteen (this volume), Lucyna Kirwil, Maialen Garmendia, Carmelo Garitaonandia and Gemma Martínez Fernández examine different strategies of parental mediation. In Europe, content filters are one of the most widespread measures taken to minimise exposure to harmful material for personal and public computers, but even when these are used, according to Price and Verhulst (2005) some basic problems will remain. One is that the user will have to select filtering criteria and the lists to choose from will need to be very long if they are to fit all kinds of family structures, cultures and values. Another issue is that the content that is filtered out is subject to ideological biases, even though this might not be transparent to the users.

Ybarra and Mitchell (2008) call for thoughtful approaches that focus on children's behaviours online and their general psycho-social profile, rather than particular technologies. We have little data on whether monitoring and filtering are effective approaches. We have seen that children in higher SES families have better internet access and use a wider range of online opportunities, *and* that they are less exposed to risk than children from lower SES households. Higher SES families have more rules concerning internet use (and media use in general), suggesting that parental mediation can have a positive effect in reducing risk. But how does this help us, knowing that the more a child is troubled offline, the more exposed the child is to risk online? In these cases, monitoring and filtering strategies are only part of any solution, and offline intervention will remain vital.

Note

[1] 'Pro-ana' refers to content encouraging anorexic behaviours and 'pro-mia' refers to similar content related to bulimia.

References

Baker, D. and Fortune, S. (2008) 'Understanding self-harm and suicide websites: a qualitative interview of young adult website users', *Crisis*, vol 29, no 3: 118-22.

Bardone-Cone, A.M. and Cass, K.M. (2007) 'What does viewing a pro-anorexia website do? An experimental examination of website exposure and moderating effects', *International Journal of Eating Disorders*, vol 40, no 6: 537-48.

Becker, K. (2004) 'Internet chat rooms and suicide', *Journal of the American Academy of Child and Adolescent Psychiatry*, vol 43, no 3: 246-7.

Biddle, L., Donovan, J., Hawton, K., Kapur, N. and Gunnel, D. (2008) 'Suicide and the internet', *British Medical Journal*, vol 336: 800-2.

Day, K. and Keys, T. (2008) 'Starving in cyberspace: a discourse analysis of pro-eating-disorder websites', *Journal of Gender Studies*, vol 17, no 1: 1-15.

Downey, S., Hayes, N. and O'Neill, B. (2007) *Play and Technology for Children aged 4-12*, Dublin: Office of the Minister for Children and Youth Affairs, www.omc.gov.ie/viewdoc.asp?fn=/documents/research/play_and_technology.pdf

Dunkels, E. (2008) 'Children's strategies on the internet', *Critical Studies in Education*, vol 49, no 2: 171-84.

EC (European Commission) (2009) 'Safer internet centres' (http://ec.europa.eu/information_society/activities/sip/projects/centres/index_en.htm).

Fox, N., Ward, K. and O'Rourke, A. (2005) 'Pro-anorexia, weight-loss, drugs and the internet: an "anti-recovery" explanatory model of anorexia', *Sociology of Health and Illness*, vol 27, no 7: 944-71.

Gross, E.F. (2004) 'Adolescent internet use: what we expect, what teens report', *Applied Developmental Psychology*, vol 25, no 6: 633-49.

Hasebrink, U., Livingstone, S., Haddon, L. and Ólafsson, K. (2009) *Comparing children's online opportunities and risks across Europe: Cross-national comparisons for EU Kids Online* (2nd edn), London: London School of Economics and Political Science, EU Kids Online (Deliverable D3.2 for the EC Safer Internet Plus Programme).

Lipczynska, S. (2007) 'Discovering the cult of Ana and Mia: a review of pro-anorexia websites', *Journal of Mental Health*, vol 16, no 4: 545-8.

Livingstone, S. (2009) *Children and the internet: Great expectations, challenging realities*, Cambridge: Polity.

Livingstone, S. and Bober, M. (2005) *UK children go online: Final report of key project findings*, London: London School of Economics and Political Science, Research online (http://eprints.lse.ac.uk/archive/00000399).

Medietilsynet (Norwegian Media Authority) (2008) *Trygg bruk-undersøkelsen 2008. En kartlegging av 8 til 18-åringers bruk av digitale medier* [*Safe Use Survey 2008. A mapping of 8 to 18 year olds' use of digital media*], Fredrikstad, Norway: Medietilsynet.

Mehlum, L. (2000) 'The internet, suicide, and suicide prevention', *Crisis*, vol 21, no 4: 186-8.

Moreno, M.A., Parks, M.R., Zimmerman, F.J., Brito, T.A. and Christakis, D.A. (2009) 'Display of health risk behaviors on MySpace by adolescents', *Archives of Pediatrics & Adolescent Medicine*, vol 163, no 1: 27-34.

Murray, C.D. and Fox, J. (2006) 'Do internet self-harm discussion groups alleviate or exacerbate self-harm behaviour?', *Australian e-Journal for the Advancement of Mental Health*, vol 5, no 3: 1-9.

Palmgren, A.C. (2007) 'Idag är jag ingenting annat än en kropp' ['Today, I'm nothing more than a body'], in S. Lindgren (ed) *Unga och nätverkskulturer – Mellan moralpanik och teknikromantik* [*Youth and network cultures – Between moral panics and romanticising technology*], Stockholm, Sweden: Ungdomsstyrelsen: 81-99.

Peebles, R., Wilson, J.L. and Lock, J.D. (2006) 'How do children with eating disorders differ from adolescents with eating disorders at initial evaluation?', *Journal of Adolescent Health*, vol 39: 800-5.

Price, M. and Verhulst, S. (2005) *Self-regulation and the internet*, The Hague, the Netherlands: Kluwer Law International.

Staksrud, E. and Livingstone, S. (2009) 'Children and online risk: powerless victims or resourceful participants?', *Information, Communication and Society*, vol 12, no 3: 364-87.

Taraszow, T., Aristodemou, E., Arsoy, A., Shitta, G. and Laouris, Y. (2009: in press) 'Disclosure of personal and contact information by young people in social networking sites: an analysis using Facebook™ profiles as an example', *International Journal of Media and Cultural Politics*.

Thompson, S. (1999) 'The internet and its potential influence on suicide', *Psychiatric Bulletin*, vol 23, no 8: 449-51.

Whitlock, J., Lader, W. and Conterio, K. (2007) 'The internet and self-injury: what psychotherapists should know', *Journal of Clinical Psychology: In session*, vol 63, no 11: 1135-43.

Wilson, J.L., Peebles, R., Hardy, K. and Litt, I.F. (2006) 'Surfing for thinness: a pilot study of pro-eating disorder web site usage in adolescents with eating disorders', *Pediatrics*, vol 118, no 6: 1635-43.

Ybarra, M. and Mitchell, K. (2008) 'How risky are social networking sites? A comparison of places online where youth sexual solicitation and harassment occurs', *Pediatrics*, vol 121, no 2: 350-8.

TWELVE

Problematic conduct: juvenile delinquency on the internet

Elisabeth Staksrud

Introduction

Children's participation in the internet revolution is regularly touted as a mixture of societal progress and an invitation to predatory adults and digital criminals. The idea that children can be active participants in a negative sense through illegal or deviant behaviour has received little attention from policy makers, awareness raisers and researchers, although issues such as 'digital bullying', 'happy slapping' and the illegal downloading of music and movies are starting to creep into the public – and official – consciousness. This chapter therefore focuses on children as online delinquents, actively *producing* online risks, such as illegal or undesired online content or conduct.

Delinquency is defined as 'conduct that is out of accord with accepted behaviour or the law' (Merriam-Webster Online Dictionary, 2008). What is considered delinquent or deviant and thereby constitutes 'risky behaviour' will naturally vary across ages, cultures, religions, nations and between people. Within the field of criminology, numerous theoretical approaches have been offered to explain the phenomenon of juvenile delinquency, often differentiated by where one places the cause of the behaviour: with individuals themselves (for example rational choice theory, somatotyping theory), peers (differential association theory), parents and school (social control theory), expectations from others (labelling theory), or the structure of society and culture (strain theory, sub-cultural theory, social ecology) (Jewkes, 2004; Muncie, 2004). The idea of *children* as potential delinquent participants in society is further complicated by the undefined and culturally fluctuating lines between what one considers 'a child', 'a juvenile', 'a youth' and 'an adolescent'. While the term 'children' is here defined to include all those below the age of 18, in line with the United Nations (UN) definition of the child, the terms have changed over time. Within the field of crime prevention it was not until the Victorian society that the idea of childhood as a separate stage of development in need of special considerations regarding punishment emerged (Jewkes, 2004: 89), thus also making the concept of childhood a social construction, dependent on the society, time and culture it is part of.

Even within the European Union (EU) countries seeking to adopt common legislation and rules where possible, the age of criminal responsibility and prosecution differs remarkably, being evenly spread from eight years old in Scotland to 18 in Belgium (Muncie, 2004: 251). In what follows, in order to shed some light on the issue, the main areas of children's negative conduct online are identified and described, some of which will be considered 'naughty' or problematic, some deviant, or delinquent, and some even illegal, depending on the national context.

Hacking

One of the earliest forms of delinquency online is hacking. While the term is used to embody various aspects of computer culture, the most common meaning given to the term in public discourse is that of a (young) computer expert and/or computer criminal breaking into someone else's computer or system. In other words the intent can be either good (as the 1976 meaning 'an expert at programming and solving problems with a computer'; Merriam-Webster, 1991) or bad ('a person who illegally gains access to and sometimes tampers with information in a computer system'; Merriam-Webster Online Dictionary, 2009). The hacker and the hacker culture have been portrayed and romanticised in books and movies such as 'WarGames' (directed by John Badham, 1983), *Count Zero* (Gibson, 1987) and 'Enemy of the State' (directed by Tony Scott, 1998). Equally, evil hackers have been used in popular fiction countless times, for example in 'Die Hard 4' (directed by Len Wiseman, 2007), 'Under Siege' (directed by Andrew Davis, 1992) and 'Goldeneye' (directed by Martin Campbell, 1995). All of these portrayals revolve around the ambiguity of the hacker's actions, where admiration for his or her skill is offset by fear of what they can do with a keyboard.

The term 'hacker' includes everyone from very young beginners (so-called 'script kiddies') to extremely skilled computer professionals, all of whom may or may not use their knowledge to commit pranks, illicitly accessing and publishing confidential information, or crimes. An example of a young hacker turning to computer crime is the story of German computer whiz Karl Koch, who started out as a computer/telephone hacker and ended up as a cold war cyberspy (Hafner and Markoff, 1995: 400, see also the movie '23', directed by Hans Christian Schmid, 1998). Most hackers concentrate on legal (or grey area) activities, such as modifying computer or game hardware (see, for instance, Grand et al, 2004; Rahimzadeh, 2006), social engineering (Mitnick and Simon, 2002), or reverse engineering and adjusting software to better meet their own needs. A famous example of the latter is the case of DeCSS, a small software program that unscrambles the encryption on DVD discs. Jon Johansen ended up as the poster child for the new generation of digital delinquents, having quit high school to work on the programme. After publishing the programme online, Johansen was prosecuted after complaints from among others the Motion Picture Association (MPA) for hacking and illegally obtaining access to protected data, but was acquitted in both of his trials (Straffesak [criminal case] nr 03-00731 M/02, Oslo lagsogn 2003).

While research is still scarce on the general magnitude of the problem among young people, the UK Children Go Online project found that among 12 to 19 year olds using the internet daily or weekly, 8% claimed to have hacked into someone else's website or email (Livingstone and Bober, 2005).

Illegal downloading and copyright infringement

Related to classic hacking, but far more within the reach of the technically unskilled, is the copying, downloading and sharing of data files containing material protected by copyright laws. Unfortunately, in much of the research involving children's activities online, the distinction between what is legal and illegal downloading is not made, nor is the distinction between listening to or viewing content and downloading it. It is clear, however, that the ability to download content online can be and is a desired digital skill that many children possess and make regular use of. For instance, in 2008, 61% of Swedish 12 to 14 year olds and 86% of 15 to 16 year olds had downloaded music online (World Internet Institute, 2008).

When it comes to (perceived) *illegal* downloading a multimethod study on Belgian teenagers (12-18 years) found that 78% admitted to downloading music from websites that 'did not demand financial contribution for copyright', while 19% considered illegal downloading to be 'bad' (Pauwels and Bauwens, 2008). A Norwegian study (Staksrud, 2008) found that 25% of 9 to 12 year olds and 64% of 13 to 16 year olds believed that it was illegal to download or share 'music they had seen in the shops'. Among those believing it was illegal, 34% of the

9 to 12 year olds and 74% of the 13 to 16 year olds still planned to do this in the future. The reasons for such planned (perceived) illegal behaviour among children needs further research, but some possible explanations can be offered. In a study among US college students, downloading activity was found to be positively related to deficient self-regulation and lessened by fear of punishment. In addition, normative beliefs affected downloading, while the perception of downloading as morally acceptable was positively related to actual downloading activity (LaRose et al, 2005).

'Happy slapping'

The online activity having received the most media attention the last few years is, perhaps ironically, also the one most closely rooted in the physical world. It is in essence unrelated to the above, although its results are distributed through the same channels. 'Happy slapping' refers to unprovoked physical attacks where the main purpose is filming or taking pictures for later distribution on the internet or via mobile phones. The phenomenon is said to have started in the UK in 2004/05, and most known offenders have been children and youth, making happy slapping a true children's 'conduct risk'. While the term refers to situations perceived as being 'comical', for example seeing people falling down, the movies produced and published have included serious incidents such as people being beaten to death and sexual assault and rape. In 2005 the British Transport Police was reported to be investigating 200 happy slapping incidents within six months in London alone (*The Guardian*, 2005), and the UK problem culminated with a victim being beaten to death by two 17 year olds in 2006 (BBC News Online, 2007). In Denmark, a 16-year-old girl was sentenced to eight months in jail for happy slapping a peer and filming the incident (*Netavisen Sjælland*, 2006), and in 2007 France introduced a new law on juvenile delinquency that included happy slapping, making it a crime to distribute images of violence (Le Président de la République Française, 2007).

Happy slapping is a prime example of how new technology might in itself encourage new forms of delinquent behaviour among young people, in this case most likely in order to receive attention and 'social credibility' within their peer group. By January 2009 almost 7,000 videos of various degrees of authenticity were listed under 'Happy Slapping' on YouTube. There have also been other similar examples of children and young people using the internet and mobile phones to publish offline delinquent behaviour, for instance in the vast number of online movies documenting serious traffic or property violations or warnings about planned high school shootings.

Digital bullying and harassment

The area of negative online conduct among children online that has received most attention from the research community in both Europe and the US, and where there are sufficient data to scope the incidence of online risk, is online bullying and harassment. The EU Kids Online project found a median response of 12% of online teenagers in Europe claiming to have sent bullying/harassing messages, ranging from 18% in Belgium to 8% in Ireland (Hasebrink et al, 2009). A study from the US of 3,767 middle school students showed that 4% had electronically bullied someone (Kowalski and Limber, 2007), while another US online study (not country representative) among 1,378 respondents under the age of 18 found 17% reported harassing others while online (Hinduja and Patchin, 2008). Existing research is inconclusive regarding gender differences in types and frequency of bullying. In a study of the prevalence of different types of bullying among young people in Colorado, USA, no gender differences were found for internet bullying activities (Williams and Guerra, 2007). However, most studies found girls to be over-represented both among perpetrators and victims of cyber-bullying (for example Kowalski and Limber, 2007). Others have shown that boys are more often engaged in directly aggressive acts in relation to traditional bullying face-to-face, while girls are more likely to be involved in indirect bullying such as gossip and exclusion (Björkqvist et al, 1992; Olweus, 1993).

Online harassment also includes harassment towards strangers, and racist/hate messages. In a representative comparative survey of children aged between nine and 16 in Denmark, Iceland, Ireland, Norway and Sweden, 10% (17% of the 13 to 16 year olds) admitted having posted comments on the internet that were hateful towards a person or group of people (Staksrud, 2003). In 2008, 22% of Norwegian children between 13-16 years admitted having posted a hateful and/or racist comment online (Staksrud, 2008).

Privacy violations

Putting photographs of one's friends and family on the internet is so common among internet users that many will not consider this behaviour deviant. At the same time, obtaining the consent of those depicted is not only common courtesy but is often also required by law. It might even be illegal to publish photographs of children without parental pre-approval, through the legal concept of 'informed consent' – where a higher degree of caution is needed when publicising personal information about young children. In a representative Norwegian study from 2008, 21% of the 13 to 16 year olds and 25% of the 17 to 18 year olds said they had posted photographs of someone else without their permission (Staksrud, 2008). Much depends on the nature of the photographs posted, and little is known of the possible adverse consequences of such actions.

Plagiarism

Increasingly common among pupils and students is plagiarism: the copying ('cut and paste') of digital material for use in school assignments without proper references to the material, passing it off as their own. In Belgium, 82% of teenagers said they had used information from the internet without referring to the source (Pauwels and Bauwens, 2008: 9). In the UK, 21% of 12- to 19-year-old regular users (daily or weekly) admitted having copied something from the internet for a school project and handed it in as their own work (Livingstone and Bober, 2005: 11).

Producing false information and dangerous advice

Online communities on the internet can provide information, help and support on all kinds of issues of concern. A negative corollary is that children and young people participating in these communities can also provide false information and advice, for example on medical issues, 'pro-ana' and 'pro-mia' sites (glorifying anorexia and bulimia), school assignments (such as through reference to Holocaust-denying materials) and racist comments and information. How often this happens is unclear (see also Chapter Eleven, this volume, for a discussion of the frequency of exposure to such content), but several empirical examples can be identified.

One example is the pro-suicide communities, easy to find both as websites and newsgroups, and listed and categorised in most search engines. A study of the availability of internet information on how to commit suicide through popular search engines (Biddle et al, 2008), found that of 240 identified sites, 90 sites and 12 chat rooms were dedicated suicide sites providing encouragement, promotion or information about various methods and their pros and cons, 44 sites provided factual information and 20 were humorous. The remaining sites focused on prevention and support. In other words, finding support both for and against suicide online is rather an easy task. Two of the most famous newsgroups – alt.suicide.holiday (ASH) and alt.suicide. methods – are known for its participants offering both moral and actual support, as well as advice to others wanting to end their lives (Galtung and Hoff, 2007). The phenomenon also includes using new technology for live streaming. In November 2008, the media all over the world reported how 19-year-old Abraham K. Biggs from Florida committed suicide in front of a live webcam after being encouraged by people online. There have also been media reports of the fulfilment of cyber-suicide pacts, where other internet users are aware of what is planned without reporting to the proper authorities; this points to a use of new technology where troubled children and young people can meet and support and even assist others to commit suicide (and take their own lives), rather than seeking adequate professional help.

In many cultures and countries the availability of the pro-suicide communities offers something new. The information offered on these sites has been restricted in traditional media due to public health concerns (for example in Ireland, the UK and Norway), and even criminalised (for example in France, Portugal and Australia) (Galtung and Hoff, 2007: 145).

Fraud

The idea that children as young as eight years old should be involved in *financial* fraud will, for most adults, sound absurd. However, with the rapid introduction of the mobile phone, also among the youngest population, more and more families are faced with this reality. The mobile phone can be used to pay for a wide range of services, and can be used like a credit card (if you have a subscription) or a wallet (if you have a pre-paid account/calling card). Commercial actors are targeting their media-converged products at young 'tweens'. Most known is perhaps the possibility of using a mobile phone to buy interactive goods such as clothes for your avatar (a computer user's representation of him/herself, or alter ego) (www.gosupermodel.com), furniture for your avatar's hotel room (www.habbo.com), or votes for your favourite 'Idol' participant. Many of these commercial sites also allow payment by credit card, and an increasing number of banks now report cases where parents have had their accounts overdrawn, claiming theft or fraud by an outsider, when in fact it has been their own child using their credit card, following the recipe for such payments on their favourite website without the parents' knowledge or consent. These violations are to a large degree facilitated by and a result of complex technical solutions and offers of the commercial companies.

One example is the aggressive marketing of mobile phone ring tones, where instead of buying a one-time product, users unwittingly sign up for a costly subscription. In 2008 one quarter of Belgian teenagers (23.7%) reported having paid more for a ring tone than they originally thought and 7.5% had subscribed to such a service without realising it (Pauwels and Bauwens, 2008). Another type of fraud is the use of gambling sites by minors, something considered illegal in many countries. In the UK Children Go Online Survey 2% of daily/weekly users admitted to having gambled online (Livingstone and Bober, 2005). A somewhat related issue is identity theft. This is especially common in bullying-related cases, where children have been reported having hacked into their victims' email or instant messaging account. In 2003, 7% of Swedish children (9-16 years) said they had used someone else's email or instant messaging without their permission. Similarly, 6% of Irish children had hacked into someone else's website (Staksrud, 2003).

Production and distribution of pornography

Finally, as noted in the introduction, much of the public concern related to children and their use of the internet has evolved around pornography, and the perceived need to protect young people from being exposed to such content. At the same time, and in line with the increased violations of privacy among peers and the quest for attention through the publication of movies and pictures as seen in the phenomenon of happy slapping, one cannot ignore the possibility and reality of children producing and distributing pornographic images online or via mobile phones. This is especially facilitated by the popularity of sites where young people are encouraged to publish nude and sexually provocative pictures of themselves, often categorised and subjected to popularity polls (see, for instance, www.deiligst.no and www.penest.no). While little research exists at this stage, it seems that this risk increases with age. In 2008, 1% of Norwegian 8 to 12 year olds, 6% of those aged 13-16 and 14% among the 17 to 18 year olds had taken a picture of themselves without their clothes and distributed it to others via their mobile phone (Staksrud, 2008).

Conclusion

While many children report what can be considered delinquent or even illegal behaviour, when looked at in retrospect, it is not clear what illegal behaviour really is. Legislation has yet – as always – to keep up with the technological developments, as technological development regularly facilitates new methods and means for delinquent behaviour not yet covered by law. This constant adjustment between young users, the market, legislation and general societal values also makes it necessary to take an open-minded view of how delinquent conduct online might be at odds with what the children themselves perceive as relevant and 'fair', realising there is great confusion about what is illegal and legal to do online. Today, most teenagers are de facto 'criminals' when doing what for them is considered 'everyday stuff' online, such as downloading music. This has created a tension between, for example, what is perceived as justifiable information rights versus copyright, a tension with political ramifications for young people, such as in Sweden, where the Pirate Party (www.piratpartiet.se) was established in 2005 to fight legislation putting restrictions on the downloading of online material for personal use.

The fact that children can be delinquent, naughty or criminal online is also an issue for awareness-raising and media literacy initiatives. The European Commission (EC) Safer Internet programmes, as well as the multiple national awareness initiatives across Europe, have rarely addressed the issue of children as potential delinquent or criminals. Neither has research, typically focusing more on the risk where children are victims rather than the situations where they are participants. Often parents are asked about their children's online experiences, reporting, for example, worries that their child is using the internet or mobile phone to 'get information about self-harm, suicide, anorexia' (EC, 2008: 24-5), but they are rarely, if ever, asked if they are worried that *their* child would *produce* such information.

The complexity of juvenile delinquency online, as demonstrated in this chapter, shows that we can expect most children at some point to do something naughty, deviant or even illegal online. The relationship between the different activities mentioned here, the motivation behind them and which children do what needs to be researched further. Ultimately this also challenges how we perceive our children. If we acknowledge that children and young people can and will use the internet for both good and bad purposes, we can start a more targeted process of research, awareness and policy development to prevent the negative behaviour when appropriate.

References

BBC News Online (2007) 'Life for "happy slap" murder boy', 26 January (http://news.bbc.co.uk/1/hi/england/southern_counties/6303599.stm).

Biddle, L., Donovan, J., Hawton, K., Kapur, N. and Gunnell, D. (2008) 'Suicide and the internet', *British Medical Journal*, vol 336, no 7648: 800-2.

Björkqvist, K., Lagerspetz, K.M.J. and Kaukiainen, A. (1992) 'Do girls manipulate and boys fight? Developmental trends in regard to direct and indirect aggression', *Aggressive Behavior*, vol 18: 117-27.

EC (European Commission) (2008) *Towards a safer use of the internet for children in the EU – A parents' perspective, Analytical report*, Flash Eurobarometer Series # 248, conducted by The Gallup Organisation, Hungary, Luxembourg: EC (http://ec.europa.eu/public_opinion/flash/fl_248_en.pdf).

Galtung, A. and Hoff, O.-K. (2007) *Selvmordsfare og Internett: Kan jussen gi beskyttelse?* [Suicide danger and the internet: Can the law protect?], Oslo, Norway: Kolofon Forlag AS.

Gibson, W. (1987) *Count Zero*, New York: Ace Books

Grand, J., Thornton, F. and Yarusso, A. (2004) *Game console hacking: Have fun while voiding your warranty*, Rockland, MA: Syngress Publishing.

Guardian, The (2005) 'Concern over risk of "happy slapping" craze, 26 April.

Hafner, K. and Markoff, J. (1995) *Cyberpunk: Outlaws and hackers on the computer frontier*, New York, NY: Touchstone Books.

Hasebrink, U., Livingstone, S., Haddon, L. and Ólafsson, K. (2009) *Comparing children's online opportunities and risks across Europe: Cross-national comparisons for EU Kids Online* (2nd edn), London: London School of Economics and Political Science, EU Kids Online (Deliverable D3.2 for the EC Safer Internet Plus Programme).

Hinduja, S. and Patchin, J. (2008) 'Cyberbullying: an exploratory analysis of factors related to offending and victimization', *Deviant Behavior*, vol 29, no 2: 129-56.

Jewkes, Y. (2004) *Media and crime*, London: Sage Publications.

Kowalski, R.M. and Limber, S.P. (2007) 'Electronic bullying among middle school students', *The Journal of Adolescent Health: Official Publication of the Society for Adolescent Medicine*, vol 41, no 6: 22-30.

LaRose, R., Lai, Y.J., Lange, R., Love, B. and Wu, Y. (2005) 'Sharing or piracy? An exploration of downloading behavior', *Journal of Computer-Mediated Communication*, vol 11, no 1: 1-21.

Le Président de la République Française, LOI n° 2007-297 du 5 mars 2007 relative à la prévention de la délinquance (1) 56 C.F.R. § 3 ter - De l'enregistrement et de la diffusion d'images de violence (2007).

Livingstone, S. and Bober, M. (2005) *UK children go online. Final Report of key project findings*, London: Department of Media and Communications, London School of Economics and Political Science (http://eprints.lse.ac.uk/399/).

Merriam-Webster (ed) (1991) *Webster's ninth new collegiate dictionary*, Springfield, MA: Merriam/Webster Inc

Merriam-Webster Online Dictionary (2008) *Juvenile delinquency* (www.merriam-webster.com/dictionary/juvenile_delinquency).

Merriam-Webster Online Dictionary (2009) *Hacker* (www.merriam-webster.com/dictionary/hacker).

Mitnick, K.D. and Simon, W.L. (2002) *The art of deception*, Indianapolis, IN: Wiley Publishing.

Muncie, J. (2004) *Youth and crime* (2nd edn), London: Sage Publications.

Netavisen Sjælland (2006) '8-måneders fængsel for "Happy slapping"', 9 November (www.netavisen-sjaelland.dk/news.php?item.326).

Olweus, D. (1993) *Bullying at school: What we know and what we can do*, Oxford: Blackwell.

Pauwels, C. and Bauwens, J. (2008) *Teens and ICT: Risk and opportunities. Final report – Summary of the research*, Brussels: Free University of Brussels.

Rahimzadeh, A. (2006) *Hacking the PSP*, Indianapolis, IN: Wiley Publishing.

Staksrud, E. (2003) 'What do SAFT kids do online?', Paper presented at the Future Kids Online – 'How to Provide Safety, Awareness, Facts and Tools', Stockholm, 20 October 2003.

Staksrud, E. (2008) 'Social networking, risk and safety – a road paved with paradoxes', Paper presented at the Safer Internet Forum, 25 September, Luxembourg (http://ec.europa.eu/information_society/activities/sip/docs/forum_september_2008/stakrud.pdf).

Williams, K.R. and Guerra, N.G. (2007) 'Prevalence and predictors of internet bullying', *The Journal of Adolescent Health: Official Publication of the Society for Adolescent Medicine*, vol 41, no 6: S14-S21.

World Internet Institute (2008) *Unga svenskar och Internet 2008* [Young Swedes and the internet 2008], Hudiksvall, Sweden: World Internet Institute.

THIRTEEN

Children and the internet in the news: agency, voices and agendas

Cristina Ponte, Joke Bauwens and Giovanna Mascheroni

Introduction

From both historical and theoretical perspectives, many have argued that media representations provide significant symbolic resources for the construction of public and political agendas and that dominant media frames are powerful in defining social problems and shaping public discourses (Griswold, 1994; Critcher, 2003; Kitzinger, 2004). When it comes to young people's engagement with the internet and how society is dealing with this, the interconnection and congruence among the public, policy and research agendas are noticeable.

Based on a systematic content analysis of news coverage in European papers, this chapter examines how the press reports children's positive and risky or harmful contacts with online technologies. Drawing on agenda-setting theories and on contemporary theories on the construction of childhood, it discusses patterns of representation of internet-related risks and opportunities, considers which social actors are given voice and investigates which role and level of agency are attributed to young people in these news narratives.

Agenda setting and conflicting discourses on children

In 2008, a survey showed that, after their closest relatives, parents see the mass media as the second most influential source of information on safer internet use (EC, 2008). Policy makers and researchers also seem to be sensitive if not susceptible to the media's discourses on young people and the internet. The case of happy slapping – 'discovered' by the British press in 2005, and now perceived as a social problem in most European countries (see Chapter Twelve, this volume) – is paradigmatic here.

The tradition of agenda-setting studies provides a useful framework to understand the effects of the news media coverage on public, policy and research agendas. Focusing mostly on the role of the media in political and public agendas, research has shown that the news media promote public and political awareness of certain issues (McCombs, 2005). Contemporary agenda-setting studies consider the effects of media coverage at two levels. Whereas the 'first level' is focused on the relative salience of issues or subjects, the 'second level' examines the relative salience of attributes of issues (Weaver, 2007: 142). Hence, the news media are first of all powerful in selecting a set of issues that resonate in the public sphere and tend to become of public concern. But they are also influential in establishing how to depict and discuss these issues. They actively set the frames of reference on the issue, employ a particular perspective and voice certain values.

As the issue of young people and the internet is of prime importance to policy makers, education, industry and research – that is, to powerful social institutions – it can be assumed that quality newspapers are particularly significant shapers of the agendas on this issue. Because of its serious and sober tone and its attention to issues traditionally deemed important to the public sphere (for example political processes, economic developments, social changes), some assert that the coverage of events and issues in the quality press is not normally framed in sensationalist and populist terms (Scannell, 2002; Schrøder, 2002; Tuchman, 2002). However, others argue that quality newspapers are also affected by market-driven journalism (Franklin, 2008). This review therefore examines newspaper depictions across Europe of young people's online experiences and analyses how they deal with the contemporary visions of children, primarily concentrating on quality newspaper coverage.

Today's media coverage of children's online activities seems to oscillate between two contradictory approaches to childhood. On the one hand, there is the emergent participatory discourse in political and academic circles, following the United Nations (UN) Convention on the Rights of the Child. Recognising children as full social actors, with their own 'youth culture', communicative rights and agency, this approach is variably endorsed throughout Europe as part of national constructions of childhood (James and James, 2008: 3).

The traditional discourse, on the other hand, conceives children as uncompleted and incompetent agents, provides values and ideas about 'proper' childhood, and, not surprisingly, it is the dominant discourse in moral panics (Critcher, 2003, 2008). With respect to interactive digital media, this perspective on young people is especially mobilised. Children's favourite online activities – for example gaming, chat rooms and social networks – are associated with negative feelings and identified as the irrational side of the internet. New communication technologies are deemed responsible for altering the relationships between young people and adults in that they promote a horizontal socialisation based on the increasing influence of peer groups. The perceived exclusion of adults from youth digital culture leads to the view of the child at risk and the adoption of a moral panic frame (Drotner, 1999; Buckingham, 2007).

The presence of the moral panic frame in the news on children and the internet must also be understood in relation to the commercialisation and marketing of news. The quality press has clearly moved toward the adoption of a more sensationalist tone and attention to scandals, crime stories and soft news. In particular, the discourse of fear, which has proved to be a successful news format worldwide, exemplifies the entanglement of the logic of the market and the dominant discourses about young people (Altheide, 2002).

Content analysis

Building on these ideas, this chapter addresses three research questions aimed at finding patterns in the way the European quality press constructs the social issue of young people and the internet. First, what types of internet-related risks and opportunities are covered? Second, what agency is attributed to young people and how is their role conceived? And third, what voices are heard in the newspaper stories on young people's encounters with the internet?

The answers to these questions are based on a dataset proceeding from a large-scale systematic content analysis of newspaper coverage in 14 European countries over a two-month period (October–November 2007). In this media analysis, which was conducted within the framework of the EU Kids Online project, news coverage about young people and online technologies was scrutinised in 51 newspapers with differing scopes (national and regional) and editorial orientations (from 'serious' to more popular and tabloid)[1].

For the majority of the countries, quality and popular newspapers appeared to have similar agendas, contradicting the assumption that the quality press is less oriented towards 'exciting' news than the popular press (Haddon and Stald, 2009b: in press). From all the newspaper articles on the subject surveyed, about half were published in quality newspapers, implying that this press, at least for the period under study, played a significant part in the media discourses on young people and the internet – popular newspapers accounted for 27% of the overall press coverage and regional newspapers 22%. Further analysis concentrated on coverage in the quality newspapers.

The corpus for detailed analysis consisted of 13 national quality newspapers across Europe (see Table 13.1), and a consistent procedure was followed in the participating countries for the sampling of the articles. For each country we selected only the newspaper that devoted most attention to young people's engagement with internet-related technologies. Throughout the 61 days under analysis, seven newspapers had news on this topic on between 16 and 23 days and published around 20-30 items in that time, suggesting a pattern of regular attention. Spanish and Estonian papers led in frequency and items, while the British, the Greek and particularly the Danish were at the bottom in both values.

Table 13.1: Quality newspapers: frequency of news and items published (1 October–30 November 2007) (absolute figures)

Country	Newspaper	Days with news	Number of items
Spain	El Pais	36	50
Estonia	Postimees	30	52
Norway	Aftenposten	23	37
Austria	Standard	20	28
Italy	Corriere della Sera	20	30
Slovenia	Dnevnik	18	21
Germany	Frankfurt Allemaine Zeitung	17	22
Ireland	Irish Times	17	25
Belgium (Flanders)	De Standaard	16	24
Portugal	Público	14	19
UK	The Independent	12	12
Greece	Kathimerini	9	11
Denmark	Jyllands Posten	3	3
Total		61	334

For our present purpose, we concentrated on a particular subset of variables indicative of the relative salience of both subjects (*first level of agenda setting*) and attributes of issues (*second level of agenda setting*). Specifically, we considered the type of online risks and opportunities, the views and voices represented and the ways these were framed through the newspaper headlines.

Relative salience of risks and opportunities in the news

The 334 newspaper stories in our corpus included 549 mentions of online risks and opportunities. Most of the mentions (69%) dealt with risks, confirming the dominance of 'bad news'. The opportunities offered by the internet received less attention (30%) and they were even absent in countries where a small number of stories cover the internet, such as in the British and Danish papers.

Internet risks relating to aggressive and sexual behaviour, two types of risks that have been at the heart of many moral panics about children as wrongdoers or victims, received disproportional press coverage, 46% and 34% respectively. The potential harmful moral and ideological consequences of the internet (18%) and online commercial risks such as stealth marketing or selling inappropriate products (15%) were significantly less prevalent, and pathological harms of the internet such as internet addiction were almost ignored (3%). As to press coverage of opportunities, the benefits for social identity and relationships were at the top (15%), far ahead of educational opportunities, civic participation and creativity, all below 10%, as shown in Table 13.2.

If we only consider the newspapers with medium to high press coverage (see Table 13.1), aggressive conduct was the main narrative in the news on young people's engagement with the internet in almost all the countries, being particularly visible in the Spanish and Estonian papers, both at the top. Sexual risks, mostly children affected by sexual content and contact, were the second most covered topic. The media's alertness to sexual crime may be shaped by national events. This was exemplified in the Belgian and British papers, both countries that lived through collective traumas with regard to sexual abuse of children and that faced intense public responses to these traumatic events.

Commercial risks were almost ignored in the Italian, Spanish and Portuguese papers, and moral and ideological risks received significantly more attention in the German, Estonian and Slovenian press. Again, these variations can be explained from the different national contexts. In the Southern Latin countries the lower rate and slower pace of internet penetration and usage seem to help explain why their quality press has yet to focus on consumer rights and privacy (Mascheroni et al, 2009: in press). On the other hand, countries like Estonia and Slovenia underwent a fast and widespread diffusion of the internet and an explosive growth of marketing to children. These countries have

Table 13.2: Risks (R) and opportunities (O) mentioned in the news (percentages) (multiple coding)

Risks and opportunities	Austria (Standard)	Belgium (The Standard)	Denmark (Jyllands Posten)	Estonia (Postimees)	Germany (Frankfurt Allgemeine Zeitung)	Greece (Kathimerini)	Ireland (Irish Times)	Italy (Corriere Della Sera)	Norway (Aftenposten)	Portugal (Público)	UK (The Independent)	Slovenia (Dnevnik)	Spain (El País)	% Total
Aggression	29	21	33	67	55	55	36	40	38	47	25	90	62	46
Sexual risks	14	79	67	23	9	27	36	27	19	42	67	0	30	34
Negative values	21	21	33	27	41	0	0	10	8	21	0	48	6	18
Social Identity (O)	14	8	0	37	9	9	12	27	35	0	0	43	6	15
Commercial risks	11	4	33	40	14	9	28	3	8	0	0	38	4	15
Education (O)	14	4	0	46	0	0	12	20	11	5	0	10	0	9
Participation (O)	14	21	0	15	14	0	4	7	5	0	0	24	4	8
Creativity (O)	11	4	0	13	9	0	16	10	0	5	0	14	10	7
Addiction	0	0	0	0	5	18	8	0	8	0	0	0	2	3

been successful in keeping pace with the rate of internet penetration in Western and Northern European countries, but are at the same time facing transitional questions and challenges, mostly related to the lack of relevant provision and content specifically aimed at children (Bauwens et al, 2009: in press).

Children's agency in news stories

Next to the relative salience of certain types of risks and opportunities, the relative salience of attributes was rather ambiguous. In particular, we focused on how the newspapers represented children's role and agency (Hasebrink et al, 2009) in the events they reported.

Figure 13.1 shows that in general children were mostly depicted in passive terms, that is, as recipients of online contents and services. When newsmakers wrote about risk experiences, in half of the cases children were portrayed as receiving or exposed to harmful content. In one third of the cases they appeared as agents acting towards other persons. The third communicative role, children participating in social contacts, received far fewer references. When journalists covered positive online experiences, the distribution of the three communicative roles was more balanced.

An ambiguous perspective on young people and the internet was clearly shown in the articles dealing with violence and sexual risks. In the case of aggression, the acting children were mainly wrongdoers,

Figure 13.1: Children's agency in quality newspaper coverage on the internet and children

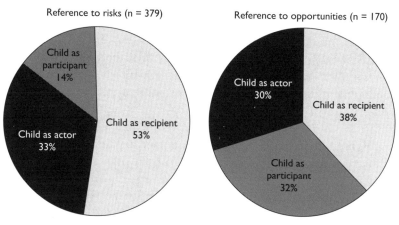

Reference to risks (n = 379)

Child as participant 14%

Child as recipient 53%

Child as actor 33%

Reference to opportunities (n = 170)

Child as actor 30%

Child as recipient 38%

Child as participant 32%

although their misbehaviour was often explained through the availability of and exposure to aggressive content. This causal linkage between content and conduct manifested itself distinctly in the coverage of a Finnish school shooting event on 7 November 2007. Except for the Danish paper, which framed the event just as 'violence at school' and therefore had no items to be included, all the others narrated the incident as a story in which the internet and YouTube encouraged deviance. In half of the headlines on 8 November 2007 the aggressive conduct by a 17 year old was explicitly linked to the internet: 'Bloody deed was announced on internet' (*Der Standard*), 'Plans of Finnish gunman on the internet?' (*De Standaard*), 'He announced his action on YouTube' (*Corriere della Sera*), 'Gunman kills eight at Finnish school after YouTube threat' (*The Independent*), 'School shooting prophecy reached YouTube' (*Postimees*), 'He heralded the massacre on YouTube' (*Kathimerini*).

In the news dealing with sexual risks young people were almost exclusively represented as victims, mainly as exposed to or exploited by pornographic content (this accounted for 80% of all news dealing with sexual risks). One in four items on sexual risks was part of a wider news story on a large-scale and a successful Interpol operation to catch a paedophile. The fact that only three papers ignored this story (*Frankfurt Allgemeine Zeitung, Corriere della Sera* and *Dvenik*) confirmed the paedophile figure as a 'genuinely universal folk devil, with perceptions and remedies which are much more uniform than in any other issue' (Critcher, 2003: 127). This narrative was framed as the 'devil hunt', a global mobilisation of readers to participate. The frame was clearly expressed in the headlines, in which the quality press shared the same emotionally charged language as the popular press: 'Interpol "unmasked" child abuser' (*Der Standard*), 'Interpol runs down identity of wanted paedophile via Internet' (*De Standaard*), 'Interpol launches the first world search for paedophile' (*El País*), 'Interpol seeks all over the world for a feared paedophile' (*Postimees*), 'Interpol issues appeal in paedophile hunt' (*The Irish Times*), 'Interpol in appeal to find prolific child abuser' (*The Independent*).

The news narrative on negative values and commercial risks highlighted children as vulnerable, ignorant and innocent receivers of harmful content and contacts, but in both risks one out of three mentions presented children as asocial or even as anti-social agents. Therefore, except for the news on sexual risks, the representation of children as wrongdoers seems to be rather robust in the media attention to young people's engagement with the internet.

Voices in the news

Not only were children largely framed as requiring discipline in discussion of their use of the internet, but the voices that were heard also show that children were spoken about and sometimes spoken for by different social institutions (see Table 13.3).

Judicial authorities were clearly the main voice, mostly connected with risk situations that framed children's online practices in terms of crime and deviance. Still, it was somewhat surprising to find out that journalists themselves and children were also in the top positions. Illustrating how quality newspapers have an active and authoritative voice in the public debate over the internet and children, journalists and editors came in second place, performing their opinion making and commentary role, but also often speaking on behalf of the parents who were rarely heard from. The weight of the journalists' voices contradicts the (dominant) perspective of a neutral presentation of facts and actors in the quality press and it equally suggests that children's engagement with the internet is becoming a media panic, even within this sector of the press. Stressing risks that threaten the moral order, such as aggressive conduct and sexual content, the quality press seemed to join their voices with other voices, such as pressure groups, individual experts and politicians outside government, constructing a 'unified discourse' that includes 'the remedy to the threat' and the 'ultimate responsibility for protection from the threat' (Critcher, 2003: 173-4).

Table 13.3: Voices in the news: who speaks about what? (absolute figures) (multiple coding)

Agency/spokesmen	Voices	About risks	About opportunities	About risks and opportunities
Police/legal representatives	119	115	2	2
Journalists	75	56	10	9
Children (up to 18)	58	40	15	3
Government, politicians	37	24	10	3
NGO, charities	32	21	7	4
Researchers, academics	31	20	7	4
Education	29	16	8	5
Internet industry	27	10	13	4
Institutions (non-commercial)	20	12	7	1
Parents	14	10	3	1

Particularly with regard to the Finnish school shooting event, journalists played an active role as commentators. While some headlines framed it in pathological terms or by explaining it through historical associations and generalisations ('Psychoanalyst: School-shooter may have had narcissist personality disorder', *Postimees*; 'What is going on with normal students?', *Frankfurter Allgemeine Zeitung*; 'Columbine generation, the web used to kill…', *Corriere della Sera*), others used a more 'problem-solving' approach ('We need services to help angry young men', *The Irish Times*; 'Mobilizing responsibility', *Aftenposten*). Still, both approaches, how different their tones may appear, seem to externalise the incident as a problem of '*the young* and their media uses that are targeted as evil' (Drotner, 1999: 612; original emphasis).

The large number of children's voices heard should not be immediately considered as a sign of recognition of their communicative rights. Children were mostly heard in association with aggression and negative values, presented much more as aggressors or as actual and potential victims than as competent and positively empowered. The high presence of children's voices among stories about risk was mainly due to the Finnish school shooting: 40% of children's voices were about this incident and its copycats.

There are a few contrasting national variations at work in the way quality papers let children have a say in the matter. While the Spanish *El País* had no children's voices, the Norwegian *Aftenposten* gave children more room to speak, their voices being the most frequent in this paper. These national differences indicate that across Europe different definitions of childhood co-exist and shape the public discourse.

Lastly, the prominent role of governments and industries in news stories dealing with the opportunities of the internet demonstrates how in the quality press' agenda the so-called good news about young people and the internet is mostly associated with announcements of public policies or technological innovations. Unsurprisingly, the internet industry was the only voice that dealt more with opportunities rather than risks associated with young people's internet use. It suggests not only that the industries play a proactive role as news promoters but also that their responsibilities in safeguarding the internet safety of children are under-stated. While the demand for industry intervention and for co-regulation is often heard from the European Commission (EC), non-governmental organisations (NGOs), scholars and educators, this is not reflected in the media agenda.

Conclusion

Although an analysis of news coverage alone cannot demonstrate how the media affects public, policy and research agendas, this snapshot of European quality press coverage about young people's engagement with the internet helps us understand in what discursive contexts parents, teachers, policy makers and scholars are dealing with the social issue of children and the internet. It also provides an insight into which voices and actors are actually heard when the public is informed about young people's online experiences.

This comparative analysis not only demonstrated how the processes of commercialism and sensationalism are affecting news coverage of these phenomena, it also identified cultural processes at work. National stories and culture shape the media's constructions of childhood and how children's online experiences are framed (for example, interconnection between news coverage on sexual risks and paedophilia). The framework focusing on the risks and negative 'side-effects' of young people's experiences online (as part of a media panic) appears to be the result of a combination of factors: the suitability of both new media and childhood to be incorporated within a moral panic discourse on the one hand, and the concurring news values that guide the selection and editing of news, on the other.

On two fronts the European quality press fails in its duty to contribute to a balanced discussion about matters of public interest. First, news stories frequently failed to balance in their coverage the enabling and restraining aspects of the internet, whereas among researchers and policy makers there seems to be a tendency to a more nuanced approach to the prominence of the internet in children's everyday life. Second, the media agenda does not give all stakeholders the same communicative entitlements. Young citizens are still rather voiceless social groups in a debate that concerns them the most. Equally parents are under-represented in public debate about their children and other adults speak on their behalf. Not only does the quality press overlook the diversity of stakeholders that are involved in the issue, it also fails to notice the diversity of online experiences of children.

Note

[1] This analysis resulted in 1,036 articles. For an account of the research design, sampling and coding, see Haddon and Stald (2009a).

References

Altheide, D.L. (2002) 'Children and the discourse of fear', *Symbolic Interaction*, vol 25, no 2: 229-50.

Bauwens, J., Lobe, B., Segers, K. and Tsaliki, L. (2009: in press) 'A shared responsibility: similarities and differences in the factors that shape online risk experiences for children in Europe', *Journal of Children and Media*.

Buckingham, D. (2007) *Beyond technology: Children's learning in the age of digital culture*, Cambridge: Polity.

Critcher, C. (2003) *Moral panics and the media*, Buckingham: Open University Press.

Critcher, C. (2008) 'Making waves: historical aspects of public debates about children and mass media', in K. Drotner and S. Livingstone (eds) *The international handbook of children, media and culture*, London: Sage Publications: 91-104.

Drotner, K. (1999) 'Dangerous media?', *Pedagogica Historia*, vol 35, no 3: 593-619.

EC (European Commission) (2008) *Towards a safer use of the internet for children in the EU – A parents' perspective, Analytical report*, Flash Eurobarometer Series # 248, conducted by The Gallup Organisation, Hungary, Luxembourg: EC (http://ec.europa.eu/information_society/activities/sip/docs/eurobarometer/analyticalreport_2008.pdf).

Franklin, B. (2008) 'The future of newspapers', *Journalism Studies*, vol 9, no 5: 630-41.

Griswold, W. (1994) *Cultures and societies in a changing world*, Thousand Oaks, CA: Pine Forge Press.

Haddon, L. and Stald, G. (eds) (2009a) *A cross-national European analysis of press coverage of children and the internet*, London: EU Kids Online, London School of Economics and Political Science (www.lse.ac.uk/collections/EUKidsOnline/Reports/MediaReport.pdf).

Haddon, L. and Stald, G. (2009b: in press) 'A comparative analysis of European press coverage of children and the internet', *Journal of Children and Media*.

Hasebrink, U., Livingstone, S., Haddon, L. and Ólafsson, K. (2009) *Comparing children's online opportunities and risks across Europe: Cross-national comparisons for EU Kids Online* (2nd edn), London: London School of Economics and Political Science, EU Kids Online (Deliverable D3.2 for the EC Safer Internet Plus Programme).

James, A. and James, A.L. (eds) (2008) *European childhoods: Cultures, politics and childhoods in Europe*, Basingstoke: Palgrave Macmillan.

Kitzinger, J. (2004) *Framing abuse*, London: Pluto Press.

McCombs, M. (2005) 'A look at agenda-setting: past, present and future', *Journalism Studies*, vol 6, no 4: 543-57.

Mascheroni, G., Ponte, C., Garmendia, M., Garitaonandia, C. and Murru, M.F. (2009: in press) 'Comparing online risks for children in South Western European Countries: Italy, Portugal and Spain', *International Journal of Media and Cultural Politics*.

Scannell, P. (2002) 'History, media and communication', in K.B. Jensen (ed) *A handbook of media and communication research*, London: Routledge: 191-205.

Schrøder, K. (2002) 'Discourses of fact', in K.B. Jensen (ed) *A handbook of media and communication research*, London: Routledge: 98-116.

Tuchman, G. (2002) 'The production of news', in K.B. Jensen (ed) *A handbook of media and communication research*, London: Routledge: 78-90.

Weaver, D. (2007) 'Thoughts on agenda setting, framing, and priming', *Journal of Communication*, vol 57, no 1: 142-7.

FOURTEEN

The role of parental mediation in explaining cross-national experiences of risk

Bojana Lobe, Katia Segers and Liza Tsaliki

Introduction

The range and incidence of risks experienced by children online varies cross-nationally, although the overall rank ordering of more or less common risks is fairly consistent (Hasebrink et al, 2009). The reasons why countries vary in online risk experience and risk perception have recently attracted concern from different academic disciplines, such as media studies and consumer research (Livingstone and Bovill, 2001; Park and Jun, 2003; Mediappro, 2006; SAFT, 2006; Livingstone and Haddon, 2008). Some authors state that challenges lay in the form of having a different primary target and a different working style in each country (for example SAFT, 2006: 3). Yet the question of how exactly cross-national differences in the degree of children's online risk experiences can be explained has rarely been examined from an international, comparative perspective. This chapter examines in detail the factors that help explain the differing likelihood of online risk experiences in different European countries. More specifically, it addresses the question of whether parental mediation, when other factors are controlled for, plays a significant role in reducing risk across 18 European countries.

The EU Kids Online network has identified cross-national diversity in the occurrence of risk experiences across Europe, and has been able to distinguish between high, medium and low-risk countries (Hasebrink et al, 2009; see also Chapters Four, Six and Fifteen, this volume). Our own work (Bauwens et al, 2009: in press) looked at the factors that shape online risk experience for children in high-risk countries by examining the combined impact of seven factors related to the spheres of government, industry, education and children. These seven factors included children's use of the internet, the national legal framework, the country's Networked Readiness Index (NRI, 2008), educational policy, the role of internet service providers (ISPs), public sector and non-profit online content provision and awareness raising.

We found that risks experienced in 18 different countries showed very different patterns, each country possessing its own specific configuration of factors (which during the process of analysis we call 'conditions'). We also concluded that expected traditional social, cultural, political and economic divides between old and new European Union (EU) member states do not coincide with the gap between high and non-high (that is, medium and low) risk countries. Overall, the situation in many European countries shows that a robust legal framework does not automatically guarantee a low degree of online risk. Especially in those countries where children are making use of or accessing the internet in a very advanced way, the efforts that governments put to set up an appropriate legal framework do not keep up with the rapid pace of young people's internet use. We also learned that even when the government is taking initiatives in different spheres of action (education, awareness campaigns, regulation), the relative lack of provision of online content that positively meets children's needs and interests has increased the risk encountered, whereas high provision has reduced it. This finding shows that in countries where children are eager to go online, but are unable to find content tailored to their competencies and interests, they are more at risk of encountering content that is irrelevant or inappropriate. Given the importance of parental mediation in the way children conduct themselves online (for example Livingstone and Helsper, 2008), we examine the role of parental mediation in children's experiences of online risk.

Parental mediation of online risks

Exploring the role of parental mediation is all the more important when we consider the present call to build parental regulation into policy, thus devolving the regulation of children's access and use onto parents (Livingstone and Bober, 2006). In spite of its importance, parental mediation of children's internet use has only recently started to attract considerable academic and research interest and attention. This is hardly surprising because, similarly, academic literature on the strategies used by parents and adults in order to modify or counteract undesirable effects of other media took a while before it flourished – in the 1980s. Then it was found that parents employ three types of regulation for their children's television viewing, which could arguably be transposed to the internet as well: restrictive mediation (for example setting rules about or restricting exposure); active mediation (for example talking to children about the medium and its content); and co-viewing with their children (Valkenburg, 2004: 54-5). Others (Livingstone, 2007) define parental regulation of children and young people's media use in terms of 'evaluative guidance' (when parents seek to influence children's reactions by means of discussion) and 'restrictive guidance' (when parents wish to regulate media access, including the time spent on particular media).

When it comes to how children and parents cope with online risks, there is considerable variation across countries: in some countries, including Sweden, the Netherlands, Denmark, Iceland and Norway, almost all children who go online have parents well acquainted with the internet. In others, including Greece, Cyprus and Portugal, where barely half of children go online, parents generally do not use the internet and hence are hard-pressed to monitor their children online (Hasebrink et al, 2009). Going deeper into the relationship between parents and children regarding parental perception of what constitutes risk for their child, the 2005/06 Eurobarometer survey reveals a negative correlation between parental perception of online risk experienced by their child and the parent's confidence that their child is able to cope with online risk (see Hasebrink et al, 2009). Thus, in Belgium, Cyprus, France, Germany, Ireland, Italy and the UK, parents tend to perceive less online risk and to have a higher estimate of their child's ability to cope, possibly because they under-estimate the need to cope with online risks. Meanwhile, in Estonia and Bulgaria followed by Poland and the Czech Republic, parents perceive more risk and either recognise their child's need to cope or perceive children to lack the necessary coping strategies.

Method and analysis

The findings offered in this chapter are based on a secondary analysis of existing qualitative and quantitative data sources and findings comparing children's online opportunities and risks (as reviewed by EU Kids Online; see Hasebrink et al, 2009) together with data from the 2008 Eurobarometer parental survey (EC, 2008). Eighteen European countries, for which sufficient data sources and findings were available, were selected for inclusion (see Table 14.1 for an overview). These well represent the diversity of Europe in historical, regional and political terms (for a more detailed description of the rationale behind this selection, see Bauwens et al, 2009: in press).

In order to perform a cross-national comparison on available secondary data we employed qualitative comparative analysis (QCA), a technique which aims to offer 'in-depth insight in the different cases and capture the complexity of the cases' while still pursuing some level of generalisation (Rihoux, 2006: 860). QCA is particularly appropriate when it is hypothesised that the phenomenon to be explained (the 'outcome variable') is shaped by the interaction of multiple conditions, possibly in different ways across the cases. Thus QCA seeks to account for the configuration (or configurations) of conditions associated with a particular outcome (here, higher or lower online risk in a country). This is achieved through a statistical analysis that clarifies patterns of similarity and difference across cases (here, across countries) in the most parsimonious manner (that is, using the fewest explanatory factors possible). Hence, QCA enables the researcher to identify the core conditions that shape the particular phenomenon under study. A distinctive feature of the analysis is that it permits multiple alternative explanations within the data set, in recognition of the specificities of the cases themselves.

The QCA procedure usually consists of five stages. First, the outcome variable is dichotomised (typically, it is assessed as present or absent) for all cases included in the analysis. Second, the range of explanatory factors (conditions) hypothesised to affect the outcome variable are identified. Third, these also are dichotomised (as high/low or present/absent, for instance). The fourth stage entails the construction of a so-called 'truth table', which displays the list of all possible combinations of conditions (with 0 or 1 values) and a particular outcome (with 0 or 1 value) for each observed case. In the fifth step, these combinations are systematically compared with each other ('long formulas') and logically simplified ('minimal formulas').

Alternative explanations of the degree of online risk in the EU Kids Online countries

Our aim is to explore the extent to which the various coping strategies employed by parents work in regulating children's online behaviour. To start with, we defined the phenomenon under study (that is, the outcome variable) as 'the degree of online risk among children' (represented as 'degree of online risk' in Table 14.1). In order to assess the degree of online risk perceived and experienced by children all over Europe, we relied on the overall classification of the EU Kids Online countries with regard to online risk perception as developed by Hasebrink et al (2009)[1]. Countries were divided into 'non-high degree of online risk countries' (Cyprus, Italy, France, Germany, Greece, Portugal, Spain, Austria, Ireland, Belgium, Denmark and Sweden) and 'countries with high degree of online risk' (Bulgaria, Czech Republic, Poland, Slovenia, Estonia, the Netherlands, Norway and the UK). We assigned a value of 1 to those countries classified as high online risk countries, and 0 to those classified as non-high degree of online risk countries. As the aim of our model is to explain what combinations of specific conditions concerned with parental mediation affect the degree of online risk, we used the following conditions, based on our previous study (Bauwens et al, 2009: in press), and on the findings from Eurobarometer's parental survey (EC, 2008):

I   *Educational policy (edu_pol):* this accounts for media education in schools (including information and communication technology [ICT] learning; other initiatives regarding ICT; and media education). If at least one of these three is affirmative, the condition value is 1, otherwise negative, or no data is 0.

II *Online content provision (provision):* this condition aims to capture a significant provision of positive online content for children. Value 1 means that the provision is 'high or between high and medium', while value 0 means the provision is 'medium or low'.

III *Restrictions set by parents (less_restrictions):* this condition measures whether parents set any conditions/restrictions regarding their children's internet use and the online activities allowed (for example giving out personal information, buying online, talking to strangers, etc) (for statistics, see EC, 2008). The lowest percentage of no restrictions set is in Germany (15%), while the highest is in Cyprus and the Czech Republic (both 52%). Based on the distribution of countries within these two values, countries with a percentage of no restrictions higher than 33% were assigned a value of 1 (less restrictions) while those with lower percentages were assigned a value of 0 (more restrictions).

IV *Less frequent talking to a child about internet use (less_talking):* this condition measures whether parents talk to their children about what they are doing online (EC, 2008). The parents that talk to their children the least are mainly in the Czech Republic (53%), whereas the UK has the smallest percentage of parents not frequently talking to their children (only 13%). Based on the distribution of countries within these two values, countries with a percentage higher than 33% were assigned a value of 1 (less frequent talking) while those with lower percentages were assigned a value of 0 (more frequent talking).

V *Non-use of monitoring and filtering software by parents (no software):* this condition measures whether parents use any software that either filters (that is, blocks certain websites) or monitors (that is, records internet activity) their children's internet use (EC, 2008). The lowest percentage of parents that do not use this software is in the UK (13%), while the highest is in Portugal (58%). Based on the distribution of countries within these two values, countries with a percentage of no software higher than 35% were assigned a value of 1 (more parents not using any software) while those with lower percentages were assigned a value of 0 (fewer parents not using any software).

VI *General risk sensitivity (GRS) score:* this score has been computed as a maximum likelihood score based on perceived likelihood of becoming a victim of crime; of terrorism; getting a serious illness, or health damage from food consumed or other source; or getting seriously injured in a car accident (Hohl and Gaskell, 2008). High values indicate high-risk sensitivity. The scores above 0.00 are assigned a value of 1 (higher risk sensitivity) and those below are assigned a value of 0 (lower risk sensitivity).

QCA analysis of online risk

In Table 14.1, the values for each condition (in columns) and for each country (in rows) are presented in the raw data table combined with the truth table. The outcome variable is displayed in the last column. The data vary sufficiently across conditions (each condition is sufficiently different from the other ones), and each condition displays sufficient variation (as the subset of 0 or 1 values is at least one third). Sufficient variation is also obtained across the cases. For more technical details, see Rihoux and de Meur (2008).

Analysis was performed by TOSMANA (version 1.3.0.0), an analysis software programme designed for small-number analyses. In order to achieve the shortest core combination of conditions out of the complex data set, the non-observed cases (logical cases) need to be included to produce one main minimal formula[2].

The following analysis reveals the combination of conditions that appear to play a role in explaining a high degree of online risk experience of children among these countries. Four distinct country groupings emerged, each accounted for by a particular configuration of conditions that lead them to a high degree of online risk. Note that, in the logical statements that follow, the upper-case letters indicate the presence of the condition and the lower case indicates its absence. Multiplication (*) indicates a specific combination of conditions

Table 14.1: Raw data and truth table for QCA

Country	Educational policy	Online content provision	No software used by parents (%)	GRS	Less frequent talking to child (%)	Parental restrictions (%)	Degree of online risk
Austria	1	1	33 (1)	−0.44 (0)	26 (0)	23 (0)	0
Belgium	1	1	32 (0)	0.13 (1)	34 (1)	24 (0)	0
Cyprus	1	0	44 (1)	−0.03 (0)	21 (0)	52 (1)	0
Czech Republic	1	0	48 (1)	0.02 (1)	53 (1)	52 (1)	1
Denmark	1	1	55 (1)	−0.08 (0)	38 (1)	22 (0)	0
Estonia	1	0	52 (1)	−0.12 (0)	50 (1)	48 (1)	1
France	1	0	25 (0)	0.27 (1)	38 (1)	30 (0)	0
Germany	1	0	17 (0)	−0.3 (0)	15 (0)	15 (0)	0
Greece	1	0	31 (0)	0.3 (1)	20 (0)	35 (1)	0
Ireland	1	1	19 (0)	−0.17 (0)	16 (0)	22 (0)	0
Italy	1	0	39 (1)	0.32 (1)	23 (0)	29 (0)	0
The Netherlands	0	1	42 (1)	−0.12 (0)	37 (1)	23 (0)	1
Poland	0	0	34 (1)	0.14 (1)	28 (0)	22 (0)	1
Portugal	1	0	58 (1)	−0.03 (0)	20 (0)	35 (1)	0
Slovenia	1	0	45 (1)	0.03 (1)	25 (0)	47 (1)	1
Spain	1	0	39 (1)	−0.18 (0)	15 (0)	16 (0)	0
Sweden	0	0	34 (1)	−0.19 (0)	39 (1)	20 (0)	0
UK	1	1	13 (0)	0.02 (1)	13 (0)	21 (0)	1

Note: This table displays percentages and dichotomised values (with 0 or 1 values).

(logical operator 'AND') while a plus sign (+) indicates the alternative combinations of conditions (logical operator 'OR'):

The first configuration, significant for **the Netherlands** (edu_pol ★ NO SOFTWARE) yields lower education efforts about appropriate ICT use among children combined with more parents not using software to monitor or filter their children's use. Hence, these two factors combined explain the high degree of online risk in this country[3].

The next configuration is significant for the **Czech Republic** and **Estonia** (LESS_TALKING ★ LESS_RESTRICTIONS). In these two countries, parents account extensively for the high degree of online risk found, as parental restrictions on children's internet use are not sufficient; discussion with children on what they do online is also lacking.

The greater online risk in **Slovenia (**GRS ★ LESS_RESTRICTIONS ★ NO SOFTWARE) is explained by a higher general risk sensitivity, combined with weak parental mediation (less restrictions) and with more parents not using any software.

Poland and the **UK** (GRS ★ less_talking ★ less_restrictions ★ no software) are countries with higher general risk sensitivity and a relatively high children's internet use ranging between 89% and 91%. The great number of children online along with, possibly, more skilled internet use, brings about additional challenges, even more so in combination with high risk sensitivity, despite strong parental mediation.

The next analysis, below, examines instead the combination of conditions that appear to play a role in explaining a low or average degree of online risk experience of children in certain countries. Again, we see countries as configurations of conditions that lead them to a low degree of online risk, and here too, four distinct country groupings emerged, each accounted for by a particular configuration of conditions that lead them to a low/average degree of online risk.

Let us now have a look at the countries with medium and low levels (non-high) of online risk. To make our interpretation easier and more parsimonious, let us have a look at the following solution[4]:

In **Austria, Ireland**, **Cyprus, Portugal, Germany** and **Spain** (grs ★ less_talking), the low level of online risk appears to be the result of general lower risk sensitivity combined with more efficient parental mediation in the form of talking to the children about their internet use.

In **Belgium**, **France** and **Sweden** (LESS_TALKING ★ no software), it seems that although fewer parents talk to children about their internet use, parents are using protective software, and this accounts for the lower degree of online risk.

Greece (LESS_RESTRICTIONS ★ no software) is a country in which parents put relatively few restrictions on children's internet usage. However, there are more parents who use protective software that seems to work towards securing a lower degree of online risk.

In **Denmark** and **Italy** (EDU_POL ★ less_restrictions ★ NO SOFTWARE), a strong educational policy and more parental restrictions on how children can use the internet at home is found to contribute to a lower degree of online risk, despite the fact that there are more parents not using protective software. In these two countries, soft strategies like talking are more popular than the use of software to regulate children's online use.

Conclusion

This chapter probed the impact of different strategies of parental mediation (talking, setting rules and restrictions, using software) across 18 different countries. The results of our QCA analysis for both the high and non-high-risk countries confirm, first of all, the significance of parental mediation. In countries where parental mediation strategies are weak or absent, children encounter high-risk experiences on the internet.

As to the question of which strategies work best, this is more difficult to answer. Our results show significant gradation in parental strategies used in high and non-high-risk countries, and the results of these different strategies are difficult to predict. Similar parental mediation strategies do not seem to work in the same way across different countries. In some countries, inter-personal mediation strategies – such as parents talking to their children and setting restrictions – have a greater effect. In other countries, the use of filtering software appears to be the strategy that may prevent children from being exposed to high online risk.

Country-specific and cultural differences thus become paramount. This means that there is no easy one-fits-all solution to parental mediation regarding children's online risks. Instead active mediation (that is, talking to children about online risk and content or setting rules) may be the most effective strategy in some countries, whereas in different cultural contexts, filtering software may be more effective.

Notes

[1] For a detailed operationalisation of the outcome variable, see Bauwens et al (2009: in press).

[2] In the analysis, two minimal formulas were obtained to explain the high degree of online risk, but after close scrutiny, the one displayed was judged to fit the data better.

[3] In our first model (see Bauwens et al, 2009: in press), the weak educational policy was hidden behind other factors.

[4] Again, the software produced three different solutions of possible combinations of conditions and we decided to explain each case based on our knowledge of the countries.

References

Bauwens, J., Lobe, B., Segers, K. and Tsaliki, L. (2009: in press) 'Looking for trouble: similarities and differences in the factors that shape online risk experiences for children in Europe', *Journal of Children and Media*, special issue.

EC (European Commission) (2008) *Towards a safer use of the internet for children in the EU – A parents' perspective, Analytical report*, Flash Eurobarometer Series # 248, conducted by The Gallup Organisation, Hungary, Luxembourg: EC (http://ec.europa.eu/public_opinion/flash/fl_248_en.pdf).

Hasebrink, U., Livingstone, S., Haddon, L. and Ólafsson, K. (2009) *Comparing children's online opportunities and risks across Europe: Cross-national comparisons for EU Kids Online* (2nd edn), London: London School of Economics and Political Science, EU Kids Online (Deliverable D3.2 for the EC Safer Internet Plus Programme).

Hohl, K. and Gaskell, G. (2008) 'European public perceptions of food risk: cross national and methodological comparisons', *Risk Analysis*, vol 28, no 2: 311-24.

Livingstone, S. (2007) 'Strategies of parental regulation in the media-rich home', *Computers in Human Behavior*, vol 23, no 3: 920-41.

Livingstone, S. and Bober, M. (2006) 'Regulating the internet at home: contrasting the perspectives of children and parents', in D. Buckingham and R. Willett (eds) *Digital generations: Children, young people and new media*, Mahwah, NJ: Lawrence Erlbaum Associates: 93-113

Livingstone, S. and Bovill, M. (2001) *Children and their changing media environment: A comparative European study*, Mahwah, NJ: Lawrence Erlbaum Associates.

Livingstone, S. and Haddon, L. (2008) 'Risky experiences for European children online: charting research strengths and research gaps', *Children & Society*, vol 22, no 4: 314-23.

Livingstone, S. and Helsper, E.J. (2008) 'Parental mediation of children's internet use', *Journal of Broadcasting & Electronic Media*, vol 52, no 4: 581-99.

Mediappro (2006) *The appropriation of new media by youth*, A European research project, Brussels: Chaptal Communication with the Support of the European Commission/Safer Internet Action Plan.

NRI (Networked Readiness Index) (2008) *Global information technology report 2007-2008*, World Economic Forum (www.insead.edu/v1/gitr/wef/main/home.cfm).

Park, C. and Jun, J.-K. (2003) 'A cross-cultural comparison of internet buying behavior. Effects of internet usage, perceived risks, and innovativeness', *International Marketing Review*, vol 20, no 5: 534-53.

Rihoux, B. (2006) 'Qualitative comparative analysis (QCA) and related systematic comparative methods: recent advances and remaining challenges for social science research', *International Sociology*, vol 21, no 5: 679-706.

Rihoux, B. and de Meur, G. (2008) 'Crisp-set qualitative comparative analysis (csQCA)', in B. Rihoux and C.C. Ragin (eds) *Configurational comparative methods: Qualitative comparative analysis (QCA) and related techniques*, Thousand Oaks, CA and London: Sage Publications: 33-67.

SAFT (Safety, Awareness, Facts and Tools) Project (2006) *SAFT 2006 Parent and Children Survey. 2004-2006*, Norwegian Action Plan for Children, Youth and the Internet and the European Commission Safer Internet Action Plan, Norwegian Media Authority.

Valkenburg, P. (2004) *Children's responses to the screen: A media psychological approach*, Marwah, NJ: Lawrence Erlbaum Associates

Section IV
Policy implications

FIFTEEN

Maximising opportunities and minimising risks for children online

Jos de Haan[1]

Protecting or inspiring our children

New and increasingly interactive technologies provide opportunities for children and young people to communicate personal textual and visual information in publicly accessible and searchable online spaces. These new uses not only potentially promote sociability, self-confidence and identity formation, they may also expose children and young people to a variety of risks to their physical and psychological well-being (Hasebrink et al, 2009). In the European Union (EU), several measures have been deployed to promote safer use of the internet by children and young people, often inspired or driven by the Safer Internet Action Plan (1999-2004), Safer Internet Plus Programme (2005-08) or Safer Internet Programme (2009-13). These EU initiatives are evaluated on a regular basis and supported by research into online risks (for example Staksrud, 2005; EC, 2006, 2007, 2008; Deloitte Enterprise Risk Services, 2008). Yet participants at the 2007 Safer Internet Forum still found it necessary to call for reliable facts and figures to inform future work on online safety.

Guided by a conceptual framework including different forms of online risks and opportunities, this chapter makes policy recommendations regarding children's use of the internet. It asks how positive uses of new technologies can be stimulated, what we can learn from existing research on how to prevent children from harm in online environments and how children can learn to cope with negative experiences. Realising that providing opportunities is one possible way to reduce risks, the classification of opportunities and risks builds on a three Cs approach: content, contact and conduct. This classification derives from the three modes of communication afforded by the internet:

- *Content:* one-to-many (child as recipient of mass distributed content)
- *Contact:* adult/child-to-child (child as participant in an interactive situation)
- *Conduct:* peer-to-peer (child as actor in an interaction in which s/he may be the initiator or perpetrator)

Using each mode of communication, children may encounter risks to their development and well-being. On the other hand, they also have access to many online opportunities such as education and learning, identity formation and social connection. With the evidence base of the EU Kids Online project as a guiding resource, and drawing on the conceptual framework developed in Hasebrink et al (2009; see also Chapter Four, this volume), the policy recommendations in this chapter address both maximising opportunities and minimising risks for children online.

Reducing risks and stimulating positive use

How can we stimulate children's positive use of the internet while reducing their exposure to risks? In this section we identify several routes for the protection and stimulation of children in an online world. We consider legislation and children's digital rights, content provision, safety by design, awareness raising, parental mediation, media literacy, education, coping and self-regulatory codes and practices.

Legislation and children's digital rights

A regulatory framework is a key building block of a national/international strategy for addressing the downside of the internet. While a regulatory framework has elements that are the responsibility of particular parties, such as internet service providers (ISPs), its overall maintenance and development is carried out by national governments. The World Economic Forum (2007) indicates that about half of the countries judge that they have adequate regulation on internet issues in general, and most of these countries can be found in the western world.

In order to achieve wider legitimacy and consistency with advances in our understanding of and respect for children's autonomy, culminating in the United Nations (UN) Convention on the Rights of the Child, regulatory frameworks should position these rights as their foundation. In general, digital rights refer to the freedom of individuals to perform actions involving the use of information and communication technologies (ICTs) and are related to the protection and realisation of existing rights, such as the right to privacy or freedom of expression. In order to strengthen the position of children in an information age we need a *digital rights charter for children* based on the UN Convention. Digital rights that encourage creativity and sociability in particular need to be supported. Furthermore, as teenagers value their privacy online and seek to protect it (especially from parents), the *right to privacy* needs to be included in such a charter.

The availability of a regulatory framework seems to be related to the level of general internet diffusion in the countries. Overall, countries with a greater proportion of internet users often also have more legislation regulating activities on the internet. As a consequence, for children in countries with high internet diffusion, online services are a normal part of their media environment and everyday life, and the availability of a regulatory framework is more likely. On the other hand, children in countries with low internet diffusion lack opportunities to use the internet, and their safety online is less likely to be guided by a regulatory framework. Internet regulation can be supported by e-inclusion strategies that improve access for all. Special attention needs to be paid to those who are excluded. It is necessary to recognise the continuing stratification in access to and use of the internet. Low socio-economic status (SES) groups and often also minority ethnic groups face the risk of digital exclusion. Research shows that the more teenagers take up online benefits, the more risks they encounter (Hasebrink et al, 2009). As far as possible children need to be protected against these online risks. However, safety initiatives to reduce risk also tend to reduce opportunities. It is therefore important to balance children's protection against children's rights (to opportunities).

In all countries, guidelines on how to reduce risks are available, although in some countries these struggle to keep up with new risks (often related to Web 2.0 applications). Governments need to pressure content providers to provide more transparency with regards to their commercial interests. For example, advertisements need to be clearly distinguishable from other content. We recommend a code of practice for internet advertising (including a ban on the commercial exploitation of children under the age of 10). Furthermore, commercial parties need to specify to users (especially children) what they do with the information users provide.

Best practice guides need to be provided to reduce risks. These should promote positive uses as well as discouraging potentially harmful ones.

Content provision

The digital rights of children can be supported by providing content that stimulates the intellectual and artistic development of children and by promoting civic information and learning opportunities. Although there is little cross-nationally comparable evidence regarding the incidence and take-up of these various opportunities, in line with the new European Commission (EC) Safer Internet Programme we would like to stress the need for positive content provision. In countries such as Denmark, the Netherlands and the UK, media content for children seems to be rich and broad, whereas other counties lag behind. In most countries, public service broadcasters seem to be the major media content providers for children, followed by some commercial broadcasters (Hasebrink et al, 2009). Increasingly, cultural heritage institutions such as museums, archives and libraries are digitising their collections and making them available to the public at large and to children in particular (de Haan et al, 2006). These digitisation efforts are supported by many different EU initiatives, but mainly depend on the funding capacity of member countries. More and more children use these materials for educational purposes (Duimel and de Haan, 2009). Research suggests that the provision of good online content for children reduces their exposure to risk (Bauwens et al, 2009: in press). A broad discussion is needed on how positive content can be provided and put to use for the benefit of children. To enable provision of high-quality content both governments and industry should support non-profit organisations.

Safety by design

In at least 10 European countries (Belgium, Denmark, Estonia, Germany, Greece, Ireland, Italy, the Netherlands, Slovenia and the UK), ISPs seem to play an active role in safeguarding online safety for children by offering the typical 'safety packages', participating in local projects to raise public awareness, collaborating with Insafe's safety nodes and producing and distributing online safety awareness-raising material for schools. ISPs in other countries appear less active in these respects. The safety packages on offer from ISPs include a wide range of services such as anti-virus and anti-spyware protection, defence against phishing attacks with URL filtering and anti-spam functions, detection of Wi-Fi intrusion, improved personal firewalls to discourage intrusions by hackers and the blocking of viruses targeting loopholes in the network (Hasebrink et al, 2009).

Although the use of safety packages is widespread, the Safer Internet Programme bench study (Deloitte Enterprise Risk Services, 2008) reveals that, notwithstanding recent improvements, the software on the market that attempts to protect children from harmful content leaves much to be desired. Furthermore, it seems hard to get a consensus on what constitutes good protection. Only just over half (59%) of parents declare that they use filtering or monitoring software (EC, 2008). However, there is a need for continued improvements to filtering technology, and a continued need to empower parents and educators to choose and use adequate filtering solutions as appropriate.

Although it is highly plausible that safety information provided by ISPs can raise awareness and reduce risks, few empirical evaluations have been conducted. However, as it is likely that safety considerations built into online spaces (such as report abuse buttons, pre-installed filters, warnings and age verification) can improve safe internet use by children, we suggest it is part of the responsibility of ISPs to implement such features in products and services used by children.

ISPs can also provide technical protection against risks related to personal blogging or to social networking. On Safer Internet Day, 10 February 2009, the EC's Safer Internet Programme presented agreed principles for guidance on social networking signed up to by all of the major industry players (EC, 2009). Following this achievement, careful implementation of practices in line with these principles is important. Furthermore, ISPs should also provide technical protection against cyber-bullying risks, by enforcing their terms and conditions of use and removing persistent abusers from their networks.

Awareness raising

Many risks arise out of ignorance. Insafe is already working to maximise awareness of online risk among parents, teachers and other stakeholders, including children. Given the development of internet use (the advent of new forms of online activity, for example social networking and other Web 2.0 applications) and the rise of new risks attached to these activities, awareness campaigns need to be continuously updated. Some countries report high levels of risk, while the internet use is relatively modest (Hasebrink et al, 2009). These countries in particular, Estonia, Poland and the Czech Republic, require urgent awareness raising.

The use of picture and video sharing, for example through social networking or blogging, gives rise to new awareness issues with regard to *personal information risks*. Awareness-raising materials should contain specific information about the danger that user-published picture and video files can reveal young people's locations and personal details. They should also address risks associated with the fact that such information, once available online, may circulate freely in networks beyond the user's control or knowledge. In particular, awareness-raising materials should focus on both the collection and dissemination of pictures and videos by adults or adolescents with a sexual interest in children, as well as their use in other forms of online abuse such as bullying and stalking. Information should also include the risks associated with producing and uploading image or video-based content that has been requested by a user whose identity the child or young person is unsure of.

Children should be educated about the fact that cyber-bullying can have far-reaching consequences for the victim. Although many victims appeared not to have been traumatised by this cyber-bullying, others felt threatened or harassed (Hasebrink et al, 2009). Children should be made aware that high-risk behaviour on the internet (such as handing passwords to peers, posting personal information online without appropriate privacy controls) increases the risk of being bullied. Because of the anonymous nature of some internet communication services, children believe that they cannot be traced and consequently cannot be punished. Parents and teachers should be made more aware of cyber-bullying, and encouraged to involve themselves with their children's use of the internet and mobile phones as well as enhancing their own knowledge of the internet. Victims should be empowered as to the actions they may or must take in order to protect themselves (for example preservation of evidence).

Parental mediation

The EU Kids Online project showed that parents practise a range of strategies for mediating their children's online activities. For the internet, as for other media, research finds that parents attempt three types of management: imposing rules and restrictions, using technical tools (such as filtering or monitoring) and using social approaches (watching, sharing, talking about the internet with their children) (Livingstone and Helsper, 2008). Parents favour time restrictions, sitting with their children as they go online and discussing internet use. They prefer these social strategies to technical mediation (filtering, monitoring software). Attention is mostly given to 10 to 11 year olds, is lower at younger ages and decreases thereafter (for further discussion, see Chapter Sixteen, this volume).

Although there have been several studies, there is as yet little empirical evidence that any of these mediation strategies is particularly effective in reducing children's exposure to risk or increasing their resilience to cope (Livingstone and Helsper, 2008). However, we know parents are concerned and in varying degrees able to help their children. It appears that they think their children encounter more online risk at home than in school and parents mediate the internet more than they do television, at least in high internet use countries. In low internet use countries (such as Cyprus, Italy, Greece, Portugal, Spain and Bulgaria), parents seem to lack either awareness or skills to mediate the internet use of their children (Hasebrink et al, 2009). In these countries it is necessary to empower parents. Still assuming that the empowerment of parents is indeed effective for the reduction of the online risks of their children, parents should be stimulated to improve their use of all the available mediation strategies.

Parents should be broadly aware of what their children do online, although this should be balanced by the child's right to privacy. For younger children, it is reasonable to expect that their parents will understand the internet sufficiently to guide their use, but this may not hold for their guidance of teenagers' use. Teenagers are often more expert than parents, especially in the use of social networking and games. Parents should know which problems their children might face when using these applications. Safety is widely accepted as a parental responsibility but parental mediation is difficult for policy makers to influence because parents have considerable autonomy when it comes to raising their children. Parental mediation might be stimulated by awareness-raising campaigns or by meetings at schools. Awareness campaigns in European countries should include materials about new risks, and also include commercial risks.

Given the parents' preference for social strategies it seems plausible to encourage dialogue about content and risk areas. Some activities assumed to be risky by adults may actually be interpreted as opportunities by teenagers (the chance to make new friends, to share intimacies, to push adult boundaries and to enjoy risk taking). Awareness-raising initiatives need to realise that these differences in the perceptions of risks exist.

In general, parents of high SES groups are more actively mediating their children's internet use than parents of lower SES groups. It also appears that children from lower-class families are more exposed to risks online (see Chapter Nine, this volume), are more often unable to cope with online risks and more often lack the guidance or control from their parents. Awareness-raising campaigns should explicitly address parents of these 'vulnerable' teenagers who are more likely to be both victims and perpetrators. Notwithstanding the difficulties in reaching low socio-economic groups, policy makers should focus on these groups not only as a part of their e-inclusion strategy, but also to raise awareness of risks in this group.

Media literacy

The evidence shows that among young people internet-related skills increase with age. This is likely to include their abilities to protect themselves from online risks. Teenagers are good in basic skills and manage handling social networking sites easily. But performing more complex tasks such as searching out information for educational purposes and estimating the reliability of this information tends to be more difficult (Duimel and de Haan, 2007). It also seems that in countries with high internet diffusion rates, risk awareness and literacy initiatives gain priority on the policy agenda. Growing interest in media literacy is in line with digital rights for children promoting positive use. In Europe, the UK, Slovenia, the Netherlands, Norway and Austria stand out as being more active in terms of media literacy, while the national reports on Germany and France include few explicit mentions of media literacy-related initiatives; other EU countries seem to have only few initiatives (Hasebrink et al, 2009; see also Chapter Eighteen, this volume).

Media literacy initiatives see children as agents and seek to empower their decisions. Evidence supports those initiatives and suggests they can enhance more complex and analytical skills that support the critical and creative capabilities of children (Buckingham, 2005). Media literacy should also support self-protection against internet risks. Media literacy initiatives for children might best be integrated with school curricula (see below). Media literacy programmes are also necessary for parents and educators, to improve their digital skills and to increase their ability for dialogue with children.

Education

The technical infrastructure of schools has been massively increased in the last few years throughout Europe, although this may not necessarily mean in practice that children are able to use the school's internet facilities frequently (see Eurydice, 2005). Notwithstanding the overall increase, there are differences between countries. Countries leading in the diffusion of internet access in households are also forerunners in digitising their educational infrastructure. This means that Scandinavian countries, the Netherlands and the UK are leading the way. Children's online use at schools is not only influenced by the technical infrastructure but also by the way the internet is integrated into curricula and everyday teaching practices. Teachers are key players in supporting the positive online experiences of children by providing access to high-quality content and in safeguarding children and young people from negative experiences. They play a central role in communicating effective strategies to reduce risks not only to children, but also to parents. We recommend the stimulation of public discourse about risks and the distribution of good practice guides (covering both risks and positive use) among parents (for more information, see Chapter Sixteen, this volume).

Educational programmes in leading countries can be used as an example to other European countries. Online safety materials (cf European Schoolnet) should also include mobile media. Schools should assume responsibility in the case of cyber-bullying, as this new form of bullying is often an extension of classic bullying behaviour. Schools should have specific policies in place to deal with cyber-bullying[2].

Coping

How do children respond once exposed to risk? Their ability to cope with online risk varies across types of risks, cultures, genders and ages. Across Europe there are demographic and national variations. These differences point to a range of factors that shape coping responses, some of which may impede appropriate self-protective actions (Staksrud and Livingstone, 2009). It seems plausible that coping strategies depend on how children perceive the risk. Findings tend to suggest that online risks may be brushed off, or disregarded, by the majority of young people. But what do children do when faced with more serious risks? They are often reluctant to tell an adult about their negative experiences on the internet and would rather tell a friend. Thus children do use strategies to cope with online risks, and results from qualitative research suggest that children feel in control and confident in using these strategies. However, whether these strategies are effective remains unknown (Hasebrink et al, 2009). Awareness-raising campaigns should be continued for all types of risk encountered by children online, but more attention should be given to how children do and should cope when they encounter such risks. We recommend that policy makers at the European and national level develop guidelines for coping strategies that go beyond the advice to 'tell a teacher or parent', which is seldom followed.

Self-regulatory codes and practices

Anglo-Saxon, Northern and Central European countries have a greater tradition of self-regulation than Latin and Southern European countries, in which legislation plays a more important role than self-regulation. Ongoing work in Europe and elsewhere (AOL/NCSA, 2004; FOSI, 2008) includes efforts to ensure that risk and safety considerations are the focus of self-regulatory actions by the industry.

Self-regulation is well established in the world of computer games. The Pan-European Game Information (PEGI) was introduced in 2003 as an age classification system in European countries in order to help parents make deliberate decisions about the acquisition of computer games in shops. The EC has also contributed to the development of PEGI Online (PO), to make online gaming as safe as possible (see www.pegionline.eu). We recommend that the EC should support the wider introduction of PO.

Conclusion

Do we protect our children in the ever more sophisticated online world? Do we empower them to safely use web services? Or do we fail our children? In an online world that is becoming more interactive and also more dangerous, surely our children need protection and guidance. In this chapter a wide variety of suggestions were put forward on how to make the internet a safer place for children. These proposals included many different partners such as the EC, national governments, ISPs, teachers, parents and not least, the children themselves. Turning away from this focus on risks we should also think about the online empowerment of children by increasing their media literacy, by providing positive content and by demonstrating the value of this content. This positive provision of opportunities might be an effective way to avoid online risks. In the coming years stimulating positive use will be a key challenge for policy makers, but this also draws on the responsibility of other groups such as teachers and parents.

Notes

[1] I would like to thank Linda Adrichem, Carmelo Garitaonandia, Simon Grehan, Maialen Garmendia, Sonia Livingstone, Jivka Marinova, Gemma Martinez, Helen McQuillan, José Alberto Simões and Elisabeth Staksrud for their valuable and highly appreciated contribution to this chapter.

[2] See the COST Action programme which aims to share expertise on cyber-bullying in educational settings at www.cost.esf.org/domains_actions/isch/Actions/Cyberbullying.

References

AOL (America Online)/NCSA (National Cyber Security Alliance) (2004) *Online safety study*, AOL/NCSA.

Bauwens, J., Lobe, B., Segers, K. and Tsaliki, L. (2009: in press) 'A shared responsibility: similarities and differences in the factors that shape online risk experiences for children in Europe', *Journal of Children and Media*, vol 3, no 4.

Buckingham, D. (2005) *The media literacy of children and young people*, London: Office of Communications.

Deloitte Enterprise Risk Services (2008) *Safer internet: Protecting our children on the net using content filtering and parental control techniques*, Report prepared for the Safer Internet Plus Programme, European Commission (www.sip-bench.eu/sipbench.php?page=results2008 &lang=en).

de Haan, J., Mast, R., Varekamp, M. and Janssen, S. (2006) *Bezoek onze site; over de digitalisering van het culturele aanbod* [*Visit our site; on the digitisation of cultural content*], The Hague: Netherlands Institute for Social Research/SCP.

Duimel, M. and de Haan, J. (2007) *Nieuwe links in het gezin* [*New links in the family*], The Hague: Netherlands Institute for Social Research/SCP.

Duimel, M. and de Haan, J. (2009) *ICT en Cultuur: het gebruik door tieners* [*ICT and culture: How teenagers use the opportunities*], The Hague: Netherlands Institute for Social Research/SCP.

EC (European Commission) (2006) *Safer internet: Eurobarometer survey on safer internet*, Special Eurobarometer 250, Brussels: EC (http://ec.europa.eu/information_society/activities/sip/docs/eurobarometer/eurobarometer_2005_25_ms.pdf).

EC (2007) 'Safer internet for children – a children's perspective', Qualitative Eurobarometer surveys (http://ec.europa.eu/information_society/activities/sip/surveys/qualitative/index_en.htm).

EC (European Commission) (2008) *Towards a safer use of the internet for children in the EU – A parents' perspective, Analytical report*, Flash Eurobarometer Series # 248, conducted by The Gallup Organisation, Hungary, Luxembourg: EC (http://ec.europa.eu/information_society/activities/sip/docs/eurobarometer/analyticalreport_2008.pdf).

EC (2009) 'Safer social networking principles for the EU' (http://ec.europa.eu/information_society/activities/social_networking/docs/sn_principles.pdf).

Eurydice (2005) *Key data on education in Europe*, Brussels: Eurydice (www.okm.gov.hu/doc/upload/200601/key_data_2005.pdf).

FOSI (Family Online Safety Institute) (2008) *State of online safety report*, Washington, DC: FOSI.

Hasebrink, U., Livingstone, S., Haddon, L. and Ólafsson, K. (2009) *Comparing children's online opportunities and risks across Europe: Cross-national comparisons for EU Kids Online* (2nd edn), London: London School of Economics and Political Science, EU Kids Online (Deliverable D3.2 for the EC Safer Internet Plus Programme).

Livingstone, S. and Helsper, E.J. (2008) 'Parental mediation of children's internet use', *Journal of Broadcasting & Electronic Media*, vol 52, no 4: 581-99.

Staksrud, E. (2005) *SAFT project final report*, Oslo: Norwegian Board of Film Classification.

Staksrud, E. and Livingstone, S. (2009) 'Children and online risk: powerless victims or resourceful participants?', *Information, Communication and Society*, vol 12, no 3: 364-87.

World Economic Forum (2007) *Executive Opinion Survey 2006 2007*, Geneva: World Economic Forum.

SIXTEEN

Parental mediation

*Lucyna Kirwil, Maialen Garmendia, Carmelo Garitaonandia
and Gemma Martínez Fernández*

Theoretical framework

Parental mediation of children's use of the internet involves the regulation of children's internet use by parents in order to maximise benefits and, in particular, to minimise the potential negative impacts of the internet on children (Livingstone, 2007; Livingstone and Helsper, 2008). The notion originates in socialisation theory that refers to the parent–child relationship as a developmental process and envisions the parental mediation of internet use through regulatory strategies that parents introduce to maximise benefits and minimise risks for their children (Kirwil, 2009a). Therefore, parental mediation of children's use of the internet involves various child-rearing strategies and practices guided by values which are important to parents and which children learn within the family. Parental mediation of internet use is influenced by such characteristics as the age, gender, internet literacy, frequency and motivation for internet use of the child and the gender, socio-economic status (SES), education, internet use and skills, awareness of online risks and theories of child development of the parents, together with the importance they give to values threatened by internet use and their attitudes towards the internet (Padilla-Walker and Thompson, 2005; Eastin et al, 2006a; Livingstone and Helsper, 2008). Moreover, there seems to be a link with child-rearing values found within a culture (Kirwil, 2009a).

The most useful theoretical framework describes parental strategies for mediating children's internet use by employing a two-dimensional approach: 'system-based' and 'user-based' parental mediation, that is, technical solutions and parental guidance for children. Other frameworks describe a 'protective' versus 'promoting' parental attitude to children's upbringing, and differentiate between general strategies of social mediation, restrictive mediation and instructive mediation. Types of parental mediation are similar to general parental styles in family socialisation, dimensions of authoritarian, authoritative, permissive and neglectful styles (Eastin et al, 2006a; Lwin et al, 2008).

Technical solutions consist of software installed on the computers used by children to monitor the way they use the internet, that is, what kinds of activities they undertake online, what websites they visit and with whom they communicate. Usually 'monitoring' means checking the computer used by the child and blocking inappropriate websites or communication forums and/or talking to the child about the unsuitability and potential negative consequences of these websites and communication forms. While the latter is a form of parental guidance ('instructive mediation') that children can understand and accept, the former could be seen as restrictive control and intruding on their privacy.

'Restrictive mediation' refers to the regulation of children's media use by rule making, while 'instructive mediation' means parents' active efforts to interpret and translate media content and messages to children (Barkin et al, 2006; Eastin et al, 2006a, 2006b; Livingstone and Helsper, 2008; Lwin et al, 2008). In rule making, parents prohibit or set limits for exposure to certain contents (typically violent or sexual) or to online interaction with certain users or internet communities (Livingstone and Helsper, 2008). We may conclude that to mediate their children's use of the internet, parents use three general strategies:

- *Social approach:* watching, talking and trying to share their children's activities online
- *Making rules about and setting restrictions on* children's online activity
- *Technical solutions* involving filtering and monitoring children's online activities

Parents' strategies for mediating their children's use of the internet

Findings on parental mediation suggest that parents favour social mediation of their children's internet use over systems-based regulation that includes the installation of protective software (Barkin et al, 2006; Eastin et al, 2006a, 2006b; Livingstone and Helsper, 2008; Lwin et al, 2008). As the Eurobarometer 2005 survey (EC, 2005) shows, parents with children aged 6-17 that use the internet at home prefer *co-use* to *rule making* and *technical restrictions* (65%, 49% and 29% respectively) (Kirwil, 2009b). Social mediation is favoured because it allows parents more insight into and more control over young internet users, if the parents have enough internet skills themselves. If not, they are better able to learn the real nature of the internet by observing their children surfing online. Parents also favour restrictive rules (56% restrict time online, 52% restrict some websites) to non-restrictive instructive rules (31%), because they make it easier to exert direct control over children's activities.

Eurobarometer 2008 (EC, 2008) provides us with more insight into strategies favoured by European parents when mediating their children's use of the internet. We will endeavour to establish if there are any particular characteristics of either the parents or of the children themselves which may influence the internet mediating patterns of the parents.

Social mediation

Here we identify if there is any relationship between mediation strategies and parents' characteristics such as parental role, level of education and their frequency of use of the internet. We have taken into consideration whether a question has been answered by the mother or the father and also the level of education of both. In order for Table 16.1 to be clear and concise, only the percentage of parents who 'usually' (always or very frequently) do the mentioned activities have been included.

The most frequent strategy is that of asking/talking to the child about his/her online activities, while staying nearby is in second place, and sitting with the child when he/she goes online is in third place. In terms of parental roles, mothers seem to play a far more active role than fathers, their percentages being above average for all types of activities, particularly those of asking/talking to the child and staying nearby. Both activities seem to be closely related to the mother's traditional role at home.

Although the level of education of the parents[1] does not provide a clear pattern in relation to social mediation strategies, parents with the highest level of education seem to be slightly less *active* than those with the lowest level of education.

Even though the frequency of parents' use of the internet is not dependent on their internet literacy in all cases, the two characteristics are clearly closely related. Parents who make daily use of the internet employ mediating activities which are very similar to those of the average. Principally, they ask their children questions or talk to them and stay nearby, whereas weekly users tend to stay nearby more and also spend more time sitting with the child. Parents who only use the internet monthly tend to watch their children more closely, either by

Table 16.1: Social mediation strategies, parental role, level of education and parents' frequency of internet use (%)

Strategies	Average	Parental role		Education			Parental frequency of internet use			
		Father	Mother	Primary	Secondary	Higher	Everyday	Once a week or more	Once a month or more	Less than once a month or never
Ask/talking about what he/she does/did	75	67	78	74	75	70	75	76	69	66
Staying nearby	61	55	63	59	61	62	60	67	64	50
Sitting with child	37	35	37	39	37	36	36	40	42	34
Total EU 27(N)	8,631	2,591	6,039	472	4,823	3,112	5,526	1,880	412	809

Source: Data for all tables in this chapter: Eurobarometer 2008. Tables by authors.

staying nearby or by actually sitting with them. The groups whose internet use is less frequent may have a lower level of education, which is perhaps related to a greater concern about controlling their children's online activities.

We have analysed the different patterns shown by parents in relation to their children's characteristics and will see whether boys' and girls' activities are mediated in the same way and whether there are differences in mediation depending on the child's age. As Table 16.2 shows, regarding parental *social* mediation patterns, parents stated that they tend to sit with, ask questions and talk to boys slightly more than they do with girls. Parents whose children are aged between 6 and 10 tend to sit with, talk to and ask their children about what they are doing on the internet more than with older children.

Table 16.2: Social mediation strategies, child's gender and age (%)

Strategies (usually used)	Average	Gender		Age		
		Boy	Girl	6-10	11-14	15-17
Ask/talking about what he/she does/did	75	75	74	86	80	59
Staying nearby	61	62	60	82	64	38
Sitting with child	37	38	36	60	36	16
Total EU 27(N)	8,631	4,462	4,168	2,602	3,227	2,801

Online activity restrictions

We identify here those activities which parents do not allow their children to participate in to determine whether there is any relation between these restrictions and the parents' characteristics and the child's characteristics (see Tables 16.3 and 16.4).

Parents do not generally seem to place many restrictions on their children's online activities, nor have they developed extensive rules with which to regulate their children's interactions online. In fact, there seems to be a lack of coherence among the restrictions. For instance, there appears to be some kind of *moral panic* related to children creating a profile for themselves on the internet, whereas very few parents have set down any rules to control their children giving out personal information online or talking to strangers whom they have met online, although the latter could involve similar risks to those of the former. Although some of the main restrictions which parents place on their children's use of the internet are related to cost (purchasing online and downloading games, films and music), they also limit the time

Table 16.3: Online activity restrictions, parental role and parents' frequency of internet use (%)

Restrictions	Average	Parental role		Frequency of parental internet use			
		Father	Mother	Everyday	Once a week or more	Once a month or more	Less than once a month or never
Create a profile	47	45	47	45	45	47	33
Buy online	19	16	20	19	18	12	15
Download games	19	17	19	19	17	11	13
Spend a lot of time	15	12	17	14	15	16	13
Use instant messaging tools	15	12	16	15	16	12	8
Download films	13	12	13	13	14	11	8
Download music	12	12	12	12	11	10	9
Give personal info	11	11	11	12	11	5	10
Access certain websites	11	12	11	11	11	8	8
Use chat rooms	9	8	10	9	9	12	5
Use e-mail	8	7	8	8	9	8	4
Talk to people they don't know offline	7	5	8	6	8	6	5
Total EU 27(N)	9,627	2,828	6,798	5,526	1,880	412	809

Table 16.4: Online activity restrictions, child's gender and age (%)

Restrictions	Average	Gender		Age (years)		
		Boy	Girl	6–10	11–14	15–17
No restrictions	27	25	29	24	22	36
Create a profile in an online community	47	49	44	49	49	42
Download/play games	19	19	18	19	20	17
Buy online	19	19	19	17	21	18
Spend a lot of time online	15	15	16	15	18	13
Use instant messaging tools	15	15	16	15	14	9
Download/play films	13	13	12	14	13	9
Give out personal information	11	13	10	14	11	9
Download/play music	12	12	12	11	10	7
Access certain websites	11	11	11	10	8	5
Use chat rooms	9	9	9	11	6	3
Use email	8	8	8	19	17	9
Talk to people they do not know in real life	7	7	7	14	11	8
Total EU 27(N)	8,631	5,013	4,613	2,959	3,627	3,042

they spend connected, perhaps in order to encourage their children to do their homework. As far as the frequency of use of the internet by parents is concerned, no clear pattern seems to emerge in relation to restricting their children's activities. Daily users tend to be slightly less restrictive than average, weekly and monthly users, who tend to be more restrictive. Those, who very seldom or never use the internet, are also less restrictive.

Regarding the rules or restrictions imposed by parents, two rules out of 12 are more frequently imposed on girls and four out of 12 are more frequently imposed on boys. Therefore, these data show that parents tend to be more restrictive with boys than girls.

Although parents set fewer restrictions or rules for their children as the children become older, there is one age group in which this pattern is not followed – 11 to 14 year olds have more restrictions placed on them than the younger group. Some studies have shown that children in this age group are most at risk as they are neither low users like the young children, nor are they wiser/more experienced users as are the older teens (Livingstone and Bober, 2004). This age group seems to take online risks, play games and experiment with identity more.

Technical restrictions

More than half of the parents surveyed said they had adopted a filtering tool in order to prevent their children visiting certain websites, whereas 42% use a monitoring tool in order to be able to see all the websites their children visit (see Table 16.5). Still, more than one out of three says they have not installed any software for tracking or controlling their children's access.

As far as parental roles are concerned, mothers' involvement is again above average. When considering the level of education of the parents, a clear pattern emerges. The higher the level of education, the more frequently they tend to install filtering software, whereas the lower the level of education the more frequently monitoring devices are adopted.

Table 16.5: Technical restrictions use and reasons for not using them, parental role and level of education (%)

	Average	Parental role		Education		
		Father	Mother	Primary	Secondary	Higher
Software used						
Filtering	55	54	55	50	57	53
Monitoring	42	40	42	45	43	39
None	34	36	34	37	32	37
Total EU 27(N)	8,631	2,591	6,039	472	4,823	3,112
Reason for not using						
No need, I trust my child	67	69	66	58	68	67
Don't know how to access	15	13	16	20	16	13
Don't believe in their efficiency	3	3	2	4	2	3
Total EU 27(N)	2,654	886	1,767	151	1,366	1,051

More than two thirds of parents state that technical restrictions are unnecessary because they trust their children. There are also some parents (15%) who state they do not know how to access this software. We can presume they would be willing to install these technological devices. Only a small minority say they do not trust their efficiency. There is a slight difference in the percentages between fathers and mothers – once again, more mothers than fathers do not know how to access this software and slightly more distrust their children.

As regards the parents' level of education, the higher the level of education, the fewer people who say they do not know how to use software to regulate or monitor, and those who have only finished their primary education seem to trust their children less. However, the level of trust which parents generally have in respect of their children's online activities is remarkable. Moreover, qualitative research carried out in Spain showed that children felt very pleased when their parents considered them responsible enough to look after themselves when surfing on the internet (Garitaonandia and Garmendia, 2007).

Table 16.6: Technical restrictions use, child's gender and age

Software		Gender		Age (years)		
	Average	Boys	Girls	6-10	11-14	15-17
Filtering	55	55	54	59	57	47
Monitoring	42	41	42	45	45	34
None	34	35	34	30	31	43
Total EU 27(N)	8,631	4,462	4,168	2,602	3,227	2,801

As far as children's characteristics are concerned, parents tend to install filtering software more often on boys' than on girls' computers. However, girls tend to have more monitoring software installed on their computers than boys. In terms of age, a clear pattern seems to emerge – the older the children the fewer technical restrictions parents place on them.

Parental mediation of children online and the socialisation culture

Analysis of parental goals gathered in the European Values Survey 2000 (see Halman, 2001) by Kirwil (2009a) reveals that European countries represent several socialisation cultures defined by different sets of values that children have to learn within a family. The sets of values differ depending on the importance given to individualistic or collectivistic orientation in child rearing. An individualistic orientation predominates in Nordic, north-western and historically Catholic countries, while a collectivistic orientation predominates in post-Communist countries (see Figure 16.1).

Parents engage more in mediating children's behaviour online, favour social mediation and use multiple strategies in the countries with a stronger individualistic orientation in child rearing in comparison

Figure 16.1: Patterns of parental mediation of children online in countries with various child-rearing orientations

Individualistic orientation in child-rearing in: AT, BE, DK, DE, EL, ES, FR, IT, NL, SE, SI and UK	Collectivistic orientation in child-rearing in: BG, CZ, EE, PL, and PT

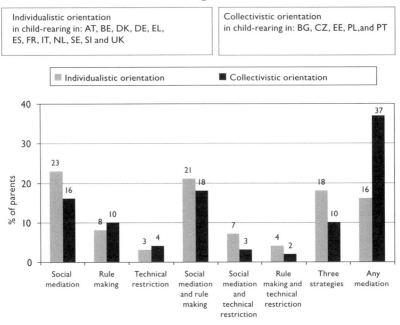

Source: EVS (2000, see Halman, 2001); EC (2005); Kirwil (2009b)

with those countries with a stronger collectivistic orientation. This mediation gives more opportunity for communication with children and for instructive mediation.

What have we learned about the effectiveness of parental mediation for internet use?

It is important for researchers, policy makers and parents themselves to learn whether any type of parental mediation protects children and, if so, what strategies are effective. The Eurobarometer 2005 survey (EC, 2005) presented a different picture for the European sample overall, namely that more parental mediation is related to more (not less) online risks for children. However, analyses conducted separately for different country groupings revealed different 'parental mediation–online risk' relationships across Europe (Kirwil, 2009a). We therefore analyse the effectiveness of parental mediation by asking whether parental mediation is effective in different types of countries (a theme that is also addressed in Chapter Fifteen, this volume). A specific parental mediation strategy for children online is considered effective when the *proportion of children that encounter online risks is significantly lower in the countries in which this strategy is widespread in comparison with the countries where it is not.* By adopting this approach we have found that, in general, the more social mediation, restrictive mediation and technical restrictions in use in a country, the less children from that country experienced content risk in their own home. Figure 16.2 illustrates how content risk experienced by children from 18 EU countries is related to website restrictions used for mediation by their parents.

Figure 16.2: In the countries where more parents restrict access to websites, fewer children experience content online risk at home

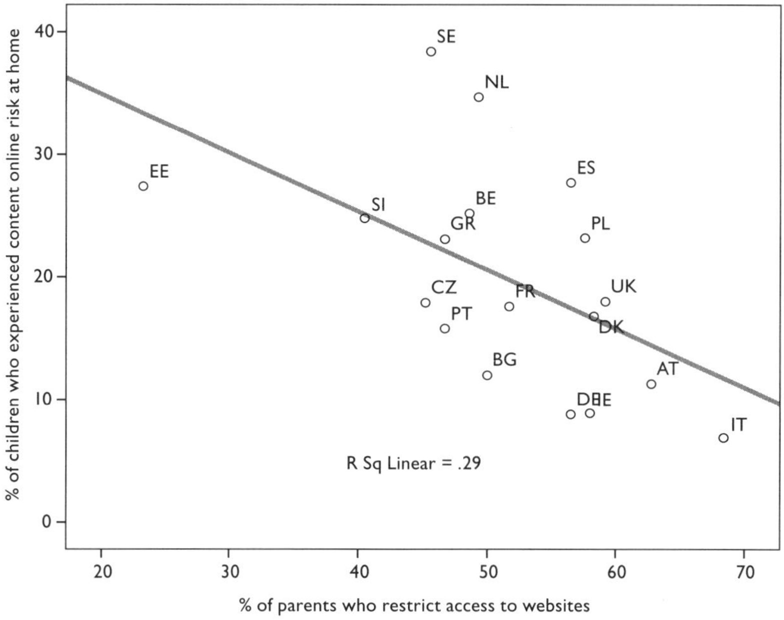

Source: EC (2005); Kirwil (2009a)

The analysis conducted for 18 EU countries shows that restrictions placed on visiting inappropriate websites may reduce the probability of children's exposure to online content risk at home[2]. Statistical analyses also suggested that children experience less online content risk to the extent that parents ask their children to report disturbing experiences encountered online[3].

Similar analyses for social mediation, for making any rule about internet use and for technical restrictions indicated that each of these strategies was associated with a lower number of children at risk from online content[4], although the effectiveness of several strategies seems to depend on the socialisation culture of the country. For instance, a closer look at the effectiveness of time restriction in various European countries shows that the significance of the strategy depends on the different socialisation cultures of the countries (see Figure 16.3).

Figure 16.3: Curvilinear relationship between parental mediation of children online with time restriction and children's experience of content online risk at home

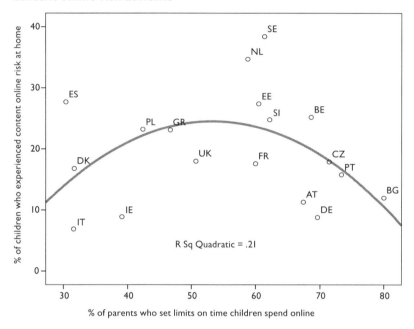

Source: EC (2005); Kirwil (2009a)

In countries such as Denmark, the Netherlands, Sweden, Belgium, Ireland and the UK (Northern Europe, mostly individualistic in child rearing), the more parents limit the time spent by children online, the more children experience online risk. In other countries such as Austria, France, Germany, Portugal, Slovenia and Spain (Catholic Europe, moderately individualistic in child rearing) and Bulgaria, the Czech Republic, Estonia and Poland (post-Communist Europe, mostly collectivistic in child-rearing), the more parents use time restrictions, the less children encountered online risk[5]. Thus, the role and the effectiveness of time restrictions to protect children from online risks appears to vary according to the country's individualistic–collectivistic orientation towards child rearing and its historical religious roots.

Conclusion

How parental mediation is related to children's experience of online risk has been a question of the greatest importance to increase internet security for children and, although there is a growing number of studies on children's internet use and parental mediation of children online, little empirical evidence is available to point to which parental strategies are effective in protecting children (Livingstone, 2007; Livingstone and Helsper, 2008). The internet enables communication and peer-to-peer interaction. It appears that parental regulation of internet use does not have comparable effects to similar regulation of television or video game playing. Restrictive parental mediation may reduce both the risks and benefits for children. Earlier studies have shown that the only way time restriction is effective in protecting children against online risk is by reducing the opportunity for this risk (SAFT, 2003; Lee and Chae, 2007). Our results confirm some previous findings about parental mediation use and provide new data which show that the effectiveness of the parental mediation of children's online activity depends on the socialisation culture in which this mediation takes place.

In summary, we found the following. First, when mediating their children's internet use parents favour social mediation over technical restrictions and restrictive rule making. Using social mediation, they prefer talking about the child's online activities subsequently to staying nearby or sitting next to the child while they are online. If they use technical restrictions, filtering software is more popular than monitoring software. When making rules on internet use, they favour restrictive rules to instructive rules.

Second, at least a quarter of parents in 2008 (one third in 2005) did not mediate their children's internet use at all. More educated parents do not use technical software because they trust their children, while less educated parents may not know how to use such software. Rules governing children's online activities are more guided by moral panics and economic reasons than by the awareness of which online activities bring which risks.

Third, parents prefer multiple mediation strategies to single ones. Fourth, parental mediation depends on parents' characteristics, that is, parental role, education and internet use:

- mothers engage in all types of parental mediation more than fathers;
- parents with higher education, as compared to parents with only secondary or primary education, use less social mediation (in general)

and monitoring software, while they more frequently stay nearby while their children are online;

- the more parents use the internet, the more they use social mediation and restrict online activities, with the exception of parents, who are daily users

Fifth, parental mediation depends on children's characteristics, with age being more important than gender:

- as children get older their parents reduce their social mediation (it becomes more non-active), technical mediation and restrictions on interactions online. More parents of early adolescents restrict their children's time and spending online (purchasing, downloading and playing games) as compared to parents of younger children and older teenagers;
- parents are more concerned about their children creating a profile in an online community than about them giving out personal information and contacting people met online.

Parents from individualistically oriented child-rearing cultures engage more in all types of mediation of their children's use of the internet, while more parents from cultures of a collectivistic orientation either do not use any mediation or favour single restrictive rules or technical restrictions.

Sixth, we have demonstrated that some parental mediation strategies may be effective in protecting children from online risks:

- selected website restriction may reduce children's experience of online risk;
- parents encouraging their children to report negative online experiences to them may reduce online risk;
- time restrictions on online use may reduce or increase risks depending on the child-rearing culture in question. In collectivistic child-rearing cultures it may reduce online risk, but in more individualistic cultures it may increase this risk.

Finally, it appears that any restrictive rules about children's internet use and technical restrictions are associated with lower online risk. However, the evidence in support of these rules being effective is not as strong as for website and time restrictions and non-restrictive rules.

As parental mediation itself is mediated by many contextual factors, we recommend that parents become more aware of the following:

- parental mediation might increase children's online safety, but this is not necessarily the case;
- multiple strategy parental mediation might be more effective than single strategy mediation;
- parental mediation should be flexible and depend on the child's level of development. New studies are required to be able to give recommendations specifically to individualistic and collectivistic child-rearing cultures;
- the effects of parental restrictions that are either too strong or too weak may themselves lead to certain risks.

It is the task of policy makers to promote parental mediation of internet use, particularly in countries with a collectivistic culture in which parental mediation tends to be lower. Policy makers should be aware that universal rules for children's security online are difficult to find, and parents should be guided in their strategies according to the socialisation of their culture, because the same strategy may function as either a protective factor against risk or one that increases it.

Notes

[1] This was operationalised by asking those surveyed to state the age at which they finished their full-time education. So, we assumed that those who were 15 at the time of finishing their education had only received primary education; those who were between 16 and 20 had also finished their secondary education; and those aged 20 at the time of ending their education were classified as having received higher education. There was another category called 'still in education', but as only 89 out of the 8,638 people polled chose this, for reasons of clarity we chose not to include it.

[2] The extent to which parents restrict access to websites explains 29% of between-country differences in children's exposure to content online risk (correlation coefficient: $r=-0.54$, $p=0.01$ one-tailed).

[3] How many parents in the country set the non-restrictive rule that a child voluntarily reports to parents about an uncomfortable experience encountered online explains 21% of differences between the countries in the amount of children's exposure to content online risk experienced at home ($r=-0.46$, $p=0.03$ one-tailed).

[4] The respective numbers for social mediation, making any rule on internet use and technical restrictions were 26%, 20% and 5% . Although correlations were non-significant the total between-country variance explained by per

cent summed up for all parental mediation strategies should be significant, because most parents tend to use multiple strategies (see Figure 16.1).

[5] This curvilinear relationship tells us that 21% of between-country differences in children's content online risk experienced at home is explained by between-country differences in how many parents set limits on the time spent by children online.

References

Barkin, S., Ip, E., Richardson, I., Klinepeter, S. and Krcmar, M. (2006) 'Parental mediation styles for children aged 2-11 years', *Archives of Pediatrics and Adolescent Medicine*, vol 160, no 4: 395-401.

Eastin, M.S., Greenberg, B.S. and Hofschire, L. (2006a) 'Parenting the internet', *Journal of Communication*, vol 56, no 3: 486-504.

Eastin, M.S., Yang, M.-S. and Nathanson, A.I. (2006b) 'Children of the net: an empirical exploration into the evaluation of internet content', *Journal of Broadcasting & Electronic Media*, vol 50, no 2: 211-30.

EC (European Commission) (2005) *Safer internet*, Eurobarometer 64.4, Special no 250, December.

EC (2008) 'Basic bilingual questionnaire: TNS opinion and social', Eurobarometer 69.2: Safer internet, March-May.

Garitaonandia, C. and Garmendia, M. (2007) *How young people use the internet: Habits, risks and parental control*, Bilbao: University of the Basque Country and EU Kids Online (www.lse.ac.uk/collections/EUKidsOnline/).

Halman, L. (2001). *The European Values Study: A Third Wave. Source book of the 1999/2000 European Values Study surveys*. EVS WORC Tilburg University WORC.

Kirwil, L. (2009a) 'Parental mediation of children's internet use in different European countries', *Journal of Children and Media*, Typescript submitted for publication.

Kirwil, L. (2009b) 'The role of individualistic-collectivistic values in childrearing culture for European parents' mediation of Internet', Typescript prepared for publication.

Lee, S.-J. and Chae, Y.-G. (2007) 'Children's internet use in a family context: influence on family relationships and parental mediation', *Cyber Psychology & Behavior*, vol 10, no 5: 640-4.

Livingstone, S. (2007) 'Strategies of parental regulation in the media-rich home', *Computers in Human Behavior*, vol 23, no 3: 920-41.

Livingstone, S. and Bober, M. (2004) *UK children go online: Surveying the experiences of young people and their parents*, London: London School of Economics and Political Science.

Livingstone, S. and Helsper, E.J. (2008) 'Parental mediation of children's internet use', *Journal of Broadcasting & Electronic Media*, vol 52, no 4: 581-99.

Lwin, M.O., Stanaland, A.J.S. and Miyazaki, A.D. (2008) 'Protecting children's privacy online: how parental mediation strategies affect website safeguard effectiveness', *Journal of Retailing*, vol 84, no 2: 205-17.

Padilla-Walker, L.M., and Thompson, R.A. (2005) 'Combating conflicting messages of values: a closer look at parental strategies', *Social Development*, vol 14, no 2: 305-23.

SAFT (Safety, Awareness, Facts and Tools) Project (2003) 'Parents know little about children's internet use' (http://web.archive.org/web/20041210145425/http://www.saftonline.org/presse/1537/).

SEVENTEEN

Making use of ICT for learning in European schools

Ingrid Paus-Hasebrink, Andrea Dürager, Christine W. Wijnen and Kadri Ugur

Introduction

Across Europe, the internet is an integral part of the lives of young people. According to the latest Eurobarometer survey on safer internet issues, three quarters of all children between 6 and 17 years in the EU27 had used the internet as of autumn 2008, with even higher figures applying to teenagers (EC, 2008: 5). There are great similarities from one country to another concerning the time spent online.

Young people use the internet mainly as an educational resource, for entertainment, games and fun, searching for information, social networking and sharing experiences with others (Hasebrink et al, 2009). They also use it for their work at school or university (Medienpädagogischer Forschungsverbund Südwest, 2007). Livingstone and Bober (2005) summarise for the UK Children Go Online project that computer access is growing, with 92% having internet access at school. Information and communication technologies (ICTs) offer many opportunities: education, participation and civic engagement, creativity as well as identity and social connection (Hasebrink et al, 2009). As the rise in new technologies leads towards network or knowledge societies, schools have an important role in strengthening children's competencies in dealing with the opportunities and risks associated with ICT.

This chapter focuses on the use of ICT in schools. First, it briefly discusses attitudes towards ICT in schools from a European perspective. Drawing on the European Union (EU) Kids Online data repository, this chapter outlines the state of research on ICT and schools. The next section focuses on the internet at school and for schools across Europe, presenting different research results of European studies on various aspects of the topic 'ICT in schools'. The concluding section starts from a constructivist perspective on learning with ICT in schools and makes proposals about best practice regarding the handling of ICT in schools.

European variation in the implementation of ICT in schools

The way that each new medium (for example books, radio, film) has been treated and integrated into schools in different European countries is strongly related to the difference in the development of the countries' media landscape (for example laws), historical and political developments, school systems and educational goals, cultural differences and concepts of childhood as well as theoretical treatments of media (for example academic or cultural discourses). In some countries such as the UK or Scandinavia, media education in school has a long tradition, while in other countries such as Italy children have primarily been taught to use new media at home (Krotz and Hasebrink, 2001; Wijnen, 2008). Historical media education discourses also influence attitudes towards ICT, the so-called 'new media' of today. Similar emphases – on inoculation and discrimination, as well as on participation and societal progress – can be found every time a 'new medium' enters society. Discussion about risks and opportunities of ICT and the way they should be integrated in school have much in common with the adoption of other media (Wijnen, 2008). The main difference is that today there is much more exchange and cooperation between single countries, and the EU plays an increasing role in setting policies for the integration of ICT in schools. Consequently, European countries now have much more in common in dealing with the challenges of new media.

Generally, the investment of European countries in ICT has grown considerably over the last years, and different attempts at implementation of ICT in schools are observable. Moreover, across Europe it has been recognised that giving access to ICT is not enough; media literacy education is also needed. There has been a significant growth in Europe in the provision of ICT equipment in schools. Data from Eurydice (2005) show that those countries where schools were not as well equipped have invested much more in computers and internet access for schools than those countries that were already up to date; the difference between countries is therefore reducing. But internet access at school still does not mean that young people can use the internet without adult control; in most European countries the internet at school cannot be used without restrictions (Hasebrink et al, 2009). Despite the fact that all European countries stress the importance of internet literacy and media education, developing internet access at school does not always go hand in hand with corresponding investments in educational programmes concerning the use of ICT. It is often not clear how internet literacy is integrated at school, but in most countries it is part of the general curriculum across all subjects. Sometimes these initiatives are strongly driven by the interest of national governments in promoting technical literacy and less concerned about risks and opportunities associated with ICT (Hasebrink et al, 2009).

At this point we provide some examples of how ICT is implemented in European schools. There is considerable national variation across educational curricula. In general, regions, school districts, schools and teachers have significant freedom to decide how the national curricula are implemented. In Finland's national curriculum (OPH, 2004: 14), ICT is handled as a part of the learning environment from the first school years onwards: 'Materials and library services must be available to the students in the way that enables active and independent learning. Learning environments must also support student's development as a member of the information society and give opportunities to use ICT and other media technology...'. By contrast, England has implemented a special subject of ICT, which is mandatory from Key Stage 1 (five year olds). Their national curriculum (National Curriculum, 1999: 36) states that 'pupils should be given opportunities to apply and develop their ICT capability through the use of ICT tools to support their learning in all subjects'. The list of required knowledge, skills and understanding about ICT is rather prescriptive, giving teachers guidelines on what to teach and which themes to discuss with pupils. In Austrian primary and secondary schools (BMUKK, 2008), media education (including ICT-related education) is integrated across the curriculum in all subjects as part of a learning environment that allows independent and individualised learning. In the national curriculum of Estonia (eRT, 2002), ICT is treated as a cross-curricular theme, and the schools are also given freedom to teach ICT separately, alongside the statutory subjects. ICT skills are mentioned in the lists of learning outcomes and competencies, and in almost all of the subject descriptions. Still, as in the English curriculum, ICT is viewed mostly as a technological tool for getting information and developing skills in handling it; consequently, its potential for developing pupils' social skills is underused. Altogether, there is little consistency in the way ICT is integrated in schools.

Research on ICT and schools

The following analysis shows the current state of research in Europe concerning ICT and schools. According to the report on data availability and research gaps in Europe within the project 'EU Kids Online', two statements can be made regarding the topic 'ICT and schools' (Staksrud et al, 2007: 19, 42). First, more research is needed on the role of teachers in various ways (for example their role in class mediating for children's computer use; their competencies and literacy with computers and the internet; or their teaching methods regarding how to improve the awareness and online safety of their pupils). Second, many European countries lack an evidence base regarding online learning.

To obtain an overview of the available studies concerning ICT and schools, relevant studies were filtered within the EU Kids Online data repository (see www.lse.ac.uk/collections/EUKidsOnline/) in terms of their research title and topic, namely 'school' or 'teacher', their target group 'teachers', and school in general. Altogether, 63 studies met these conditions more or less. Most of the relevant studies are from the UK (16) and 15 further European countries have 1–10 relevant projects.

There are several 'main research foci' that could be categorised into five main research fields (see Table 17.1). The analysis shows that the most researched focus is on access and usage of ICT in schools followed by the roles of schools and teachers.

Table 17.1: Main research foci of studies of ICT and schools (multicoded)

Research-category	Examples (number of studies)
Access and usage of ICT in schools	Media-infrastructure of schools / access to Computer; use of computers/internet in school (also in early education); for schoolwork (34)
Tasks for schools and teachers	ICT socialisation; teaching competencies/ literacy/ internet safety; improving awareness for online risks; regulation/mediation (23)
Teachers' awareness of ICT	Training for teachers in terms of ICT literacy; teachers' ICT usage/competencies/skills/ literacy; teachers' awareness of risk; teachers' attitudes towards media use of pupils (14)
Learning with ICT	Online learning; learning with media; learning software; (16)
Educational value	Effects/impact of ICT in schools; e-maturity; literacy (18)

Source: EU Kids Online data repository (Dec. 2008), www.eukidsonline.net

Altogether there is a lack of research into online learning, teaching internet literacy and the assessment of the educational value of ICT in schools.

Using the internet in and for school: a pan-European comparison

On average, European children use the internet more in the home (67%) than in school (57%); moreover, the more they use it at home, the more they also use it at school ($r=0.574$; $p<0.002$) (EC, 2008). But there are differences in children's internet access at school in Europe – countries can be grouped into four categories. In the countries with the least in-school internet access – Lithuania, Greece, Romania, Bulgaria, Italy and Spain – the proportion accessing the internet varies between 25% and 37%. In Estonia, Cyprus, Latvia, Belgium, Slovenia, Ireland, Germany, Portugal, France and Malta, the proportions are between 44% and 56%, and in Poland, Austria, Finland, Slovak Republic, Sweden, Czech Republic, the Netherlands and Hungary, between 61% and 75% access the internet at school. Denmark and the UK are the highest, with 81% and 89% respectively.

Whether children have access to information technology (IT) equipment at home is correlated with whether they have access at school (Eurydice, 2004: 34). Concerning the equipment of European schools, Eurydice (2004) states that in most of the European countries there are no central regulations fixing a maximum number of pupils per computer, and decisions concerning investments in IT equipment are taken at a local level. According to PISA data (Programme for International Student Assessment), in 2000 the average European ration was around 16 pupils aged 15 years per computer compared to 10 in 2003. But there are differences between countries as well as within countries, and countries that have a better pupil to computer ratio have a higher rate of internet access (see Figure 17.1).

Opportunities presented by the internet

In most European countries children use the internet as an educational resource and for school-related purposes alongside other activities such as playing games. European pupils use the internet often for searching out information to do their schoolwork at home. Moreover, Greek teachers observed that students use computers to deepen computer and internet literacy (91%); to prepare homework (78%); to play games (52%); to get in touch with other schools (25%); and to communicate

Figure 17.1: Relation between access to the internet in schools (%) and the number of pupils per computer

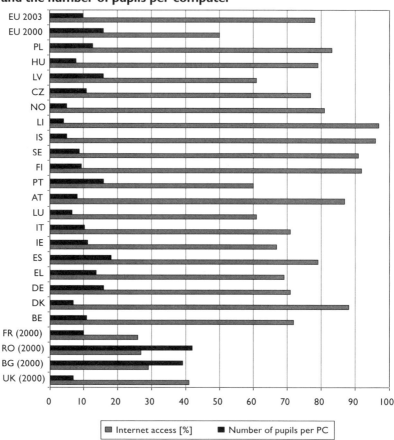

Source: Eurydice (2004)

with other students/teachers (22%) (Tsaliki, 2008). Further, in Italy online learning in school or universities is used by 11% of 6 to 10 year olds, 18% of 11 to 14 year olds, 25% of 15 to 17 year olds and 42% of 18 to 19 year olds (Murru and Mascheroni, 2008).

There are gender-related differences in using the internet for school related work – girls use the internet more often for school purposes than boys (for example in Bulgaria, Norway and Spain). In general, it seems that older children are more likely to use the internet for school-related work than younger ones (for example in Denmark, Iceland and Sweden) (see EU Kids Online, 2008; Hasebrink et al, 2009).

Moreover, the EU Kids Online national reports point out that there are differences in using the internet depending on young people's education and social status: pupils with a higher education and of higher social status use the internet more for school-related information and work while pupils with lower education and of lower social status are more likely to use it for playing games or for downloading music and movies (for example in Spain, Sweden and the Netherlands).

There are several studies that point out the relevance of schools and teachers for the development of internet literacy and awareness of online risks. Data from the Eurobarometer (EC, 2008) show 88% of European parents think that more/better teaching and guidance on internet use in schools would contribute to safer internet use. A Czech study notes that according to children media are the most important source for them to raise their awareness of online risks, followed by being taught about online risks in schools by their teachers (45%) and by their parents (39%). In Estonia among 12 to 18 year olds, 8% of girls and 5% of boys find out about new things to do on the internet from teachers; 19% of Spanish pupils say they have learned how to use the internet from their teachers at school or college compared to 21% who were taught by their parents or another relative (see EU Kids Online, 2008).

One potential benefit of using the internet at schools is that it appears that students have less risk of encountering alarming websites there than at home. Of children who use the internet at home, 12% encountered questionable or risky content compared with 5% of those who used it at school. The Cypriot national report mentions as an advantage of schools that they have controlled access to the internet, providing children with a safer environment for use, and in the French report it is stated that use at school is very restricted, so that pupils cannot surf the web freely, chat or visit blogs and therefore risks encountered at school appear limited (see EU Kids Online, 2008).

Best practice proposals for dealing with ICT in schools

To empower students to learn with ICT in an effective way it seems reasonable to reflect on the constructivist paradigm. In contrast to former pedagogical assumptions, especially behaviourist approaches, learners are now understood as agents, selecting and processing information on their own, having only to be encouraged to ask questions and to discover new information. The constructivist approach can serve as a basis for pedagogical theory and practice in dealing with ICT. According to this view, knowledge is constructed by learners using their own strategies for learning (McCormick and Paechter, 1999). Pupils live in a mediated world, where the internet with all its opportunities and risks is part of their everyday life. Thus, learning processes should be conceptualised in the context of the social cultural environments and the living experiences of young people (Paus-Hasebrink, 2006).

The Austrian pilot study, 'Learning with Web 2.0'[1] (Paus-Hasebrink et al, 2007), identified various opportunities for learning with ICT (for example wikis) at schools and suggested that dealing with learning topics in a pupil-related way could help to strengthen motivation processes at school both among teachers and students. Overall, projects like this provide many possibilities for children to gain competencies in relation to privacy, ownership and authorship, credibility and participation. At school, young people can learn how to recognise risks, how to deal with them and how to profit from the opportunities the internet offers. In the following we offer some best practice proposals for dealing with ICT in schools:

- Schools should provide a learning environment where pupils deal with topics that fit in their 'life worlds', wherein media play a relevant role and an authentic information and communication space is provided (Paus-Hasebrink et al, 2007: 89). 'Fascinating students with the reality of media techniques' (McCannon, 2009: 547) through using wikis in schools, for example, can strengthen their motivation of learning.
- Schools should provide a learning structure that involves students affectively as well as logically (McCannon, 2009) and makes them feel 'like they are central to the process of investigation' (McCannon, 2009: 547).
- There is a need for adequate pedagogical strategies relating to the topics of interest and to the needs of children as well as for diversified ways to integrate them into class.
- This means – in contrast to former pedagogical assumptions – that learners must be understood as being active individuals who select and process information independently in a self-determining fashion, needing only to be encouraged to ask questions and to discover new information.
- To support learning to use ICT in schools based on constructivist environments – which means learning both how to conduct relevant learning and to work collaboratively (for example with ICT) – Jonassen (1999) suggests scaffolding, coaching and modelling as instructional methods. Scaffolding is an approach to help learners handle tasks. Coaching is a teaching strategy that focuses on the motivation of learners and on giving adequate help and feedback.

Modelling means either behavioural or cognitive modelling. In that sense, teachers have to be coaches who are able to encourage pupils to use strategies involving self-determined learning appropriation.

- Teachers should give feedback on learning progress and recognise students' individual pace of learning.
- Teaching should be primarily student-centred (Slavin, 2006) and exercise-based. Different, multiple learning materials such as books, computers and experts should be involved in the learning exercise (Moser, 2000).
- As the Austrian pilot study showed (Paus-Hasebrink et al, 2007: 89), an efficient use of ICT (for example wikis) within classes requires a change in school structures and teaching. According to the teachers interviewed, a non-bureaucratic working environment is of particular importance in order to have time to meet the pupils' needs. That means a flexible time schedule and the opportunity to practise teaching in interdisciplinary teams).

ICT in schools require a learner-centred approach

Children and young people deal with an impressive media repertoire in their everyday life wherein ICTs play a central part. Schools are challenged to empower children in a double way: first, to help young people deal with ICT-dominated media environments in an adequate and self-determined way; and second, to use ICT in learning contexts to offer them the best competencies to meet their needs in a knowledge-based society. Schools are challenged to minimise risks and enhance opportunities from ICT use because all children – irrespective from which milieu they come – have to go to school. In this sense, schools can reduce the digital divide. This chapter has discussed a way to combine these tasks. Bearing this in mind it reflects various attitudes towards ICT from a European perspective. Against this background it provided both an overview of the state of research on ICT and schools and of the usage of the internet in and for schools in order to make some best practice proposals to deal with them effectively in a learner-centred way.

Note

[1] In the project, nine schools (including nine school principals, 27 teachers and 169 pupils aged 11-13) worked together in a school-embracing wiki on the topic 'Austrian National Parks'. In addition, the teachers were given the option of exchanging experiences and ideas in a project-based weblog.

References

BMUKK (Bundesministerium für Unterricht, Kunst und Kultur – Austrian Federal Ministry for Education, Arts and Culture) (www. bmukk.gv.at/schulen/unterricht/lp/Volkschullehrplan3911.xml).

EC (European Commission) (2008) *Towards a safer use of the internet for children in the EU – A parents' perspective, Analytical report*, Flash Eurobarometer Series # 248, conducted by The Gallup Organisation, Hungary, Luxembourg: EC (http://ec.europa.eu/information_society/activities/sip/docs/eurobarometer/analyticalreport_2008. pdf).

eRT (Elektrooniline Riigi Teataja) (www.riigiteataja.ee/ert/act. jsp?id=174787).

EU Kids Online (2008) *National reports for the cross-national comparisons*, London: EU Kids Online (Deliverable D3.2) (www.lse.ac.uk/ collections/EUKidsOnline/).

Eurydice (2004) *Key data on information and communication technology in schools in Europe*, Luxembourg: Eurydice European Unit with the financial support of the European Commission (http://eacea. ec.europa.eu/ressources/eurydice/pdf/0_integral/048EN.pdf).

Euridyce (2005) *Key data on education in Europe 2005*, Luxembourg: European Commission (http://digm.meb.gov.tr/belge/EU_ KeyData_Eurydice_2005.pdf).

Hasebrink, U., Livingstone, S., Haddon, L. and Ólafsson, K. (2009) *Comparing children's online opportunities and risks across Europe: Cross-national comparisons for EU Kids Online* (2nd edn), London: London School of Economics and Political Science, EU Kids Online (Deliverable D3.2 for the EC Safer Internet Plus Programme).

Jonassen, D. (1999) 'Designing constructivist learning environments', in C. Reigeluth (ed) *Instructional-design theories and models, Vol II: A new paradigm of instructional theory*, Mahwah, NJ: Lawrence Erlbaum Associates: 217-39.

Krotz, F. and Hasebrink, U. (2001) 'Who are the new media users?', in S. Livingstone and M. Bovill (eds) *Children and their changing media environment: A comparative European study*, Mahwah, NJ: Lawrence Erlbaum Associates: 245-62.

Livingstone, S. and Bober, M. (2005) *UK children go online. Final Report of key project findings*, London: Department of Media and Communications, London School of Economics (http://eprints.lse. ac.uk/399/).

McCannon, R. (2009) 'Media literacy/media education: solution to big media?', in V. Strasburger, B. Wilson and A. Jordan (eds) *Children, adolescents, and the media* (2nd edn), Thousand Oaks, CA: Sage Publications: 519-69.

McCormick, R. and Paechter, C. (1999) *Learning and knowledge*, London: The Open University and Paul Chapman Publishing.

Medienpädagogischer Forschungsverbund Südwest (2007) *JIM-Studie 2007: Jugend, Information, (Multi-) Media. Basisstudie zum Medienumgang 12- bis 19-Jähriger in Deutschland* [*JIM-study 2007. Youth, information, (multi) media. Basic study on the media use of 12- to 19-year-olds*], Stuttgart: Medienpädagogischer Forschungsverbund Südwest (www.mpfs.de/fileadmin/JIM-pdf07/JIM-Studie2007.pdf).

Moser, H. (2000) *Abenteuer Internet. Lernen mit WebQuests* [*Adventure Internet. Learning with WebQuest*], Zürich/Donauwörth: Pestalozzianum.

Murru, M. and Mascheroni, G. (2008) *National reports for the cross-national comparisons: National report for Italy*, London: EU Kids Online (Deliverable D3.2) (www.lse.ac.uk/collections/EUKidsOnline/).

National Curriculum (http://curriculum.qca.org.uk/).

OPH (Opetushallitus – Finnish National Board of Education, or FNBE) (1999) 'Prospectus' (www.oph.fi/SubPage.asp?path=1,17627,1558).

Paus-Hasebrink, I. (2006) 'Medienpädagogische Forschung braucht gesellschaftskritischen Handlungsbezug: Besondere Verantwortung gebührt sozial benachteiligten Kindern und Jugendlichen' [*Research in media education needs to critically refer to society. There is a need for responsibility concerning socially disadvantaged children and youth*], *Medien & Erziehung*, vol 5: 22-8.

Paus-Hasebrink, I., Jadin, T. and Wijnen, C.W. (2007) *Lernen mit Web 2.0: Bericht zur Evaluation des Projekts Web 2.0-Klasse* [*Learning with web 2.0. Report on the evaluation of the project 'Web 2.0 Class'*], Salzburg: Abteilung für Audiovisuelle Kommunikation am Fachbereich KommunikationswissenschaftvUniversität Salzburg (www.telekom.at/Content.Node/verantwortung/sponsoring/projekte/web20klasse-evaluationsbericht.pdf).

Slavin, R.E. (2006) *Educational psychology: Theory and practice*, Boston, MA: Pearson and Allyn and Bacon.

Staksrud, E., Livingstone, S. and Haddon, L. (2007) *What do we know about children's use of online technologies? A report on data availability and research gaps in Europe*, London: London School of Economics and Political Science, EU Kids Online (Deliverable D1.1 for the EC Safer Internet Plus Programme).

Tsaliki, L. (2008) *National reports for the cross-national comparisons: National report for Greece*, London: EU Kids Online.

Wijnen, C. (2008) *Medien und Pädagogik international: Positionen, Ansätze und Zukunftsperspektiven in Europa und den USA* [*Media and pedagogy international. Positions, approaches and future perspectives in Europe and the USA*], Munich: Kopaed.

EIGHTEEN

Media literacy

Brian O'Neill and Ingunn Hagen

Introduction

Across Europe and beyond, the promotion of media literacy for both children and adults has acquired an important public urgency. Traditional literacy is no longer seen to be sufficient for participation in today's society. Citizens need to be media literate, it is claimed, to enable them to cope more effectively with the flood of information in today's highly mediated societies. As teachers, politicians and policy makers everywhere struggle with this rapid shift in media culture, greater responsibility is placed on citizens for their own welfare in the new media environment. Media literacy is therefore all the more essential in enabling citizens to make sense of the opportunities available to them and to be alerted to the risks involved.

How media literacy might be achieved is the subject of this chapter, and three main themes are addressed. First, we examine how media literacy has been defined with particular reference to the growing importance of *digital* literacy. Second, we examine how media literacy has been adopted within policy frameworks as a response to rapid technological change. Third, we critique the 'technological literacy' that dominates much of the current policy agenda (Hasebrink et al, 2007), and argue for a new approach based on better knowledge about children and young people's media and internet habits.

Defining media literacy

The debate about what media literacy means is a long-standing one. It is frequently acknowledged as a good thing, although we are not always agreed on what it is (O'Neill and Barnes, 2008). A growing consensus around its key conceptual parameters is emerging with the definition 'the ability to access, understand and create communications in a variety of contexts' (Livingstone, 2004: 5; CEC, 2007a: 6). Drawing on Aufderheide (1997), the objective of media literacy, so defined, is a 'critical autonomy relationship to all media', organised around a set of common beliefs or precepts recognising that the media are constructed and that they have commercial, ideological and political implications. Digital literacy is one of a host of new literacies (Coiro et al, 2007), including computer or technological literacy associated with the information society (CEC, 2009) that now join the debate on the need for media literacy.

It is important to remember that the concept of literacy itself remains a contested one (Luke, 1989; Livingstone, 2004). Referring traditionally to reading and writing ability, literacy carries advantages and disadvantages when used in the context of media or digital literacy (Livingstone, 2008). Positively, it draws on a rich tradition of extending access to knowledge and culture. More negatively, the term does not always translate from education to policy discourses; neither does it always translate well into other languages. The equivalent Norwegian terms, for instance, *digital kompetanse* and *mediekompetanse*, both refer to more technical aspects of literacy. Digital literacy in its popular English usage is similarly associated with competence or skill and loses the original sense of reading and writing. Buckingham's reference to *digital media literacy* (2007), his preferred term, foregrounds literacy as the outcome – in terms of acquired knowledge and skills – in contrast to media education, which he defines as the process of teaching and learning about media.

An assumption of digital media literacy is that children and young people should be equipped with the necessary critical and conceptual tools that allow them to deal with, rather than be protected from, the media culture that surrounds them. Drawing on Bazalgette (1989), Buckingham (2007) argues that the aim of digital media literacy is to ensure that young people are able to both understand and participate in the media, and in so doing secure their democratic rights. As now widely promoted, digital literacy further assumes that such competence is vital for our lives and for society (CEC, 2007b). The internet as a common network for information, communication, entertainment and trade extends such social interaction to a global level.

To explore the different dimensions of this debate, it is worth examining briefly the four key components of the definition of media literacy: to be able to *access, analyse, evaluate* and *create* messages in a variety of communication contexts.

Access

This refers in the first instance to the skills and competencies required to find media content. With digital literacy, the focus is often on its functional aspects – whether people have physical access or not to the internet, or are able to operate a personal computer and navigate websites to do very basic functions. The major concern in this respect has been with the so-called digital divide. As observed by Livingstone (2004), however, evaluating and using available media content and services are dynamic social processes for which hardware provision alone is insufficient. For Buckingham (2007), access similarly includes the ability to self-regulate media use through awareness of the potential risks involved. In this context, the internet is a highly complex technological system, but it is also extremely accessible in the sense of being easy to use. However, while it may be very easy to get on to the internet, more sophisticated uses require higher degrees of competence (Gentikow, 2009).

Analyse

Analysis goes beyond the ability to decode audio-visual media messages (Hall, 1980). While knowledge of genre and media rhetorical strategies is useful, analysis also requires 'being competent in and motivated toward relevant cultural traditions and values' (Livingstone, 2004: 6). Analysis also includes being able to deconstruct production processes, issues of media ownership, institutional power and media representations (Buckingham, 2007). Livingstone (2004), building on Bazalgette (1989) and Buckingham (2003), suggests that insight into questions of media agency, media categories, media technologies, media languages, media audiences and media representations are central elements of analytic competence, but crucially are categories that need to be adjusted for new media.

Evaluate

Evaluation is a key aspect of digital literacy sometimes overlooked in favour of technical dimensions. Evaluation requires critical and analytical skills, but also knowledge of the cultural, political, economic and historical context in which the particular content is produced. Given the extraordinary breadth of opinion, information and propaganda on the internet, the ability to question authority and to assess objectivity and trustworthiness is critical. Livingstone puts it eloquently: 'Imagine the World Wide Web user who cannot distinguish dated, biased, or exploitative sources, unable to select intelligently when overwhelmed by an abundance of information and services' (2004: 6).

Create

This refers to the ability to use different media tools to communicate, to produce content for self-expression, to participate in public debates and to interact with others. A defining feature of so-called 'Web 2.0', both in terms of the accessibility of communication channels and the wide availability of everyday media production technologies, a veneer of easy access may mask an underlying complexity in which media education has a central role to play. Buckingham (2007) notes growing research that suggests that children experience empowerment as a result of being able to represent their own experiences and concerns through media creation. Practical production is a first step, but children and young people need to be familiar with and master different cultural forms of expression and communication in order to become effective readers and writers in the digital age. Erstad (2008) refers to 'trajectories of remixing' as an important aspect of content creation and the increased possibilities offered by the World Wide Web to enable young people to remix content and create something new, not predefined.

What is distinctive about digital literacy?

What, then, distinguishes digital literacy from media literacy from the literacy required to read written texts or television, for that matter? On one level, the additional elements of interactivity, hypertextuality and multimedia suggest new modes of reading beyond the linear conventions of print and audio-visual media. Beyond this, however, media literacy in the digital context must also incorporate the full range of users' engagement with digital media from information searching, entertainment and game playing, to communicating and creating content, and not the received versions of literacy inherited from print or audio-visual literacy. While useful as a starting point, the imperative for digital media literacy is to learn from users' actual experience, and to develop on the basis of evidence of everyday experience the modalities of media literacy in the digital environment.

Buckingham (2007) emphasises that definitions of literacy are necessarily challenging as they have normative and evaluative implications for questions of power and control and need to be open to negotiation and debate. Digital literacy has a critical potential, for example, if taken to include the economic and political forces that have shaped the development of the internet as well as the commercial pressures within which it operates. At its best, digital media literacy can provide young people with reading, writing, evaluative and creative skills that are a fundamental basis for empowerment in today's society. Yet within the policy realm, all too often literacy loses this sense of democratising potential (Livingstone, 2008), and is instead restricted to more limited objectives.

Media literacy and public policy

While communication in a societal context has always been a central feature of the concept of media literacy, only more recently has it become a matter of public policy. The responsibility of the UK's media regulator, Ofcom (the Office of Communications), to promote media literacy provides one of the first European examples of a recognition of the state's duty to encourage a better public understanding and awareness of media content and processes (Ofcom, 2004). This arises in the context of wider trends in media regulation away from efforts to control the industries directly to a model of co- or self-regulation whereby media industries themselves are viewed as best suited to managing the provision of media content (Penman and Turnbull, 2007). In an increasingly complex environment of new distribution channels and modes of access, this 'lighter-touch' regulation is deemed more appropriate to harnessing the potential of new media platforms (Helberger, 2007). The policy enabling such a liberalisation of market conditions is most visibly expressed in the European Union's (EU) *Audiovisual Media Services* (AVMS) Directive in which a flexible regulatory system with fewer constraints on advertising and content will operate across Europe for existing and emerging audio–visual media services (CEC, 2007c). As a counterbalance to the loosening of controls, the Directive promotes media literacy or 'skills, knowledge and understanding that allow consumers to use media effectively and safely' (CEC, 2007c: 31). Significantly, the AVMS Directive requires the European Commission (EC) to report on levels of media literacy in all member states from 2011 onwards.

In addition to the AVMS Directive, a number of other bodies involved with European media policy have adopted media literacy promotion as a strategic goal. The European Parliament, for instance (Council of the European Union, 2006a), has advocated the development of national public awareness programmes, as well as training for professionals, teachers and child protection agencies on safe internet use in schools.

They also emphasise specific internet training initiatives aimed at children, and an integrated educational approach aimed at using the internet responsibly. European policy on lifelong learning similarly emphasises the confident and critical use of information society technology among its key competencies (Council of the European Union, 2006b) and the EC's communication on media literacy in the digital environment in 2008 advocates greater promotion of media literacy as a social and educational priority (CEC, 2007b). Specifically, it invites European member states to ensure that all appropriate authorities promote media literacy, encourage research and awareness raising of the use of information and communication technology (ICT) by young people, and promote media literacy within the framework of lifelong learning.

In parallel with this sometimes surprising adoption of media literacy within media policy frameworks ostensibly geared towards market liberalisation (Goodwin and Spittle, 2002) there is a growing consensus that media or digital literacy is best understood through the lens of human rights (Frau-Meigs, 2006). The 60th anniversary in 2008 of the Universal Declaration of Human Rights provides one such context for foregrounding rights-based policies on the protection of minors and the promotion of citizens' interests in the digital environment. The Council of Europe, for instance, has proposed separate policies on the public service value of the internet (2007a), empowering children in the new communications environment (2006), and promoting freedom of expression and information (2007b). Such policy interventions have acted as a call to arms for 'a coherent information literacy and training strategy which is conducive to empowering children and their educators in order for them to make the best possible use of information and communication services and technologies' (Council of Europe, 2006).

Historically, UNESCO support for media literacy has also been decisive, having initiated the concept of media education in the 1970s and argued for its adoption by all developed countries (Zgrabljic-Rotar, 2006: 10). The 1982 Grünwald Declaration provided the first platform for concerted international action on media education (UNESCO, 1982) and UNESCO continues to promote media and information literacy as an integral part of people's lifelong learning.

Media literacy in the digital environment

Despite this enhanced profile, media literacy in its current formulation retains a number of unresolved tensions, such as its technological bias and the 'light touch' regulation of which it has become a part. In the first case, digital literacy is frequently characterised by a strong underlying technological bias, evident for instance in the EC's communication on *media literacy in the digital environment* (CEC, 2007b), the first formal statement of media literacy policy at a European level. Drawing on i2010, the EU policy for a strong internal European marketplace for the information society and media services, media literacy is closely linked with the acquisition of technical skills, and suggests that better knowledge and understanding of how media work in the digital world will lead to wider take-up of ICT, and thus help Europe become a global leader in media and information technologies.

This technology bias is repeated in the widely promoted notion of digital literacy as user competence, reinforced by the need to measure attainment in quantitative form (Ala-Mutka et al, 2008). Relatedly, there is an expectation that children and young people as the subjects of media literacy are the new experts or pioneers in the digital age (Tapscott, 1998; Prensky, 2001; see Bennett et al, 2008). Because young people are so immersed in technology, it is sometimes assumed that this new generation possesses sophisticated skills and requires a qualitatively different approach to traditional education (see Buckingham, 1998). In contrast, we concur with Dunkels (2007) that it is essential to avoid romanticising children's competence, while at the same time acknowledging their experiences and skills with regard to digital media. Children's experiences and opinions about the internet are quite different from adults, and highlight the gap in knowledge between young people as internet users and adults who make up the rules and control its access.

The second aspect of concern with media literacy, currently defined, is the 'light touch' regulation within which it is framed. Whether in relation to codes of practice for internet service providers (ISPs) or with regard to classification of video game content (the PEGI [Pan-European Game Information] rating system), the model of European media regulation is one of voluntary co- or self-regulation, invariably prioritising the needs of industry over citizens or consumers. Like many aspects of European policy, media literacy is also subject to the subsidiarity principle where individual member states make provision for media literacy at a local or national level. As a consequence, media literacy efforts remain dispersed and uncoordinated, and dependent on individual organisations to promote them, varying according to the availability of resources and the prevailing cultural and political environment.

Conclusion

The high profile of media literacy in policy discussions arises in the context of wide-ranging debates about social inclusion in the information society – ensuring no one is left behind in a fast-moving technological landscape – as well as in relation to growing concerns about the implications of greatly increased access to unregulated content and potentially harmful material, particularly on the internet. In addressing these concerns, there is a danger, particularly in the case of digital literacy, that an all too narrow approach may be adopted, restricted to measurable aspects of digital competence or technical skill. The expectation is that these skills will be developed within the school context, with teachers being trained for the task. However, the overriding interests of current policy suggest that the outcomes will more often than not be functional or instrumental. We argue that in order to move beyond the 'technological literacy' that dominates much of the current policy agenda, a new approach based on knowledge about children and young people's media and internet habits, and on research on media and digital literacy, is required. This will necessitate a more developed curriculum on media and digital literacy for children to be able to benefit from the opportunities and to manoeuvre around the risks related to media and internet use.

It will be important in this context to reflect on whether the notion of digital literacy is in danger of becoming intertwined with norms for middle-class childhood. Initiatives in support of digital literacy will have to consider broader processes of social inclusion and exclusion, particularly with respect to class and gender, and the danger that increased marginalisation could result as an unintended side-effect of school digital literacy programmes (Sefton-Green et al, 2009). Digital literacy is not a neutral empowering process but an entry point for a number of specific social opportunities.

The aim to create a flourishing digital literacy as advocated within European policy or by the Council of Europe (2006) remains an important and positive one. The ambition that all children should be familiarised with, and skilled in, the new information and communications environment, have the necessary skills to create, produce and distribute content and communications, and that such skills should better enable them to deal with content that may be harmful in nature is one of the key educational priorities of our time. To be effective, such initiatives must have both a bottom-up and a top-down level of knowledge and input. On the one hand, media and digital literacy education needs to be based on children's actual experiences, needs and wishes, and informed by knowledge and research about how young people use ICTs and the internet. On the other hand, it also needs to be informed by relevant sociological perspectives of media and internet use, as well as by a robust ethical and legal understanding of the new communications environment. Prioritising curricula that encourage digital media literacy in the sense elaborated above poses an enormous challenge for educational policy makers and schools in an era of scarce public resources and ever-increasing pressures for economic relevance. Yet, as Buckingham reminds us (2007), media education, more than most other aspects of the curriculum, promotes skills and learning that have far-reaching implications beyond the confines of the classroom and which go to the heart of exercising rights and freedoms in contemporary societies.

References

Ala-Mutka, K., Punie, Y. and Redecker, C. (2008) *Digital competence for lifelong learning. Policy Brief JRC48708-2008*, Brussels: European Commission (http://ftp.jrc.es/EURdoc/JRC48708.TN.pdf).

Aufderheide, P. (1997) 'Media literacy: from a report of the National Leadership Conference on media literacy', in R. Kubey (ed) *Media literacy in the information age*, New Brunswick, NJ: Transaction Publishers: 79-86.

Bazalgette, C. (1989) *Primary media education: A curriculum statement*, London: British Film Institute.

Bennett, S., Maton, K. and Kervin, L. (2008) 'The "digital natives" debate: a critical review of the evidence', *British Journal of Educational Technology*, vol 39, no 5: 775-86.

Buckingham, D. (1998) 'Children of the electronic age? Digital media and the new generational rhetoric', *European Journal of Communication*, vol 13, no 4: 557-66.

Buckingham, D. (2003) *Media education: Literacy, learning and contemporary culture*, Cambridge: Polity.

Buckingham, D. (2007) *Beyond technology: Children's learning in the age of digital culture*, Cambridge: Polity.

CEC (Commission of the European Communities) (2007a) *Report on the results of the public consultation on media literacy*, Brussels: European Commission.

CEC (2007b) *A European approach to media literacy in the digital environment. Communication from the Commission to the European Parliament, the Council, the European Economic and Social Committee and the Committee of the Regions*, Brussels: European Commission.

CEC (2007c) *Audiovisual Media Services Directive (AVMSD)*, Brussels: European Commission.

CEC (2009) *Citizens speak out: A louder call for European E-participation*, Brussels: European Commission.

Coiro, J., Knobel, M., Lankshear, C. and Leu, D. (eds) (2007) *Handbook of research on new literacies*, London: Routledge.

Council of Europe (2006) *Recommendation Rec(2006)12 of the Committee of Ministers to member states on empowering children in the new information and communications environment Council of Europe*, Strasbourg: Council of Europe.

Council of Europe (2007a) *Recommendation CM/Rec(2007)16 of the Committee of Ministers to member states on measures to promote the public service value of the Internet Council of Europe*, Strasbourg: Council of Europe.

Council of Europe (2007b) *Recommendation CM/Rec(2007)11 of the Committee of Ministers to member states on promoting freedom of expression and information in the new information and communications environment Council of Europe*, Strasbourg: Council of Europe.

Council of the European Union (2006a) *Recommendation of the European Parliament and of the Council of 20 December 2006 on the protection of minors and human dignity and on the right of reply in relation to the competitiveness of the European audiovisual and on-line information services industry*, Brussels: Council of the European Union.

Council of the European Union (2006b) *Recommendation of the European Parliament and of the Council of 18 December 2006 on key competences for lifelong learning*, Brussels: Council of the European Union.

Dunkels, E. (2007) Bridging the distance: children's strategies on the internet', Unpublished PhD dissertation, Umeå, Sweden: University of Umeå.

Erstad, O. (2008) 'Trajectories of remixing – digital literacies, media production and schooling', in C. Lankshear and M. Knobel (eds) *Digital literacies. Concepts, policies and practices*, New York, NY: Peter Lang: 177-202.

Frau-Meigs, D. (2006) *General report. Pan-European forum on human rights in the information society: Empowering children and young people*, Strasbourg: Council of Europe.

Gentikow, B. (2009) 'Media literacy for det 21 Århundre' ['Media literacy for the 21st century'], *Medievitenskap*, vol 3, no 2, Bergen: Fagbokforlaget.

Goodwin, I. and Spittle, S. (2002) 'The European Union and the information society: discourse, power and policy', *New Media Society*, vol 4, no 2: 225-49.

Hall, S. (1980) 'Encoding/decoding', in *Culture, media, language: Working papers in cultural studies, 1972-79*, London: Hutchinson: 128-38.

Hasebrink, U., Livingstone, S., Haddon, L., Kirwil, L. and Ponte, C. (2007) *Comparing children's online activities and risks across Europe: A preliminary report comparing findings for Poland, Portugal and UK*, London: EU Kids Online (Deliverable D3.1 for the EC Safer Internet Plus Programme).

Helberger, N. (2007) 'The changing role of the user in the "Television Without Frontiers Directive"', *IRIS Special: Legal Aspects of Video on Demand*, Strasbourg: European Audiovisual Observatory.

Livingstone, S. (2004) 'Media literacy and the challenge of new information and communication technologies', *The Communication Review*, vol 7: 3-14.

Livingstone, S. (2008) 'Engaging with media – a matter of literacy?', *Communication, Culture & Critique*, vol 1, no 1: 51-62.

Luke, C. (1989) *Pedagogy, printing, and protestantism: The discourse on childhood*, New York, NY: State University of New York Press.

O'Neill, B. and Barnes, C. (2008) *Media literacy and the public sphere: A contextual study for public media literacy promotion in Ireland*, Dublin: Broadcasting Commission of Ireland.

Ofcom (Office of Communications) (2004) *Ofcom's strategy and priorities for the promotion of media literacy – A statement*, London: Ofcom.

Penman, R. and Turnbull, S. (2007) *Media literacy – Concepts, research and regulatory issues*, Canberra, Australia: Australian Communications and Media Authority.

Prensky, M. (2001) 'Digital natives, digital immigrants', *On the Horizon*, vol 9, no 5: 1-2.

Sefton-Green, J., Nixon, H. and Erstad, O. (2009) 'Reviewing approaches and rerspectives on "digital literacy"', *Pedagogies: An International Journal*, vol 4, no 2: 107-25.

Tapscott, D. (1998) *Growing up digital: The rise of the net generation*, New York, NY: McGraw-Hill.

UNESCO (1982) *The Grünwald Declaration on media education*, Grünwald, Germany: UNESCO.

Zgrabljic-Rotar, N. (2006) *Media literacy and civil society*, Sarajevo: Mediacentar.

NINETEEN

Conclusion

Sonia Livingstone and Leslie Haddon

Researching children and young people online

After the first decade or so of research, what do we now know about children and young people online? The number and range of empirical studies of children and the internet has increased steadily over recent years, although many studies are largely descriptive – charting statistics on access, use and activities online. One theoretically informed strand of research draws on the tradition of studying children and television, extending knowledge of children's engagement with a dominant, usually national mass medium to their activities in the globalised digital age. Another strand of research seeks to position the internet within the wider context of children's lives, as long analysed by theorists of childhood, youth and the family. Others draw on particular specialisms as appropriate to the research focus – framing research in terms of theories of formal and informal learning, or information systems and digital literacies, or child welfare and protection. Ideally, these multiple theories and perspectives would complement each other, combining to generate a multidimensional account of children's relation to online technologies. In practice, research is characterised by a diversity of assumptions and insights that may or may not intersect constructively, resulting in some lively debates in this newly established field. But it can no longer be said that little is known, as was the case just a few years ago (Livingstone, 2003).

Yet it seems that the more we know, the more we know we do not know, especially for so fast-moving a target as 'the internet'. In particular, most research addresses the 'fixed internet', although in many countries, children already go online via other platforms such as their mobile phone, games machines or other devices, raising new questions of autonomy, privacy and risk (Ito et al, 2008; Ling and Haddon, 2008). And most research concerns what in retrospect we can call 'Web 1.0' – searching for and visiting websites, rather than creating information or engaging with the range of diverse applications emerging under the umbrella label 'Web.2.0'. More positively, research on creating content (Chapter Six, this volume), social networking (Chapter Seven) and new forms of learning (Chapter Seventeen), as well as children's problematic activities online (Chapter Twelve), begins to scope a promising research agenda. As Verónica Donoso, Kjartan Ólafsson and Thorbjörn Broddason comment (Chapter Two), although researchers always believe 'more research is needed', in this field such a conclusion is unavoidable; having up-to-date and relevant findings is especially important when, as in this volume, the evidence base is mined to guide policy developments (see Section IV).

Research methodology regarding the study of children online has advanced considerably in recent years, with emerging good practice in conducting research with children, especially in relation to the online environment (Chapter Three), and especially across cultures, putting countries into a comparative framework (Chapter Four). Particularly, research on children has often wrong-footed researchers by forcing them to recognise that their very adult status risks evoking social desirability biases from young interviewees, that adult implicit assumptions and inappropriate wordings risk misunderstanding what children have to say, and that some of children's lives is quite simply inaccessible to an adult gaze. Added to this is the ethical challenges of asking children about such potentially upsetting topics as bullying or sexual harassment and, furthermore, about such fast-changing phenomena as practices of online communication, especially as these multiply across fixed, mobile and convergent platforms. In response to such challenges, experienced researchers urge working 'with' rather than working 'on' children (Greig and Taylor, 1999), as demonstrated in the EU Kids Online's *Best practice research guide* (Lobe et al, 2008) and in Chapter Three of this volume.

Key gaps in the evidence base remain. Most research concentrates on teenagers, leaving a critical evidence gap regarding the many primary school-aged children who are now rapidly going online (Chapter Two). Also, albeit for good methodological and ethical reasons, research on younger children tends to use qualitative methods or to rely on parents' accounts of children's activity, making it difficult to estimate the frequency of certain practices among younger children or to compare age, gender or other groupings. Meanwhile, since teenagers are mainly surveyed, one problem is findings that tend to lack contextualisation in terms of the experiences and perceptions of young people themselves, as would be revealed by qualitative research. As discussed in Chapter Five, some features of the evidence base are shaped less by theory or methodology than by the particular cultural, political and economic contexts in which researchers work, this influencing the basis on which research is funded and the climate within which evidence is expected to inform policy.

Going online: new opportunities?

As the research reviewed in this volume makes clear, when opportunities permit, children and young people engage enthusiastically with many online activities, including entertainment, learning, participation, creativity, the expression of identity and, especially, communication and social connection. Most commonplace of all is information seeking, this sometimes in support of educational activities but most valued for supporting musical or sporting interests and hobbies, as well as practical tasks such as travel, shopping and local services. Also very common, often practised daily, are the various communication opportunities – social networking, instant messaging, emailing and so forth – that complement face-to-face communication by enabling a welcome measure of control over the management of intimacy in peer networks (Chapter Seven). Least practised are opportunities for civic participation online, despite public policy optimism regarding the internet's potential to overcome so-called youthful political apathy. Also, perhaps more surprisingly, it seems that the many opportunities to create and promote one's own webpages, blogs, artwork, stories or music are not taken up by a large proportion of young people (Chapter Six).

To understand the differential adoption of online activities, several contributors to Section II invoke Livingstone and Helsper's (2007) 'ladder of opportunities' which, echoing citizenship studies' 'ladder of participation', outlines four steps. For new users, the first step is generally information seeking, whether for leisure and school. Most children go beyond this, becoming 'moderate users' by adding in email and games. While many younger children stay at this step, frequent users and also older children take the third step to become 'broad users' by expanding their peer-to-peer engagement (for example, through music or film downloading and instant messaging). Last, it is mainly the daily users, mostly teenagers, who become 'all rounders' by adding such interactive, creative or civic activities as creating sites, images or stories for others, contributing to message boards, doing quizzes, voting or signing petitions. Two implications follow. First, the simple fact of using the internet may not mean that a child achieves their potential or gets the most from it, and further support and encouragement to progress or expand their activities may be required. Second, the fact that a child plays games online may not be, as worried adults are tempted to judge, a 'waste of time', for this may represent a step towards further activities, one that is fun, gives confidence and develops skills (Jenkins, 2006; Ito et al, 2008).

The more complex and exciting online opportunities become, the more it seems that the vision of all children as 'digital natives' or 'cyber-experts' must be qualified. Empirical research reveals considerable differentiation within the category 'children and young people', partly because not all children choose to engage with the internet in a highly sophisticated manner. As discussed in Chapter Six, children vary in their interests, being skilled and motivated agents who make thoughtful decisions about what they consider the internet can offer them. On the other hand, children are also constrained in their online activities by some familiar structural factors shaping their offline lives, and this may account for why several chapters in Section II are a little downbeat. Indeed, despite a decade of public and private sector investment to get online technologies into homes, schools and communities, the structural constraints in children's lives remain influential, perpetuating long-standing differences and inequalities. As Panayiota Tsatsou, Pille Pruulmann-Vengerfeldt and Maria Francesca Murru state in Chapter Nine, digital divides are hardly the fault of the individual for they result from unequal social and contextual resources shaping children's environments. Yet it is individuals who bear the consequences – hence the widespread support for media literacy (Chapter Eighteen).

In recent years, the analysis of digital inclusion has shifted from a focus on the simple binary of the haves and have-nots to a more nuanced recognition of the stratified 'opportunity structures' that enable or inhibit activities online (as, indeed, offline), these placing particular and often unfeasible demands on people's emerging and variable digital literacies (Livingstone, 2009). From the available research across Europe and elsewhere (van Dijk, 2005), divides remain striking both across and within countries. Cross-nationally, it seems that many children, especially those in countries where the internet has only recently become accessible, use the internet in relatively infrequent or restricted ways compared with those in whose country the internet is now thoroughly embedded in domestic, school and community settings. Within countries, persistent socio-economic differences, long correlated with educational, regional and other sources of inequality, enable children from middle-class families to take up more opportunities online than children from lower-class families, even once basic access has become available to all.

The end of digital inequalities, should this be feasible, need not mean homogeneity, for one hardly expects all children and young people to use the internet in the same way. Helen McQuillan and Leen d'Haenens (Chapter Eight) consider whether observed differences really matter – do they reflect inequalities of opportunity or merely different preferences (see also Peter and Valkenburg, 2006)? Age differences in online activities and, therefore, in literacies and opportunities, are obviously to be expected as young children develop into older teenagers, as explained by cognitive and sociological theories of child socialisation. But, while age differences do not seem to reflect either inequalities or differences in preference, gender differences pose a contrasting case. When computers were first introduced some years ago, research found girls to be systematically disadvantaged in access, time spent, technical knowledge, teacher and parent support and, not surprisingly in those circumstances, motivation and self-confidence (Bird and Jorgenson, 2003). Today, access to the internet is, in most countries, already more or less equivalent for girls and boys at home and school, although small differences persist. Beyond this, there are differences in use, which may simply reflect divergent gender preferences, and in confidence or self-perceived skills – arguably a case of inequality. Possibly, boys' preference for playing games and girls' preference for expressive and communicative activities will advantage boys in the future, but the reverse may instead be the case; it is not yet clear which online skills will be of benefit in the adult labour market.

Going online: new risks?

If educators, parents, policy makers and industry are to encourage a wider and deeper engagement with the internet on the part of children and young people, they must be confident that this is not simultaneously a recipe for harm. From the outset, EU Kids Online has sought to critically evaluate the nature and degree of risk associated with children's internet use, well aware that, as Marika Lüders, Petter Bae Brandtzæg and Elza Dunkels comment (Chapter Ten), risk is simultaneously an objective reality and a social construct. The possibility of genuine harm to a child must be addressed seriously. However, the fear of such harm, especially if amplified by the mass media (Chapter Thirteen), may bring its own problems (Smith and McCloskey, 1998), as may an over-simple labelling of certain groups as 'at risk' (Kelly, 2000). Defining risk as 'the possibility that human actions or natural events lead to consequences that affect aspects of what humans value', Klinke and Renn (2001: 159) usefully distinguish risk assessment (the calculation of risk probability and magnitude), risk evaluation (determining the acceptability of a given risk) and risk management (the process of reducing risks to a level deemed tolerable by society). In effect, the EU Kids Online network sought to undertake a risk assessment for children's use of online technologies (Hasebrink et al, 2009). Putting together the findings reviewed in Section III of this volume, the following picture emerges regarding children's online risk experiences in Europe (see ISTTF, 2008, for a comparable US review).

First, it appears that the rank ordering of risks is fairly similar across countries, notwithstanding limitations on the quality, scope and comparability of the available evidence base (see Hasebrink et al, 2009) and the fact that several risks are yet to be researched comparatively, such as 'race' hate, commercial exploitation and self-harm (although see Chapter Eleven). Giving out personal information is the most common risk (approximately half of online teenagers), although perhaps it is better treated as a condition that enables risk rather than risky in and of itself. Immediately, the complexity of risk becomes apparent for, as Marika Lüders et al (Chapter Ten) point out, the simple advice not to give out personal information online makes little sense for children using social networking sites or similar, precisely because these are based on the use of real names and other personal details. More significantly, communicating anonymously may be no less risky because it 'deindividuates' participants, removing conventional constraints on communication and thus potentially even increasing risk.

Seeing pornography online is the second most common risk for around four in ten teenagers across Europe, although ambivalence over the potential harm involved is higher than for the other risks. Seeing violent or hateful content is the third most common risk, experienced by approximately one third of teenagers and being bullied or harassed is fourth, affecting some one in five or six teenagers online. Receiving unwanted sexual comments is experienced by between one in ten teenagers (Germany, Ireland and Portugal) but closer to one in three or four teenagers in Iceland, Norway, the UK and Sweden, rising to one in two in Poland. Last, meeting an online contact offline appears the least common although arguably the most dangerous risk, showing considerable consistency in the figures across Europe at around 9% (one in eleven) online teenagers going to such meetings, although this rises to one in five in Poland, Sweden and the Czech Republic.

Qualifying this overall picture, the heterogeneity of 'children and young people' must be recognised. Although, unfortunately, little is known regarding young children and online risk, it is clear that gender and socio-economic status (SES) differentiate among children's risk experiences. Thus, in most countries, it seems that children from lower-class families are more exposed to risk (see Chapter Eleven), suggesting that safety awareness programmes and media literacy interventions could usefully target less privileged families, schools and neighbourhoods. Further, there are also gender differences in risk, mainly the unintended consequences of the choices that girls and boys make regarding preferred online activities. Boys seek out pornographic or violent content more and are more likely to meet somebody offline that they have met online and to give out personal information, while girls are more upset by violent and pornographic content, are more likely to chat online with strangers, receive unwanted sexual comments and are asked for personal information; both appear at risk of online harassment and bullying.

While the above applies, more or less, across Europe and beyond, EU Kids Online also compared national findings so as to recognise cross-national differences in, particularly, the extent to which children use the internet in each country and the level of online risk faced by children (as reviewed by the network). The resulting classification (see Table 19.1) suggests a positive correlation between use and risk. High-use, high-risk countries are, it seems, either wealthy Northern European countries or new entrants to the European Union (EU). Southern European countries tend to be relatively lower in risk, partly because they provide fewer opportunities for use. Further, high use of the internet is rarely if ever associated with low risk, thus setting a challenge for public policy ambitions of maximising opportunities while minimising risks. Average use may, it seems, be associated with high risk, suggesting particular problems in some new entrant (Eastern European) countries where the regulatory infrastructure and safety awareness are under-developed. More promisingly for public policy, high use may also be associated with only average risk, notably in some Nordic countries where both regulation and awareness are most developed.

There are clearly many possible factors that may account for cross-national differences in Table 19.1, each affording different possibilities for intervention and so with particular implications for policy (see Chapter Fourteen; and as discussed in Hasebrink et al, 2009). But it is hard to take the present analysis much further when risk assessment in this domain is hampered by lack of sufficient robust and directly comparable evidence, making the findings summarised here tentative rather than definitive.

However, the next steps in risk analysis – of risk evaluation and risk management – are even more contentious. Risk evaluation raises a particularly difficult question, for in popular and, especially, media discourses, it often seems that no risk to a child is acceptable. But, on the other hand, there is also growing recognition that a risk-free

Table 19.1: Classification of countries by children's online use and online risk

Online risk	Children's internet use		
	Below EU average (< 65%)	Average (65%-85%)	Above EU average (> 85%)
Low	Cyprus Italy	France Germany	
Medium	Greece	Austria Belgium Ireland Portugal Spain	Denmark Sweden
High		Bulgaria Czech Republic	Estonia Iceland Netherlands Norway Poland Slovenia UK

Source: Hasebrink et al (2009)

environment, even if feasible, would deny children the chance to learn to manage risk through experience. Thus it would carry unacceptable costs to children (by overly restricting their opportunities) as well as to adults (by overburdening parents, curtailing legitimate adult freedoms and increasing the regulation of firms). In seeking a balance between children's rights to online opportunities and the need to protect them from online risk, it must also be acknowledged that evidence of risk is not, in and of itself, direct evidence of actual harm. Research does show in several countries that some one in five online teenagers report a degree of distress or of having felt threatened, and research from clinicians, medics and law enforcement all suggest such harms to be real, at least for a minority of children (Finkelhor, 2008; Quayle et al, 2008; Livingstone and Millwood Hargrave, 2009). But a sound picture of the extent, distribution and consequences of risky experiences online remains elusive. When it comes to risk management, then, one must build policy on a somewhat unsteady foundation.

Policy implications

A parallel analysis in which online opportunities for children are also assessed, evaluated and managed has not been attempted here because the research literature provides separate reviews and recommendations associated with, say, online education, participation or communication but offers little by way of an overall picture. This is partly because common measures of online activities have not been developed as they have for online risks. It is also because the 'opportunities agenda' is still largely preoccupied with the prerequisites of digital literacy and digital inclusion. However, as we have stressed throughout this volume, neither children's experiences online nor the mediated environment more broadly permits a neat dividing line between risks and opportunities. This is for several important reasons, the first of which is the psychological imperative noted already, namely, that children and teenagers in particular must push against boundaries to discover their strengths and learn what they can and cannot cope with. In this sense, risks are, truly, opportunities for learning.

Another is a matter of definition: as noted in Chapter One, children perceive as opportunities some activities that adults perceive as risks (making new friends, sharing intimacy, disclosing personal information, downloading music, giving sexual or health advice and so forth). This in and of itself occasions misunderstanding within families and poses difficulties for framing sensible safety guidance. These difficulties are in turn compounded by poor specifications of the severity of risk: when does teasing become bullying, or self-posing become pornography, or the 'friend of a friend' become a 'stranger'? Yet another reason points to matters of design. Search engines, for example, do not generally distinguish sexual advice from pornography and a search for 'teenage sex' will produce both. The same applies to 'drugs' and 'anorexia', although the corporate social responsibility departments of major search companies are making some improvements in this respect. Into this design category one might also put such 'unthinking' practices as reputable sites requesting personal information (Children's BBC is a case in point) in so far as this then 'teaches' children that one can disregard adult advice 'never to give out your name online'.

It is hardly surprising, then, that empirical research shows children's experiences of opportunities and risks to be positively correlated (Livingstone and Helsper, in press). Without a subtle awareness of these interrelations, policies designed to minimise risk may impact unduly on opportunities, and policies designed to enhance opportunities may, inadvertently, carry consequences for risks. Achieving an acceptable balance is a daunting but important task. This volume has, in essence, identified two ways ahead. The first is to survey the array of policy tools available to various stakeholders in order to identify whether evidence supports particular initiatives or directions. Elisabeth Staksrud's call for policy makers to rethink their positioning of children solely as victims of risk, or Marika Lüders et al's challenge to popular advice to stay anonymous online, represent examples of this approach, as reviewed by Jos de Haan (Chapter Fifteen). The second, less common, way ahead examines the predictive value of competing explanations for online risk in order to prioritise some initiatives over others. This approach, in effect, examines where online risks or, perhaps, online opportunities, are greater so as to determine which factors make the difference. In the case of Chapter Fourteen, for example, the purpose was to compare high and low-risk countries to identify whether and when parental mediation works to reduce children's online risks (see also Chapter Sixteen).

For better or for worse, 'children are growing up in an immersive media culture that has become a constant and pervasive presence in their lives' (Montgomery, 2007: 212). We have given considerable attention to the risks in this volume, for the use of online technologies brings experiences that were once fairly inaccessible within the scope of children's daily experience – more graphic pornographic images than previously accessible, harassment reaching from the school gates into the child's bedroom, specialist knowledge about suicide methods, the celebration of anorexia or 'race' hate, modes of privacy invasion which are hard to detect and many interactions in which trust and authenticity is uncertain and easily manipulated.

But we conclude by also calling for more public debate over the opportunities for children. These are, perhaps surprisingly, often taken for granted rather than specified clearly, and when one or another advocate sets out their vision of 'positive' or 'beneficial' provision for children online, this is readily critiqued as adult-centred, commercially biased or elitist (Livingstone, 2008). Yet the same features of the online environment which exacerbate risk – the ease of creating and manipulating representations, the ready searchability and persistence of images, the speed and reach of interactions, the possibilities for both anonymity and privacy, the provisional and experimental nature of online communication – all this and more is precisely what affords the many opportunities of that same environment (boyd, 2008). Ensuring that these, rather than the risks, feature at the top of the public agenda, truly benefiting children in a host of diverse ways as suits their interests, rights and needs, is surely the central task facing researchers and policy makers in the coming decade.

References

Bird, S.E. and Jorgenson, J. (2003) 'Extending the school day: gender, class and the incorporation of technology in everyday life', in M. Consalvo and S. Paasonen (eds) *Women and everyday uses of the internet: Agency and identity*, New York, NY: Peter Lang: 255-74.

boyd, d.m. (2008) 'Why youth ♥ social network sites: the role of networked publics in teenage social life', in D. Buckingham (ed) *Youth, identity, and digital media*, vol 6: 119-42, Cambridge, MA: MIT Press.

Finkelhor, D. (2008) *Childhood victimization: Violence, crime, and abuse in the lives of young people*, Oxford: Oxford University Press.

Greig, A. and Taylor, J. (1999) *Doing research with children*, London: Sage Publications.

Hasebrink, U., Livingstone, S., Haddon, L. and Ólafsson, K. (2009) *Comparing children's online opportunities and risks across Europe: Cross-national comparisons for EU Kids Online* (2nd edn), London: London School of Economics and Political Science, EU Kids Online (Deliverable D3.2 for the EC Safer Internet Plus Programme).

ISTTF (Internet Safety Technical Task Force) (2008) *Enhancing child safety and online technologies: Final Report of the ISTTF to the Multi-state Working Group on Social Networking of State Attorney Generals of the United States*, Cambridge, MA: Berkman Center for Internet and Society, Harvard University (http://cyber.law.harvard.edu/node/4021).

Ito, M., Horst, H., Bittanti, M., boyd, d., Herr-Stephenson, B., Lange, P.G. et al (2008) *Living and learning with new media: Summary of findings from the digital youth project*, Chicago, IL: The John D. and Catherine T. MacArthur Foundation.

Jenkins, H. (2006) *An Occasional Paper on digital media and learning. Confronting the challenges of participatory culture: Media education for the 21st century*, Chicago, IL: The John D. and Catherine T. MacArthur Foundation.

Kelly, P. (2000) 'The dangerousness of youth-at-risk: the possibilities of surveillance and intervention in uncertain times', *Journal of Adolescence*, vol 23, no 4: 463-76.

Klinke, A. and Renn, O. (2001) 'Precautionary principle and discursive strategies: classifying and managing risks', *Journal of Risk Research*, vol 4, no 2: 159-74.

Ling, R. and Haddon, L. (2008) 'Children, youth and the mobile phone', in K. Drotner and S. Livingstone (eds) *International handbook of children, media and culture*, London: Sage Publications: 137-51.

Livingstone, S. (2003) 'Children's use of the internet: reflections on the emerging research agenda', *New Media & Society*, vol 5, no 2: 147-66.

Livingstone, S. (2008) 'Eine Bestandsaufnahme der Möglichkeiten für vorteilhafte, kindgerechte Online-Ressourcen: Die Gesichtspunkte Vertrauen, Risiken und Medienkompetenz' ('Mapping the possibilities for beneficial online resources for children: issues of trust, risk and media literacy'), in W. Schulz and T. Held (eds) *Mehr Vertrauen in Inhalte: Das Potenzial von Ko- und Selbstregulierung in den digitalen Medien* [*More trust in contents: The potential for co- and self-regulation in digital media*], Berlin: Verlag: 19-57.

Livingstone, S. (2009) *Children and the internet: Great expectations, challenging realities*, Cambridge: Polity.

Livingstone, S. and Helsper, E.J. (2007) 'Gradations in digital inclusion: children, young people and the digital divide', *New Media & Society*, vol 9, no 4: 671-96.

Livingstone, S. and Helsper, E.J. (in press) 'Balancing opportunities and risks in teenagers' use of the internet: the role of online skills and family context', *New Media & Society*.

Livingstone, S. and Millwood Hargrave, A. (2009) *Harm and offence in media content: A review of the empirical literature* (2nd edn), Bristol: Intellect.

Lobe, B., Livingstone, S., Olafsson, K. and Simoes, J.A. (2008) *Best practice research guide: How to research children and online technologies in comparative perspective* (Deliverable D4.2), London: London School of Economics and Political Science, EU Kids Online.

Montgomery, K.C. (2007) *Generation digital: Politics, commerce, and childhood in the age of the internet*, Cambridge, MA: MIT Press.

Peter, J. and Valkenburg, P.M. (2006) 'Adolescents' internet use: testing the "disappearing digital divide" versus the "emerging differentiation" approach', *Poetics*, vol 34, nos 4-5: 293-305.

Quayle, E., Loof, L. and Palmer, T. (2008) *Child pornography and sexual exploitation of children online: A contribution of ECPAT International to the World Congress III against Sexual Exploitation of Children and Adolescents*, Rio de Janeiro, 25-28 November.

Smith, D. and McCloskey, J. (1998) 'Risk communication and the social amplification of public sector risk', *Public Money and Management*, vol 18, no 4: 41-50.

van Dijk, J. (2005) *The deepening divide: Inequality in the information society*, London: Sage Publications.

List of country codes

AT	Austria
BE	Belgium
BG	Bulgaria
CH	Switzerland
CY	Cyprus
CZ	Czech Republic
DE	Germany
DK	Denmark
EE	Estonia
EL	Greece
ES	Spain
FI	Finland
FR	France
HU	Hungary
IE	Ireland
I	Iceland
IT	Italy
LT	Lithuania
LU	Luxumbourg
LV	Latvia
MT	Malta
NL	Netherlands
NO	Norway
PL	Poland
PT	Portugal
RO	Romania
RUS	Russia
SE	Sweden
SI	Slovenia
SK	Slovak Republic
UK	United Kingdom

Children and parents online, by country

Country	Population[1] (est. millions)	Internet[2] (Broadband[3]) penetration	Child internet use, by age[4] 2008 (2005)[5]					Parents' internet use, 2008[6] (2005)
			All	6–10	11–14	15–17		
EU 27	489.1	60.7 (31.6)	75 (70)	60	84	86		84 (66)
Austria (AT)	8.2	68.3 (32.8)	77 (66)	49	90	93		87 (76)
Belgium (BE)	10.4	67.3 (48.1)	71 (84)	58	75	80		92 (80)
Bulgaria (BG)	7.3	32.6 (10.0)	81 (41)	64	89	93		84 (34)
Cyprus (CY)	0.8	41.0 (12.6)	50 (44)	28	57	64		57 (35)
Czech Republic (CZ)	10.2	48.8 (16.5)	84 (78)	58	94	97		91 (73)
Denmark (DK)	5.5	80.4 (63.2)	93 (95)	83	98	99		98 (96)
Estonia (EE)	1.3	65.4 (36.8)	93 (90)	85	97	96		92 (83)
Finland (FI)	5.2	83.0 (53.3)	94 (89)	87	98	100		98 (96)
France (FR)	62.2	64.6 (30.3)	76 (78)	53	86	91		85 (67)
Germany (DE)	82.4	67.0 (33.5)	75 (65)	56	88	94		89 (75)
Greece (EL)	10.7	46.0 (3.90)	50 (39)	25	59	79		54 (24)
Hungary (HU)	10	52.5 (21.8)	88 (65)	68	95	95		80 (41)
Ireland (IE)	4.2	58.0 (13.9)	81 (61)	61	94	96		89 (60)
Italy (IT)	58.1	48.6 (16.4)	45 (52)	34	48	54		82 (62)

Country	Population[1] (est. millions)	Internet[2] (Broadband[3]) penetration	Child internet use, by age[4] 2008 (2005)[5]				Parents' internet use, 2008[6] (2005)
			All	6–10	11–14	15–17	
Latvia (LV)	2.2	59.0 (22.3)	83 (73)	59	92	99	87 (54)
Lithuania (LT)	3.6	59.0 (19.6)	86 (70)	69	94	96	83 (45)
Luxembourg (LU)	0.5	74.9 (44.1)	75 (88)	47	89	93	92 (87)
Malta (MT)	0.4	23.5 (20.6)	88 (68)	71	93	97	63 (41)
Netherlands (NL)	16.6	82.9 (65.6)	93 (92)	83	96	100	97 (97)
Poland (PL)	38.5	52.0 (21.6)	89 (62)	72	97	98	82 (44)
Portugal (PT)	10.7	39.8 (23.8)	68 (54)	54	81	75	65 (37)
Romania (RO)	22.2	33.4 (n / a)	70 (42)	57	72	82	58 (35)
Slovak Republic (SK)	5.5	49.6 (11.6)	78 (68)	55	87	86	76 (59)
Slovenia (SI)	2	64.8 (33.5)	88 (81)	73	95	96	84 (74)
Spain (ES)	40.5	66.8 (29.3)	70 (52)	52	86	79	72 (50)
Sweden (SE)	9	80.7 (50.8)	91 (86)	77	97	100	97 (98)
United Kingdom (UK)	60.9	70.9 (44.1)	91 (90)	87	94	95	92 (72)
Other							
Iceland (IS)[7]	0.3	90 (72.2)	94(93)	87	97	100	98(98)
Norway (NO)[8]	4.6	86 (57.3)	93	n/a	n/a	n/a	n/a(97)

continued .../

Notes:

[a] Source: www.census.gov. Internet statistics (dated 31 December 2008) retrieved 6 March 2009 from www.internetworldstats.com/stats9.htm#eu.

[b] EU internet statistics updated for 31 December 2008. Usage figures from sources published by Nielsen//NetRatings, ITU (International Telecommunication Union), GfK, local NICs (Newly Industrialising Countries) retrieved 6 March 2009 from www.internetworldstats.com/stats9.htm#eu.

[c] Eurostat, January 2007.

[d] EU27 figures (from parents of 6 to 17 year olds) from EC (2008). (European Commission) (2008) *Towards a safer use of the internet for children in the EU – A parents' perspective*. *Analytical report*, Flash Eurobarometer Series # 248, conducted by The Gallup Organisation, Hungary, Luxembourg: EC (http://ec.europa.eu/information_society/activities/sip/docs/eurobarometer/analyticalreport_2008.pdf).

[e] EU25 data (from guardians of 6 to 17 year olds), EC (2005). EC. (2005/6). Eurobarometer survey on Safer Internet. Brussels: Special Eurobarometer 250. Safer Internet, Brussels. Retrieved from: http://ec.europa.eu/information_society/activities/sip/docs/eurobarometer/eurobarometer_2005_25_ms.pdf

[f] EU27 figures (use frequency recalculated as ever/never) – EC (2008). EU25 figures – EC (2005). EC. (2005/6). Eurobarometer survey on Safer Internet. Brussels: Special Eurobarometer 250. Safer Internet, Brussels. Retrieved from: http://ec.europa.eu/information_society/activities/sip/docs/eurobarometer/eurobarometer_2005_25_ms.pdf

[g] Capacent Gallup (2009) *Örugg internetnotkun hjá barnafjölskyldum – Viðhorfskönnun* [*Safe internet use in families with children – A survey*], Reykjavik: Capacent Gallup.

[h] For children, see Medietilsynet (2008) *Trygg bruk undersøkelsen 2008* [*Safe use of the internet 2008*], Fredrikstad: Medietilsynet. For parents, see SAFT (Safety, Awareness, Facts and Tools) Project (2006) *SAFT 2006 Parent and Children Survey, 2004-2006*, Norwegian Action Plan for Children, Youth and the Internet and the European Commission Safer Internet Action Plan, Norwegian Media Authority.

The EU Kids Online network

Aims and overview

EU Kids Online (2006–09) is a thematic network examining European research on cultural, contextual and risk issues in children's safe use of the internet and online technologies. It was funded by the European Commission's Safer Internet Plus Programme (Directorate-General Information Society and Media), coordinated by the London School of Economics and Political Science and guided by international and national policy advisers. The aim was to identify, compare and draw conclusions from existing and ongoing research at the intersection of three domains:

- Children (up to 18 years old) and their families.
- Online technologies, especially the internet.
- European empirical research and policy on risk and safety.

Research teams from 21 member states were chosen for diversity across countries and research expertise: Austria, Belgium, Bulgaria, Cyprus, Czech Republic, Denmark, Estonia, France, Germany, Greece, Iceland, Ireland, Italy, the Netherlands, Norway, Poland, Portugal, Slovenia, Spain, Sweden and the UK.

Specific objectives

The objectives, achieved via seven work packages, were:
- *Data availability:* identify and evaluate available data on children's/families' use of the internet and online technologies, noting key gaps in the evidence base.
- *Research contexts:* understand the national and institutional contexts of research and inform the future research agenda.
- *Cross-national comparisons:* compare findings across diverse European countries, contextualising similarities and differences so as to identify opportunities, risks and safety issues.

- *Methodologies for good research practice:* guide researchers in meeting the methodological challenge of studying children online cross-nationally.
- *Policy recommendations:* develop evidence-based policy recommendations for awareness raising, media literacy and other actions promoting safer internet use.
- *Dissemination:* disseminate research findings, methods guidance, recommendations and all outputs to public, academic and policy audiences.
- *Network management:* network researchers across Europe to share and compare data, findings, theory, disciplines and methodological approaches.

Online database (data repository)

The EU Kids Online network constructed a publicly accessible and fully searchable database of all empirical studies conducted and identified across Europe, provided they meet a certain quality threshold. The data repository is available online at www.lse.ac.uk/collections/EUKidsOnline/. It contains the details of almost 400 separate studies (355 of them single country studies; if findings for each country in a multicountry study are counted separately, the total is over 600 studies).

Each is coded by country, topic, age of child, method, sample and so forth. References and links to original sources are provided where available, generating a resource for research users in government, academia, policy, funding, regulation and non-governmental organisations (NGOs).

The collection policy describes what is included and not included (see the project website for full details: www.eukidsonline.net). In brief, these are as follows:

- The unit of analysis is an empirical research project (not a publication) conducted in Europe.
- The report must be available and read by the coder, with sufficient methodological details to evaluate its quality.
- Relevant research includes, as a priority: (a) empirical projects concerning children + internet/online; (b) research on risks experienced by children online; (c) research on mediation or regulatory practices (by parents, teachers, etc) for children's online activities. It also includes, with more partial coverage: (d) research

on parental internet experiences; and (e) research on children's use of other technologies.

- Definitions: (a) 'Europe' includes the EU25, with priority for the 18 nations of EU Kids Online; (b) 'children' includes those under 18 years old; (c) 'online' includes internet, online games, online mobile, e-learning, etc.

Certain quality control criteria have guided these decisions, although we cannot guarantee that all research included here is of the highest quality. Each study (or project) is described according to its main features – sample, methods, topics researched, countries studied, publication details etc. These features, or a free text search, may be used to search the database.

Network members

Country	Institution	Researcher
Austria	University of Salzburg	Ingrid Paus-Hasebrink
		Andrea Dürager
		Christina Ortner
		Manfred Rathmoser
		Christine W.Wijnen
Belgium	Catholic University of Leuven	Leen d'Haenens
		Verónica Donoso
		Bieke Zaman
	Free University of Brussels	Joke Bauwens
		Nico Carpentier
		Katia Segers
Bulgaria	GERT (Gender, Education, Research and Technologies)	Jivka Marinova
		Maria Dimitrova
		Christina Haralanova
		Maria Gencheva
		Diana Boteva
Cyprus	Cyprus Neuroscience & Technology Institute	Yiannis Laouris
		Tatjana Taraszow
		Elena Aristodemou
Czech Republic	Masaryk University	Václav Štětka
Denmark	IT University of Copenhagen	Gitte Stald
		Jeppe Jensen
Estonia	University of Tartu	Veronika Kalmus
		Pille Pruulmann-Vengerfeldt
		Pille Runnel
		Andra Siibak
		Kadri Ugur
		Anda Zule-Lapima
France	France Telecom R&D	Benoit Lelong
	University of Charles-de-Gualle Lille 3	Cédric Fluckiger
Germany	Hans Bredow Institute for Media Research at the University of Hamburg	Uwe Hasebrink
		Claudia Lampert
Greece	Athens University	Liza Tsaliki
Iceland	University of Iceland	Thorbjörn Broddason
		Gudberg Jónsson
	University of Akureyri	Kjartan Ólafsson
Ireland	Dublin Institute of Technology	Brian O'Neill
		Helen McQuillan

Country	Institution	Researcher
	National Centre for Technology in Education	Simon Grehan
Italy	Osservatorio sulla Comunicazione	Fausto Colombo
	Università Cattolica del Sacro Cuore	Piermarco Aroldi
		Barbara Scifo
		Giovanna Mascheroni
		Maria Francesca Murru
Norway	University of Oslo	Elisabeth Staksrud
		Petter Bae Brandtzæg
	Norwegian University of Science and Technology (NTNU)	Ingunn Hagen
		Thomas Wold
Poland	Warsaw School of Social Psychology	Wiesław Godzic
		Lucyna Kirwil
		Barbara Giza
		Tomasz Łysakowski
Portugal	New University of Lisbon	Cristina Ponte
		Cátia Candeias
		José Alberto Simões
		Nelson Vieira
		Daniel Cordoso
		Ana Jorge
		Tomas Patrocinio
		Sofia Viseu
		Ema Sofia Leitao
Slovenia	University of Ljubljana	Bojana Lobe
Spain	University of the Basque Country	Carmelo Garitaonandia
		Maialen Garmendia
		Gemma Martínez Fernández
Sweden	The International Clearinghouse on Children, Youth & Media, University of Gothenburg	Cecilia von Felitzen
	Umeå University	Elza Dunkels
The Netherlands	Netherlands Institute for Social Research (SCP)	Jos de Haan Marion Duimel Linda Adrichem
	Amsterdam School of Communications	Patti M. Valkenburg Jochen Peter
United Kingdom	London School of Economics and Political Science	Sonia Livingstone
		Leslie Haddon
		Ranjana Das
	Swansea University	Panayiota Tsatsou

Index

Page references for notes are followed by n